CELEBRATION

CELEBRATION

A Ceremonial and Philosophic Guide for Humanists and Humanistic Jews

SHERWIN T. WINE

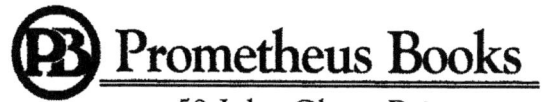

Prometheus Books
59 John Glenn Drive
Amherst, New York 14228-2119

Published 2003 by Prometheus Books

Celebration: A Ceremonial and Philosophic Guide for Humanists and Humanistic Jews. Copyright © 1988 by Sherwin T. Wine. All rights reserved. No part of this publication may be reproduced, stored in a retrieval system, or transmitted in any form or by any means, digital, electronic, mechanical, photocopying, recording, or otherwise, or conveyed via the Internet or a Web site without prior written permission of the publisher, except in the case of brief quotations embodied in critical articles and reviews.

Inquiries should be addressed to
Prometheus Books
59 John Glenn Drive
Amherst, New York 14228–2119
VOICE: 716–691–0133. ext. 210
FAX: 716–691-0137
WWW.PROMETHEUSBOOKS.COM

12 11 10 09   10 9 8 7 6

Library of Congress Cataloging-in-Publication Data

Wine, Sherwin T..
  Celebration : a ceremonial and philosophic guide for humanists and humanistic Jews / by Sherwin T. Wine.
      p. cm.
  Originally published in hardcover.
  ISBN 13: 978-1-59102-166-7
  ISBN 10: 1-59102-166-9

  1. Humanistic Judaism. I. Title.

BM 197.8.W56 1988
390'.089924—dc19

88-19160

Printed in the United States of America on acid-free paper

CONTENTS

Preface   9

Introduction   11

PART I
HUMANISM

1. Ambition   17
2. Autonomy   22
3. Believing   26
4. Community   33
5. Courage   38
6. Desire   42
7. Dignity   46
8. Emotion   50
9. Equality   55
10. Ethics   59
11. Family   63
12. Feminism   68
13. Freedom   72
14. Friendship   75
15. Happiness   78
16. Honesty   82
17. Hope   86
18. Humanism   90
19. Humanity   93
20. Humor   98
21. Idealism   102
22. Individualism   106
23. Justice   110
24. Leadership   115
25. Light   119

26. Love   122
27. Loyalty   126
28. Maturity   130
29. Peace   134
30. People   138
31. Philosophy   142
32. Realism   147
33. Reason   151
34. Science   155
35. Secularism   159
36. Self-Respect   163
37. Strength   166
38. Universalism   169
39. Wonder   173

PART II
JUDAISM

1. Anti-Semitism   179
2. Jewish History   184
3. Jewish Humanism   190
4. Jewish Survival   194
5. Secular Humanistic Judaism   199
6. Zionism   203

PART III
JEWISH HOLIDAYS

1. Rosh Hashana   209
2. Rosh Hashana Youth Service   215
3. Yom Kippur   220
4. Yom Kippur Memorial   226
5. Yom Kippur Youth Service   233
6. Sukkot   238
7. Sukkot Youth Service   241
8. Hanukka   245
9. Hanukka Youth Service   250
10. Hanukka Home Celebration   255
11. Israel Day Youth Service   257
12. Purim   262
13. Purim Youth Service   265
14. Pesakh   269
15. Remembrance Day   273

Contents 7

16. Shavuot   *278*
17. Shavuot Youth Service   *281*
18. Shabbat Home Service   *287*

PART IV
HUMANIST HOLIDAYS

1. New Year's Day Service   *291*
2. People Day   *295*
3. Humanism Day   *300*
4. World Day Service   *304*
5. Thanksgiving Service   *308*

PART V
LIFE CYCLE

1. Birth   *317*
2. Growing Up (Mitsva)   *330*
   Mitsva I (Ethics)   *330*
   Mitsva II (Self-Esteem)   *335*
   Mitsva III (Lifestyle)   *339*
   Mitsva IV (Humanism)   *344*
   Mitsva V (Women)   *349*
3. Educational Achievement   *355*
4. Confirmation (Celebration of Commitment)   *359*
5. Marriage   *365*
6. Death   *377*
7. Memorial Stone Dedication   *389*

SONGS   *391*

PREFACE

This book is the product of practical experience. It arose out of twenty years of providing all kinds of celebrations for a secular Jewish community. Weekly meetings, holidays, and life-cycle events became the opportunity to develop new themes and to write new material.

The celebration material in this book is obviously verbal. The content is also strongly intellectual and ideological, as well as reflective and sentimental. The style rests on the firm conviction that celebration events can touch both the mind and the heart. An awareness of shared beliefs is as much a part of community solidarity as holding hands and hugging.

It has become fashionable in recent years to denigrate the intellectual and to praise the emotional, as though the two were opposed to each other. *Rational people are cold. Emotional people are warm.* This nonsense has often sponsored a mushy togetherness that lacks the strength of shared convictions. Humanism and a secular humanistic Judaism are philosophies of life that go beyond being nice to other people. They derive their emotional impact from the boldness of their vision of the human condition. Articulating this vision in private reflection or community celebration provides its own emotional power. If the ideas are exciting, then the response to these ideas can be equally exciting.

This book can be used in several ways. It can be a meditation book for private reflection. Readers can learn about humanism and Jewish humanism. They can clarify their own convictions. They can renew their commitment to a humanistic lifestyle.

It also can be a celebration for public meetings and services. The prose poetry and song themes are intended to provide opportunities for inspiration and community solidarity. Both ordinary and special occasions are included.

It can be a resource book for a variety of events, meetings, or celebrations. Readers may decide to pick and choose and to create their own combinations. A little from here and a little from there may result in a more satisfactory mixture than the present arrangement allows.

Finally, it can be a textbook for humanism and humanistic Judaism. Without the songs the book becomes a summary of the highlights and perspective of a secular philosophy of life. In fact, because the ideas are presented in a tighter format than an ordinary textbook, it may be easier to focus on basic ideas and concepts.

With the exception of the songs, all the celebration materials are original. They make no claim to being the only way to articulate and celebrate a secular Judaism. This collection is *one* alternative among many. It reflects my personal style and the experience of the Birmingham Temple in Detroit, where these words have been tested.

What follows is a labor of love. I hope that you will find it useful, intellectually convincing, and emotionally satisfying.

Sherwin Wine
January, 1988

INTRODUCTION

HUMANISTIC JUDAISM

Humanistic Judaism is a philosophy of life which has been part of the Jewish experience for over one hundred years. However, it grew out of attitudes and beliefs which were part of the "underground" of Jewish life for the past two thousand years. It is very distinct from Orthodox Judaism in rejecting the authority of the rabbinic tradition. It is also very distinct from the three non-Orthodox "liberal" alternatives—Conservative, Reform, and Reconstructionism—in rejecting the need for theistic language. The age of science, capitalism, and the secular revolution have so transformed Jewish life that it has become impossible, without a dogmatic arbitrariness, to maintain conviction in traditional beliefs. The main issue is whether to dress up the new beliefs in the clothing of rabbinic Judaism or to choose a more direct and a more honest approach.

Humanistic Jews prefer a more direct approach. They deplore the fact that so much time is devoted to "kosherizing" belief and so little time to clarifying it. What is most important is to allow contemporary Jews to say what they really think and feel without the necessity of finding ancestral approval.

Combining humanism, a people-centered philosophy of life, and Judaism, the culture of the Jewish nation, creates humanistic Judaism. The marriage of these two commitments is very natural, since the real experience of the Jewish people has humanistic significance. Jewish history, more than any other national history, testifies to the moral indifference of the universe and to the necessity of human beings to take control of their own fate.

For most secular and humanistic Jews, their secularism and their humanism do not derive from some abstract philosophic investigation of empirical science and naturalism. It arises from their own experience as Jews in the century of the Holocaust.

CELEBRATION

Celebration is the humanist alternative to ritual. It is less compulsive than ritual, preferring that forms serve people and not the reverse.

12   Introduction

Celebration is the act of dramatizing our commitments to people and ideas. It helps us to focus on what is most important in our lives, on what is worthy of our energy and enthusiasm. Symbols are indispensable to the drama of celebration. They turn abstractions and indescribable feelings into something more concrete, more vivid. Visual design, music, and poetry give expression to our hearts and minds.

Celebration can be private. But it is usually public, a way of reinforcing community bonds. The experience of group solidarity is one of the traditional "highs" of celebration. For those of us who are humanists, it is an important experience since we often suffer from a rebellious individualism. This individualism enables us to think freely and to maintain our integrity, but it also frequently prevents us from joining groups and participating in the human connection we say we admire.

There are many ideal times for celebrations, significant moments in the calendar year or in the cycle of personal and community life. There are the transitions from season to season, the anniversaries of important events, the weekly or monthly meetings, the "passages" in each individual life. For the imaginative mind there is no dearth of celebration opportunities.

Many humanists discourage celebrations because they are reminders of the ritual they discarded. They fail to realize that the need to celebrate is a human need which would continue to exist even if all memory of traditional religion vanished. Rationality has nothing to do with avoiding celebrations. Reasonable people pay attention to human needs. They know that a "warm" religion does not have to be either traditional or theistic. It simply has to provide opportunities for communities to feel like communities. Faith without symbols would be as "cold" as reason without symbols.

The celebration material in this book is primarily verbal. It is the result of the need, in a non-humanistic world, to reinforce the humanistic commitments of people who are seeking to clarify their personal philosophies of life and to discover fellow believers in the context of a caring community. We have to say aloud what we already believe in order to fully understand it and to establish a connection with those who share our convictions.

If there is any kind of humanistic "spiritual" experience, it lies in the sense of transcendence which comes from deeply feeling part of something greater than ourselves. This something is natural and human. It is the family, the nation, the community of believers which rescues us from alienation. A successful celebration provides that sense of transcendence—whether the vehicle be words, songs, dance, or the silent holding of hands. It acknowledges the importance of being an individual, but it also recognizes that being truly human involves much more than that.

There are five kinds of celebrations in this book:
  1. Celebrations of humanistic values. These values are embraced by secular

and humanistic Jews. But they also are embraced by other secularists and humanists.
2. Celebrations of Jewish identity and Jewish culture.
3. Celebrations of Jewish holidays.
4. Celebrations of humanistic holidays which can be shared by both Jews and non-Jews.
5. Celebrations of the personal life-cycle.

All of these celebrations are based on the conviction that reason and emotion, inspiration and integrity, humanism and Judaism, do not need to be separated. They complement each other.

PART I
HUMANISM

Although there are many distinct humanist organizations and many varieties of humanism, humanism in modern times has come to stand for a set of shared approaches to the nature of reality and moral behavior. While humanist thinkers existed as far back as ancient Greece (e.g., Democritus and Epicurus), a bold articulation of humanism to a receptive public had to wait for the eighteenth and nineteenth centuries. The age of science and the overthrow of the old religious establishment allowed humanism to become a popular option.

Classical humanism was presented to the public of Europe and the Americas by many famous thinkers. Virtually all the great philosophers of modern times—from Auguste Comte to John Stuart Mill, from Bertrand Russell to John Dewey, from Friedrich Nietzsche to Jean-Paul Sartre—have been humanists.

The mood of humanism is quite different from that of the old religion. Faith encourages belief without evidence, but reason prefers no conclusion to an impulsive conclusion. While scientific evidence provides us with many strong beliefs about the world, it certainly avoids absolute beliefs. It also makes agnosticism respectable where evidence is insufficient. For humanists, "I don't know" is a sign of strength, not a sign of weakness and confusion.

The world of humanism is less harmonious than that of traditional philosophy. Most classical philosophers and theologians disliked the natural world because it was always changing. They preferred the serene eternity of supernatural realms. Humanists, on the other hand, live with the reality of continuous change. They also live with the awareness that the vast universe in which we struggle to survive is morally aloof: it does not care whether we live or die. There is no harmony between the laws of nature and the ethical agenda of human beings.

The humanist epic of creation is longer and more complex than the creation stories of established religion. The evolution of the universe and the evolution of life have taken a long time to bring us to the present state of the world. Over billions of years chance has written a script that would not have been easily predicted along the way.

The vision of human nature has also changed with humanism. *Hutspa* has replaced worship and resignation as a guideline to behavior. Authorities must forego reverence and demonstrate that their moral demands have some connection to the basic human needs of happiness, survival, and dignity.

When it first emerged, humanism was a radical new way of approaching life and decision making. Today the secular perspective seems much more conventional, even though religious fundamentalists continue to target humanism for abuse and rejection. As a way of life humanism initially seems less satisfying than the "glitz" of supernatural religion. It provides no loving God, no happy ending for the good and the righteous, no perfect order for the universe, no immortality for the soul. But, in the end, it rewards its "believers" with the special pleasure of dignity. Despite the harshness of reality, humanists know that they have the right and the power to be the masters of their own lives, that they have the strength to confront the world as it is and not as fantasy makes it appear, and that they have the opportunity to serve the future and not the past.

The humanist themes that follow represent some of the basic ideas and values which a humanist embraces. Each theme is expressed in four to eight prose reflections. These "meditation services" can be used for weekly meetings. They can serve as introductions to lectures, open discussions, or dramatic presentations. For humanistic Jews they can be integrated into a Shabbat celebration. The recommended Hebrew, Yiddish, and English songs which follow each prose reflection will enhance the emotional power of each experience. And the memorial meditation which concludes each celebration is an opportunity to pay tribute to our roots and to the important people of our past.

1
AMBITION

SONG: V'SHOOV ITKHEM (No. 95)

MEANING OF LIFE

Where does the meaning of life lie?

For some people, the meaning of life lies in peace and quiet. They dream of heaven, a place where problems cease and struggle ends, where all is serene. No challenge intrudes on this landscape of pleasure and leisure. No anxiety mars this scene of bliss and tranquility. Worry becomes a fading memory.

For other people, the meaning of life lies in safety and security. They dream of salvation, a dramatic rescue from all enemies and dangers. The world is transformed into a vision of childhood. A protective spirit engulfs every living creature and makes it warm and comfortable. Fear retreats into oblivion.

For people who call themselves humanists neither of these alternatives is very appealing. They prefer more excitement and more challenge. Womb-like tranquility and parental rescue are not enough for their dignity. Although striving and struggle may bring pain as well as pleasure, they are the stuff out of which the good life is made. They rescue us from the dullness of apathy and the boredom of needing nothing. They give dignity to ambition.

If we are humanists, we do not seek to scale the final peak. The meaning of life is in the climbing.

SONG: LAM'TSAPPEEM (No. 56)

REALISM

Successful ambition starts with the courage to face reality.

Illusions are very dangerous to people planning their lives. If we underestimate the height of the mountain we have to climb, if we overestimate our talents and abilities, if we deny our power to do what we are able to do, we will endure the pain of disappointment, frustration, regret, and despair.

We need the courage to face the fact that no one cares as much about our future as we do. Family and friends can love us deeply. They can provide help, support, and empathy. But their needs are not fully our needs. Their dreams are not exactly our dreams. In the end, no one can really do our living, or our dying, for us.

We need the courage to face the fact that what we do well is more important than what we imagine we do well. Competence is good for self-esteem. A good carpenter is more significant than a bad poet, no matter how hard the poet strives. A good accountant is more successful than a bad philosopher, no matter how hard the philosopher yearns to be profound. Training is happiest when it is married to talent.

SONG: MEE HAHAM (No. 65)

CHOICE

Successful ambition starts with personal responsibility.

Responsibility is never easy, just as growing up is never easy. When we are children, we find it so convenient to blame others for what we choose to do that we are reluctant to give up this privilege when adulthood arrives. Even though we say the opposite, we prefer to be the victims, rather than the masters, of our lives.

If we claim to be adults, we do not deny our freedom. We do not run away from the fact that nothing we do really happens without our consent. No threat or intimidation can work if we are willing to face the consequences. In the end, we do what we choose to do. And no one else is responsible for the decisions we make.

If we claim to be adults, we do not romanticize the fates. We do not invent directives from destiny. We do not wait for our "assignment" to be revealed.

Each one of us is able to do many things well. Each one of us is able to enjoy many pleasures intensely. But we cannot do everything we want to do. We cannot experience everything we want to experience. We have to make choices.

Our life, our "destiny," is what we choose to do. Nothing more, nothing less.

SONG: HATOV O HARA (No. 41)

DISCIPLINE

Successful ambition starts with the power to discipline our energies.

Many people have trouble distinguishing between wishing and reality. They prefer infant fantasies. They firmly believe that if they want something badly enough they will get it. Enthusiasm becomes the substitute for training and hard work. Intense desire becomes the alternative to persistence and scheduled learning.

Many people have trouble distinguishing between freedom and dignity. They imagine that self-esteem is the power to resist the demands of others, no matter how reasonable these demands may be. They maintain that self-respect comes from what we are and not from what we do, even though there is no real distinction between the two. In their eyes, dignity is only freedom, not the discipline of useful achievement. But true dignity comes from the awareness that choosing a goal is only the beginning of ambition. Using our will to resist our fear and laziness is the rest of the story.

No goal worth pursuing provides us with a path free of pain and tedium. No career worth developing promises us training free of frustration and temporary failure. Success means that our will is as strong as our desire.

SONG: HALBEESHEENEE (No. 35)

PERSPECTIVE

Successful ambition needs the wisdom of long-range vision.

In an age of affluence, we grow accustomed to immediate gratification. So many of our needs find instant satisfaction that we easily forget the struggle for survival. We find it hard to understand why our plans do not quickly come to fulfillment. We find it difficult to imagine that frustration and disappointment are natural parts of human development. In our narrow vision, bumps become unassailable mountains. Obstacles become impenetrable barriers.

Perspective is the power to put stumbling blocks in their proper place, to see them by their real dimensions. Sometimes life needs an aerial view, a vision of the trees that makes us notice the forest. Our imagination rises up above the present trouble and connects it to our past success and to future possibilities. We perceive that what appears to be the ultimate disaster is only a stepping stone to future acceptance. We do not panic when unwelcome events surprise us.

Perspective is the ability to keep the landscape of our life in scale. We are willing to climb again and again because we know that the peaks are not as high as we once imagined.

SONG: BASHANA HABAA (No. 21)

RISK

Successful ambition needs the willingness to live with risk.

The desire for safety and security is a very strong human desire. In a world filled with failure and danger, memories of babyhood linger in our psyche. How nice it would be if every decision we made was attached to a guarantee for success! How comforting it would be if every project we planned was insured by destiny! In a decent world, everything would be as reliable as our mother's womb.

But the desire for adventure is also a human desire. It feeds on our insatiable curiosity and on our need for self-reliance. It resists predictable pleasure and uninterrupted coziness. Surprise and spontaneity make it come alive and give it room to breathe. A little fear feeds it with energy and rescues life from the boredom of guarantees.

Whenever we strive for what we are not sure of achieving, we run the risk of losing. We also run the risk of winning. If our talents are appropriate, if our discipline is real, no game is more exciting.

To know that destiny insures nothing and to love that scary fact is to embrace all that life can offer.

SONG: AYFO OREE (No. 14)

MEMORIAL

Successful ambition also needs heroes of ambition.

Human culture does not really thrive when everything is comfortable. Great civilizations have never emerged in the paradise of tropical islands and lush lagoons. Instead, they tend to grow where problems challenge human ingenuity. Flooded river valleys and rock-faced harbors, wintry plains and storm-assaulted coastlines—these are the settings for human progress and achievement. Where life is too easy, where leisure dulls ambition, the weather is more interesting than the people.

Our own striving builds on the striving of past generations. We are here today because pioneers crossed an ocean to build a new life in a new world, because immigrants believed that their lives and the lives of their children could be improved through dreams and hard work, because parents and grandparents disciplined their fear and their skepticism to risk new ventures and new careers. Although they talked a lot about safety and security, they were far bolder than they would choose to admit.

We can learn from their legacy of courage.

SONG: ZAYKHER (No. 103)

2
AUTONOMY

SONG: MA TOVOO (No. 64)

LIGHT

The sun is the light of our world. Thrust into the infinity of space, it warms its planetary children as a mother shelters her young. Confident in its glory it exudes a fiery power and sends its burning rays to heal the darkness.

This orb is very special to us, for through it we find our life. The outer galaxies are twinkles in the night. But the wonders of daylight quicken our vitality. Even the counting of time is the sun's dependent. Day follows night in an endless succession. Year pursues year by the earth's revolution. Relentlessly the sun burns while people mark the calendar of their present. Light and life are one. The wonder of light is the wonder of life.

SONG: ZEMER LAKH (No. 104)

INDIVIDUALITY

We are all part of a single species. In this way we resemble all other animals. Like them we share both form and behavior with fellow members of our race. Like them we feel and act by the tyranny of instinct and impulsively serve the survival of the group. Yet the sameness of the species is less important in us than in any other creature. In our psychic makeup we enjoy the oppportunity of genuine personality and the special thrill of the individual sense. Our very thoughts and drives are so undetermined by birth that our behavior defies prediction and reduces human history to a farcical science. Biography is only possible among men and women. Only we sense the person before we feel the race.

To be an individual, to be committed to our uniqueness is to be, in some way, lonely. It is to acknowledge that we are distinct and separate, deriving our reality from no group or species. It is to affirm the value of difference so that personal decision may challenge social dictation with integrity. It is to defy the clichés of history, and to deny the claim of family or nation to ultimate loyalty and obedience. The conscience of every one of us is supremely important. It gives us reality.

CONGREGATION

Who are the wise? People who understand themselves.
Who are the strong? People who rule themselves.
Who are the beautiful? People of wisdom and strength.

SONG: MEE HAHAM (No. 65)

INTEGRITY

We all play many roles and belong to many groups. In the family we are father or mother, son or daughter. In the arena of business we act the employer or employee, doctor or patient, lawyer or client. In every sphere of life we search for the part that we must play. When the directions are less than clear, we feel uncomfortable. Rigid dramatic rules are often reassuring. There is security in a carefully edited script.

Smiling in time, controlling anger, looking dignified and serving those we dislike are difficult achievements. But they are part of the training. Hard theater demands hard discipline. When we prepare for life in society, we prepare for a thousand and one taxing dramas. The result is often confusion. We mix our roles and lose ourselves on a vast stage with many directors. Our personality gives up its unity and becomes a series of parts. The script of the moment defines our essence. We search for our integrity and we cannot find it.

To have integrity is to experience ourselves as distinct from the roles we play, to know ourselves to be real, even when the audience vanishes.

SONG: AYZE HOO GIBBOR (No. 18)

AUTONOMY

All of us live with the threat of our own incompetence. All of us experience weakness and despair. It is hard to stand alone and to rely on the hesitant strength of inner conviction to meet the crisis of living. How we long for stable props that will support our faltering and will ease the pain of being an individual! How comfortable it is to lose oneself in family or country and to find oneself the obedient part and not the autonomous whole. When the ordinary mortal yearns to be serenely dependent, then omnipotent fathers and all-powerful kings are preferable to freedom.

The sadness of life is the outer clutching rather than the inner reliance. To beg and lean is the common fate of most men and women. To find the source of life's power within ourselves is the rare discovery. Yet no insight is more important than this revelation. The fiber of zestful living is an individuality too firm to break. Only when we become aware that each of us is independently real do we uncover our strength.

SONG: BAMAKOM (No. 19)

SELF-RESPECT

We all strive for many things—for love, for power, for the prestige of social station. But no goal is more precious than the integrity of self-respect. To sense our wholeness and consistency is to discover an order within that can bravely confront the disorder without. To feel deeply that each of us is the ruler of himself and not the helpless victim of passion and whim is to understand the essence of humanness and the virtues of heroism. Courage is a fault when it merely thrives on the enthusiasm of others. It becomes the ally of maturity when it proceeds from the fire of personal conviction.

SONG: AYFO OREE (No. 14)

MEMORIAL

The history of humanity is a testimonial to the person of integrity. Micah and Isaiah defied the power of the state and the prejudice of the public with the security of their inner sureness. Freud encountered the laughter of a thousand skeptics and met their onslaught with the power of his reasoning mind. Even Lincoln knew the hatred of the timid and confronted their hysteria with his consistent vision of the goal. It is the boldness of these leaders, even more than their words, that reaches across the years to enrich our own conviction.

In the intimate world of our loved ones, persons of integrity have also touched our years and made us stronger by their strength. Their memory evokes the struggle of pioneers in a new world and new society. Expelled from the hell of the old continent, they thrust themselves bravely into the adventure of seeking a new home. To uproot and transplant themselves and to retain their sense of personal identity was their act of bravery. The special grace of parents and grandparents who faced and mastered the ordeal of newness becomes a model for the courage we need.

SONG: SHEEM'OO (No. 83)

3
BELIEVING

SONG: V'SHOOV ITKHEM (No. 95)

TRUTH

I believe.

I believe in people.

I believe in people who search for truth.

I believe in people who search for truth with open hearts and open minds.

Hearts and minds are not easy to open. Life is less difficult if we memorize an answer and pretend to believe in it. There is comfort in faith, the comfort that comes from acts of loving loyalty. There is strength in dogma, the strength that flows from unquestioning obedience.

The path of dignity is harder to follow. It proceeds along no well-defined route hallowed by the agreement of centuries. It finds no joy in the safety of familiar faces and familiar places. Boldly it seeks out the danger of surprise, the surprise of new ideas and new experiences, the surprise of new discoveries and new adventures. The road is not fixed. It changes with the facts. And we, the explorers on the way, taste the excitement of the search and the fear of never knowing what we will find.

CONGREGATION

I believe.

I believe in people.

I believe in people who search for truth.

I believe in people who search for truth with open hearts and open minds.

SONG: SAHAKEE (No. 78)

STRENGTH

I believe.

I believe in people.

I believe in people who are strong.

I believe in people who are strong enough to live with questions which still have no answers.

Believing can be therapy. It can calm our fears. It can tame our anxieties. It can help us hide from the fact that we do not know what we think we know. Uncertainty is so threatening that we often invent answers just to avoid living with it.

There are many questions which have good answers. There are answers about growing food and building houses. There are answers about making friends and staying healthy. There are answers about nature's laws and the evolution of life. Some come from men and women of genius. Others come from ordinary people in the struggle for survival.

But there are many questions which still have no answers. They hover in the realms of speculation and opposing theories. They tease us with the challenge of how much more we have to learn about people, life, and the universe. They leave us with the unwanted gift of uncertainty. They force us to say "I don't know" and to confess that we are agnostics. Yet, the strength to live with this uncertainty rescues us from cheap rewards and enables us to wait for the truth.

CONGREGATION

I believe.

I believe in people.

I believe in people who are strong.

I believe in people who are strong enough to live with questions which still have no answers.

SONG: OUT OF THE NIGHT (No. 76)

COURAGE

I believe.

I believe in people.

I believe in people who are brave.

I believe in people who are brave enough to stand face to face with reality.

What we want to hear is quite different from what we need to hear. We want to hear that the universe loves us, that the world is just, that what happens happens for the best, that love conquers all. But these imaginings are fantasies. They are excuses we invent to keep us from the painful task of being responsible for our own lives.

What we need to hear is the voice of reality. We need to confront the world as it is so that we can make it better. Courage is more than the power to withstand physical pain. It is the mental strength to look the universe in its realistic face and say "I know who you are. I know that your ways and my desires are not always compatible. I know that you do not care whether I live or die. But I do. And I accept responsibility for my life."

CONGREGATION

I believe.

I believe in people.

I believe in people who are brave.

I believe in people who are brave enough to stand face to face with reality.

SONG: LAM'TSAPPEEM (No. 56)

POWER

I believe.

I believe in people.

I believe in people who are wise.

I believe in people who are wise enough to know their own power and to grow with it.

It is very easy to feel weak and helpless. Our childhood is so long that it takes many years for us to discover our strength. Our challenges are sometimes so overwhelming that it is easier to run away than to confront the danger. But our fears distort the reality of our power. We are stronger than we imagine ourselves to be. We are more skillful than we give ourselves credit for.

Wise people do not underestimate their strength. Nor do they exaggerate it. They simply recognize how convenient it is to be weak. Strong people carry a special burden. They know that strength comes as much from an act of will as from some inner reserve of power. They know that talent wasted is talent betrayed. They know that the risk of success goes together with the risk of failure. If they acknowledge their fear, they also acknowledge their power to control their fear.

CONGREGATION

I believe.

I believe in people.

I believe in people who are wise.

I believe in people who are wise enough to know their own power and to grow with it.

SONG: B'AYLE HAYADIEYIM (No. 22)

LOVE

I believe.

I believe in people.

I believe in people who love.

I believe in people who love others with the passion of their own self-esteem.

Some people love with words. Their mouths breathe affection. Their tongues speak loyalty and caring. But they are not able to move from loving words to loving deeds. They feel deficient. They do not trust their own power. They believe that giving to others is giving up their own safety and security. Promises of love are all that their frightened spirit will allow.

Some people love with deeds. They nurture through what they do and not merely by what they say. If they give to others, they do not feel diminished. If they help others, they have no sense of martyrdom. They know that love is more than addition and subtraction. They know that selfishness and self-esteem are incompatible. They know that helping others to feel strong makes them feel strong. Love is not sacrifice. Love is the affirmation of our own power through the act of nurturing others.

CONGREGATION

I believe.

I believe in people.

I believe in people who love.

I believe in people who love others with the passion of their own self-esteem.

SONG: SHEEM'OO (No. 83)

HOPE

I believe.

I believe in hope.

I believe in hope that chooses—that chooses self-respect above pity.

I believe in hope that dismisses—that dismisses the petty fears of petty people.

I believe in hope that feels—that feels distant pleasure as much as momentary pain.

I believe in hope that acts—that acts without the guarantee of success.

I believe in hope that kisses—that kisses the future with the transforming power of its will.

> Hope is a choice,
> never found,
> never given,
> always taken.
>
> Some wait for hope to capture them.
> They act as the prisoners of despair.
>
> Others go searching for hope.
> They find nothing but the reflection of their own anger.
>
> Hope is an act of will,
> affirming, in the presence of evil,
> that good things will happen,
> preferring, in the face of failure, self-esteem to pity.
>
> Optimists laugh, even in the dark
> They know that
> hope is a life style—
> not a guarantee.

—Sherwin Wine

CONGREGATION

I believe.

I believe in hope.

I believe in hope that chooses—that chooses self-respect above self-pity.

Believing

I believe in hope that dismisses—that dismisses the petty fears of petty people.

I believe in hope that feels—that feels distant pleasure as well as momentary pain.

I believe in hope that acts—that acts without the guarantee of success.

I believe in hope that kisses—that kisses the future with the transforming power of its will.

SONG: TIKVA B'HEERA (No. 89)

4
COMMUNITY

SONG: V'SHOOV ITKHEM (No. 95)

UNITY

Our congregation is more than a congregation. It is more than a collection of people. It is a community of friends, an alliance of believers. We are engaged in shared work. We are moved by shared ideals. There is a solidarity of purpose, a union of goals. When we celebrate, we celebrate together. And when we need support, we support each other.

Our congregation is more than an institution. It is more than a casual assumption. It is a family of choice, a fellowship of like-minded people. Our bonds are more than convenience and tradition. We have chosen to be here because we want to be here. We have chosen to be here because we need to be here—because standing alone is never as inspiring as standing together.

SONG: HINNAY MA TOV (No. 47)

PHILOSOPHY

A strong community needs a strong purpose. It needs a focus of intention to mobilize its energies.

Our purpose is our philosophy. Our purpose is a unique set of ideas which we call humanistic Judaism. We do not have fixed beliefs, but we do have strong beliefs. We believe in the use of human reason. We believe in the necessity of human dignity. We believe in the value of Jewish identity. If we look at human problems, we also look for the human power to solve them. If we look at Jewish history, we also look for the human ingenuity that made it all possible.

The philosophy gives meaning to all the things we do together. It explains the words we say, the tributes we make, the projects we choose. It explains the literature we love, the songs we sing, the causes we embrace. It is our message and self-image, defining the essence of our community. Although it is a barrier to those who do not share our convictions, it is an open door to those who do.

Our philosophy is our integrity.

SONG: SAHAKEE (No. 78)

COMMITMENT

A strong community needs strong commitment. It needs the willingness to turn easy phrases into reality.

Commitment has very little to do with intention. It has everything to do with action. Communities work because their members make them work. They give their time, their talents, and their money. They give their energy, their enthusiasm, and their caring. If risky ventures have to be undertaken, they undertake them. If menial work has to be done, they do it. If compromises have to be endured, they endure them. They do not live off the labor of others. They choose to do what needs to be done.

Without commitment, life is dull. It suffers the boredom of too much watching and too little doing. It offers the guilt of promising but never completing. Intensity may sometimes exhaust us. It may sometimes fill our days with unbearable worry. But it is the sign of our vitality, our capacity to achieve what we want to achieve.

Believers alone did not make the community. Workers did.

SONG: EEM AYN (No. 28)

TRAINING

A strong community needs strong training. It needs the discipline of integrity.

Our philosophy praises certain ideals, but they are of no value if they only remain ideals, the pious preaching of the lazy. Praising reason is no substitute for being rational. Loving dignity is no replacement for having dignity. Affirming Jewish identity is no alternative to understanding it. Making the ideal real is more than an act of wishing. It is more than enthusiasm. It is self-discipline. It is pushing ourselves to be what we aspire to be.

A humanistic Jew is always in training. He strives to be more rational, more autonomous and more sensibly Jewish than he presently is. He does not expect to change by some miraculous intervention. He knows that his character will ultimately depend on his own sincerity and determination. There is so much to be studied. There is so much to be done. There are so many skills of character to be practiced.

Believers start communities. Trainers give them integrity.

SONG: HATOV O HARA (No. 41)

FRIENDSHIP

A strong community needs strong friendship. It needs the pleasure of mutual support.

Each of us is more than a philosophy, more than a message about life. Each of us is a person, a total being. We have needs and desires. We have hopes and fears. When we join groups, we need more than ideas. We need human connection and human support. We need listening and loving concern. We need to share both our laughter and our tears.

Friendship is the special plus of the good community. It warms our ideas and ideals with the power of mutual enjoyment. Our private thoughts make us lonely. They reflect our uniqueness and individuality. But friendship helps us reach out beyond ourselves to others. It helps us discover that others share our wants and desires, that others share our hopes and fears.

Communities need convictions. And convictions need friendship to make them human.

SONG: ZEMER LAKH (No. 104)

LEADERSHIP

A strong community needs strong leadership. It needs intelligent guidance.

Leadership is unavoidable. Communities need direction. They need planning. They need pushing. They need pulling things together. In working communities, even where no formal procedure is made to choose leaders, they will arise spontaneously. True leaders are willing to assume a special responsibility for the welfare of the group. They are willing to solve difficult problems and to make difficult decisions. They are willing to be role models of action to others and to mobilize the community by their own example. They are especially willing to represent what they say they believe in to the outside world.

Good leaders are not masters. Neither are they servants. They are generous guides. They have strong opinions, but not inflexible ones. They have integrity, but not self-righteousness. They never ask others to do what they are unwilling to do themselves. Preferring inspiration to dictation, they lead other people with the gentle power of respect and admiration.

Good leaders keep strong communities strong.

SONG: AYFO OREE (No. 14)

ROOTS

A strong community needs a strong sense of roots.

Our community has its own unique memories. They are part of our family history. They define our tradition. They give us depth. Without their support, we would always have to start from the beginning. Without their support, we could never build on the achievements of the past. Just as our dreams show us how far we have yet to go, our memories show us how far we have already climbed.

Our community family memories are years old. They point to many experiences, include many events and embrace many achievements. They especially involve many people. Some of these people were good leaders. Some of them were good workers. Most of them are still living. Some of them have died. All of them have made this celebration possible.

SONG: HAYAMEEM HOL'FEEM (No. 43)

WELCOME

It is important for us to stay young, to keep ourselves curious, creative, and full of adventure. We always need new faces, new people, new ideas, new enthusiasm. Otherwise we shall grow stale from the ritual of familiar action. We shall become too comfortable with our own success and too smug with our own achievement. Our old friendships become richer when we do not feed on them all the time, when we open our hearts to new ones. Our old convictions become more interesting when we do not repeat them to old audiences, when we have to explain them to new listeners. If we have something important to give to those who join us, we have even more to receive.

We welcome into our community all the men and women who have recently chosen to become part of our religious adventure. We need them as much as they may need us. We need the opportunity of their friendship. We need the freshness of their commitment. We need the power of their imagination. We need the work of their hands. As we recall on this anniversary day the symbols of our past, we know that they are the reality of our future. They make us feel alive and significant. They give us the pleasure of hope.

SONG: KEE V'SIMHA (No. 54)

5
COURAGE

SONG: SHALOM LARAHOK (No. 81)

COURAGE

Life is filled with danger. It lingers everywhere and will not go away.

There are so many things to fear: poverty and disease, storms and earthquakes, violence and war. They intrude on human history and cannot wait to return. Some people dream of utopia and imagine that some day there will be no fear. Other people speak of heaven and promise another place, in another world, where danger will vanish.

But worlds without danger are fantasies. Death is real. Pain persists. Hatred is as popular as love. To live life honestly, with no attempt to deny the darker side of its reality, is hard. To face the truth, with no effort to hide from the facts of human nature and human existence, is frightening. Yet what else is the life of courage? We cannot be brave if danger is an illusion.

Courage begins with honesty, the willingness to confront the world as it is and not merely as we want it to be.

SONG: MEE YITT'NAYNEE OF (No. 66)

FEAR

Some people are embarrassed by fear. They regard fear as a weakness, an emotion without dignity. They seek to dismiss it, to drive it out of their minds and their hearts. They strive to be fearless, to face danger without being afraid.

Some people are afraid of fear. Anxiety reminds them of all the perils in this world. It makes them notice all the harmful things which threaten their existence. They seek to run away from their fear, to pretend that it is not there. They hope that by denying its presence it will vanish and give them peace of mind.

But truly brave people are neither embarrassed by their fear nor are they afraid of it. If dangers are real, fear is normal and rational. If perils are authentic, being afraid is the first step we take to rescue ourselves. Brave men and women never lose their fear. They discipline it. They control its energy. They direct it to useful ends.

Courage is the power to make fear our servant and not our master.

SONG: OUT OF THE NIGHT (No. 76)

DEFIANCE

Resignation is a comfortable lifestyle. It makes decision making so easy. We simply accept what the fates deliver and praise them for what we have not requested. Surrendering to destiny makes us feel more secure, especially if we think the fates are angry.

Defiance is less comfortable. It is so abrasive. It is so insulting to the powers that be. It refuses to accept what is morally unacceptable. It refuses to praise what is undeserving of honor. Even if success seems unattainable, it persists in trying. It resists surrender.

Bravery is a style of living that wants more out of life than quiet survival and quiet death. It demands the dignity of self-esteem, the willingness to challenge when others conform, the power to hope when others are hopeless.

Courage is the determination to climb mountains even when the peak cannot be scaled.

SONG: ZOG NIT KAYNMOL (No. 105)

UNCERTAINTY

Many people need guarantees. They want to be sure that success is certain. When prophets speak of eternal promises, when wise teachers discuss the iron laws of history, when visionaries forecast the future that must be, they are reassured. They are prepared to take action.

Some people are bolder. They are wary of people who see what cannot really be seen. They are skeptical of experts who know what cannot really be known. Although others may need to believe that all will be well, they do not require false reassurance. They feel strong enough to live with uncertainty.

To live courageously is to live without guarantees, to make decisions without waiting for every fact, to take action without knowing all the consequences. Brave people do not need the illusions of absolute certainty. They will think before acting. But they will never think so much and so long that it is too late to act.

Courage is the refusal to wait for what will never come. It is the willingness to choose when it is time to choose.

SONG: AL HOMOTIEYIKH (No. 5)

GENEROSITY

Self-absorption comes easily to many of us. We have enough needs and desires to use most of our effort. Finding our own happiness is exhausting enough. We do not have the time or the will to worry about the happiness of others.

Yet for some of us, self-absorption is too safe and too petty to be significant. The energy of life demands that we reach out beyond ourselves to wider goals and broader needs. Living requires more openness, more grandeur, more nobility of purpose.

Brave people are willing to share. They are eager to reach out to others. They are able to give because the act of giving affirms their own power. Selfishness demeans them. It is a reminder of how easy it is for us to do nothing more than to please ourselves.

Courage is the adventure of going beyond our familiar world to serve the needs of others.

SONG: EEM AYN (No. 28)

INTEGRITY

When we are too eager for approval, we lose our courage. We say what other people want us to say. We do what other people want us to do. We become what other people want us to become.

Many men and women choose to wear the masks that public opinion fashions for them. They never tell others what they really believe; they never act out their private convictions; they never feel comfortable with controversy. They prefer to be safe, even if safety makes them the prisoners of convention.

Integrity is the courage to be one person instead of two—the bravery to let our private self mold our public image, the determination to be the master and not the victim of life—even though disapproval and anger may be the rewards of our honesty.

Courage is the search for respect, not agreement.

SONG: AYFO OREE (No. 14)

MEMORIAL

Danger gives meaning to life. It gives us problems. It puts us on the alert. It fills us with anxiety. A life without danger is more boring than death. If we are never afraid of losing anything, if we are always safe, if we are never threatened by challenge, then indeed we are in paradise—and paradise is bland.

Human purpose thrives on danger. When human survival and dignity are no longer safely guaranteed, they bring an intensity to living, a meaning to existence. Challenge gives us focus and direction. It mobilizes our energies. It releases our passions.

Courage is the partner of danger. We frighten ourselves with new demands and then strive all the harder to achieve them. If the goal is noble enough, even the threat of death will not deter us.

SONG: ZAYKHER (No. 103)

6
DESIRE

SONG: SHALOM L'YISRAEL (No. 82)

AMBIVALENCE

The world reflects the soul of any human being. Within its bounds it shelters both the chill of darkness and the warm promise of light. Within its heart it embraces the iciness of death and the fervent fire of life. Our universe is the pawn of contradiction. Destruction and dissolution display their terrifying might while the vitality of growing things struggles to assert itself. The war between life and death, light and darkness, is the drama of nature. Mother earth is the helpless victim of this unending battle where neither victory nor surrender find their place.

If the human psyche features the same eternal conflict, it breeds an act of imitation. We daily face the ruthless night within our own desire and grope for the tender light of our redemption.

SONG: BAROOKH HAOR (No. 20)

REALITY

Out of the long story of Israel emerges a bittersweet saga of suffering and joy. In the life of our people the taste of the world is sharp and vivid. Human wisdom has bestowed upon our passing years its finest moments. Human cruelty has also drained its lust upon the prostrate body of our dreams. The experience of love and security has been soured by the trauma of vinegar hate. The stench of agony rises from the pages of our martyrdom. We have seen the two faces of our universe: We have embraced the smile of pleasant destiny; we have cowered before the sneer of malicious fate.

Good and evil lie deep within the human soul. We have tasted the power of both. The songs of our people are melodies of laughter and tears. They seize our heart with the remembrance of pain and the hope of love.

SONG: V'RAK ANAKNOO (No. 94)

UNCONSCIOUS

Our personality is deeper than we imagine. Under the pleasant veneer of public conformity there lies the abyss of private desire. Desires and needs that shun exposure mingle with the passions that arouse our shame. To be aware of them is acutely discomforting. They seem to flay our self-respect and to stab our waking moments with a dagger of guilt. How we desire not to want what we so desperately wish for! The mental deep is a reservoir of danger. Desires of little respectability are flung from our frightened knowledge to hide in inaccessible places. From time to time they emerge with all their power to fill our being with a nameless terror. We are afraid and we cannot define our fear. We cry and we cannot describe our grief.

Each of us is a network of electric wants. Each of us is a well bottomless to the probe. Each of us is a fragile combination of good and evil. Society loves one side of our desire and cringes before the possibility of the other. But both parts are equally real and equally human. They cannot be denied. If the wonder of love is ours to give, sadistic cruelty is also our talent. If the warmth of compassion is ours to invoke, cold hate is no strange intruder. We cannot control what we do not recognize.

SONG: HAEMET YOTSAYT (No. 32)

CONFLICT

We choose life. We choose happiness. At least, we think we do. It seems so natural to assume that what we desire is the pursuit of life itself. If we blunder and make mistakes, if we harm ourselves and others, it is only because our ignorance keeps us from finding the best way to our destination. Happiness is such a normal goal that it is hard to imagine that we would want something else. The difference between virtue and vice seems to be in the weakness of our wisdom.

But the reality of our soul objects to this illusion. The love of life is only part of our being. Its pulse beats time with the rhythm of death. We sometimes want to die even though we cannot face the wanting. We sometimes want to hurt ourselves even though we cannot bear the hurt of knowing. To pursue death is absurd. Yet human behavior is the prisoner of this contradiction. Two mighty forces pervade our desire and strive to pull us in opposite ways. Two mighty powers confront each other within our soul and battle for victory. The enemy of life is not only unenlightened thinking but also the grim energy of death.

COMMUNITY

Good or evil. That is the question.
That is the problem. The decision is ours.

SONG: HATOV O HARA (No. 41)

SELF-DESTRUCTION

Our mistakes are often not mistakes at all. They are the rational pursuit of desires that our sanity rejects. When we blunder we are sometimes more dangerous to ourselves than we dare admit. We soothe our troubled guilt with easy confessions of dullness and inadequacy. We reproach ourselves with the conventional charges of stupidity and lethargy. But deep within we know that the crime is not always incompetence. The sin is, rather, a well-developed skill for succeeding at failure. How we love to destroy ourselves, and how wonderfully well we do it! The trouble is that we are much too clever at self-extinction. How to live is less the challenge than wanting to live. Our tragedy does not lie in the continuing cruelty of people to people, but in the infinite capacity of people to be cruel to themselves. We love death too fervently and delight in the joys of suffering. How easily we maneuver ourselves into trouble and revel in the martyrdom of having it. The pleasure of pain and the pain of pleasure define our destruction. Our will to live stands as a lonely hero against the assaults of our inner enemies.

COMMUNITY

Who are the strong?
People who subdue their evil desire.
People who subdue their anger's fire.
They are strong.

Desire 45

SONG: AYZE HOO GIBBOR (No. 18)

CHOICE

History is not only the tale of our experience in the outer world. It is also a reflection of the war within. Human nature stages a battle of formidable opponents and summons each of us to choose his side. Will we embrace the failure of death? Or will we seize the standard of life? Only our personal decision will resolve this controversy of purposes. To choose happiness is to defy death and to mock the cowardice of feeble suicide. Our talents offer us the promise of the good life. We must be neither afraid nor ashamed to pursue this fate.

SONG: AYFO OREE (No. 14)

MEMORIAL

The heroes of our Jewish past were men and women of flesh and blood who did not hesitate to be human in every way. Jacob practiced the art of deception. David succumbed to the call of illegal passion. Moses was consumed by the fire of his anger. Jeremiah longed for vengeance. The pages of our history are filled with the stories of heroes who were more than saints. They went beyond mere virtue to embrace the fullness of life.

Even the parents and friends whom we admired and honored were more than whitewashed respectability. The fire of life burned within their spirit. They knew the breadth of the human heart. Because they understood the power of their passions, they responded to others with a special grace. Love arises from experiencing in others what we feel within ourselves. We are bound together by mutual need.

SONG: SHEEM'OO (No. 83)

7
DIGNITY

SONG: SHALOM L'YISRAEL (No. 82)

PURPOSE

What is the purpose of life? What is the goal of moral behavior?

Some people believe that the purpose of life is obedience to God. Since obedience can never be an end in itself, the pleasures of the afterlife are offered as ultimate rewards. But what if the routine of paradise seems less than pleasurable? What if the fear of punishment seems an undignified motivation? What if a divine dictatorship seems an affront to human dignity?

Other people believe that the purpose of life is human survival. The preservation of our individual existence takes on a sacred character. But is mere survival a worthy goal? Is the quantity of life more important than its quality? Are there no circumstances when it is appropriate to risk death?

Still others maintain that the purpose of life is human happiness. Striving for pleasure and contentment becomes a compelling virtue. Yet is the life of pleasure satisfying enough? Are all pleasures of equal value? Is there no time when pain and suffering are appropriate options?

We humanists believe that the purpose of life is human dignity. Enabling people to become the masters of their own lives and to respect this potential in others is the moral enterprise. Where human dignity is at stake, it is appropriate to defy tradition, it is ethical to risk death, it is moral to choose painful challenge.

SONG: SAHAKEE (No. 78)

AUTONOMY

Human dignity means human autonomy.

Human autonomy begins with the individual. It begins with personal self-esteem. All of us have the right to be the master of our fate. All of us have the power to be the captains of our souls.

Human autonomy begins with equality. We are not servants. We are not the slaves of any master. We are not naïve children too dumb to understand the purpose of rules and regulations. We are not fearful defectives, grateful for the protection of strong leaders who would impose their will upon us.

If we have dignity, we do not refuse our own power. We do not cringe before unreasonable authority. We do not praise unkind fates. We assume the responsibility for our own actions. We fashion new rules to meet new needs. We choose to confront reality with courage.

SONG: OUT OF THE NIGHT (No. 76)

FREEDOM

Human dignity means freedom.

Freedom begins with choice. It begins with the anxiety of human decisions. Even though we are part of the animal kingdom, even though we are the product of a long evolutionary history, even though our genes determine our behavior, we possess a liberty that other living creatures do not possess. We do not have unlimited options, but we have enough to give us self-awareness and to make us the judges of our own behavior.

Freedom begins with honesty. It begins with a realistic admission of our differences. We are not automatons. We are not condemned to give the same response to the same provocation. We are not the prisoners of relentless programming. We are the owners of a liberty we often seek to deny.

If we have dignity, we do not refuse our own freedom. We do not confuse our fear with necessity. We do not blame others for our cowardice. We face up to our options. We discipline our fear. We cultivate our bravery.

SONG: HATOV O HARA (No. 41)

48   *Dignity*

COMPETENCE

Human dignity means competence.

Competence begins with reason and with respect for the truth. Every day brings us new experience. Every day brings us new facts. Old beliefs sometimes need to be changed. Old skills sometimes need to be improved.

Competence begins with knowledge. It begins with the ability to understand ourselves and to understand the world we live in. Faith is never enough. Repeating the answers of the past is never adequate. We need to be flexible enough to learn.

If we have dignity, we do not run away from the truth. We do not turn the world into a reflection of our fantasies. We do not plead our intentions when our deeds fail. We strive for knowledge. We weigh our beliefs on the scales of evidence. We train ourselves to turn desires into deeds.

SONG: AYZE HOO GIBBOR (No. 18)

RESPECT

Human dignity means respect.

Respect begins with empathy. It begins with a sense of our common struggle. Each one of us is unique, and yet we are all human. We have so many things in common: We share our form, our basic needs, our fundamental desires; we share our fears, our hopes, our dependency on others.

Respect begins with generosity. It begins with our willingness to give to others what we insist they give to us. If we wish to be the masters of our own lives, we cannot teach others to be servants, for we know that their self-esteem reinforces our own.

If we have dignity, we do not deny the dignity of others. We do not elevate ourselves by lowering the self-worth of our friends and neighbors. We are not afraid of sharing power. We help others to become human in the way we wish to be human. We prefer competent equals to cowering servants. We take pride in the strength of every person.

SONG: HINNAY MA TOV (No. 47)

HOPE

Human dignity means hope.

Hope begins with determination. It begins with a refusal to surrender to the assaults of destiny. Nature is sometimes a good friend: it gives us youth, strength, and pleasure. It is also a clever enemy. It persists in the creation of aging, disease, and undeserved disaster. Despair is easy if we indulge it.

Hope begins with imagination. It begins with the ability to notice alternatives. Opportunities are useless if they are never seen. Options are empty if we never look for them. Despair thrives on narrow vision.

If we have dignity, we do not dwell on the shady side of nature. We do not rush to resignation. We take no pleasure in defeat. We remember our strength. We allow our sense of humor to tease our imagination. We know that there are many kinds of victory.

SONG: AYFO OREE (No. 14)

MEMORIAL

Dignity is the monopoly of no single people. The pages of Jewish history, like the pages of the histories of many peoples, record the stories of many men and women who led lives of self-esteem and who are messages of dignity from the past to the present.

The prophets risked death to proclaim their warnings. The Maccabees dared rebellion even when there was no prospect of victory. The resistance heroes, during the time of the Holocaust, offered their defiance in the face of certain destruction. The Zionist pioneers acted on their dream when the world believed it only to be a dream.

In our personal lives, there have also been people from our past who taught us the lesson of dignity. We honor them as we honor all the heroes of self-esteem.

SONG: SHEEM'OO (No. 83)

8
EMOTION

SONG: V'SHOOV ITKHEM (No. 95)

FEELINGS

Feelings make life worthwhile. Without needs and desires, there would be no purpose to living, no goals to strive for. Without needs and desires, there would be no meaning to existence, no passion to inspire us.

Feelings make the world a treasure house of opportunity. There are so many things we want to touch. There are so many experiences we want to have. There are so many people we want to be near.

Feelings also make the world a place of danger and dread. There are so many things we want to avoid. There are so many experiences we want to push away. There are so many perils we want to escape from.

Attraction and avoidance, running to and running away, attachment and separation—these are the recurring themes of human existence. They fill our lives with ecstasy and despair. They infuse our spirit and make us human.

SONG: ZEMER LAKH (No. 104)

POSITIVE AND NEGATIVE

No feeling is all good or all bad. Every emotion we have started out as a strategy for survival. It drew us near to what was good for us or made us move away from what was bad for us.

Emotion 51

When anger emerged, it defended our territory; it protected our family; it drove out intruders. When love began, it nurtured our children; it fed the helpless; it guarded the young. When sadness appeared, it made us slow down; it gave us time to think; it allowed healing to take place. When joy exploded, it mobilized our energies; it announced our strength; it reinforced our bond with others.

When we are defending our dignity, anger may be necessary. When we are building a community, love is essential. When we are faced with defeat, sadness is appropriate. When we are planning our future, joy is our friend.

There is a time and place for every feeling. Angry sadists do not understand. Loving masochists do not comprehend. But healthy people do.

SONG: AYIT (No. 15)

SELF-AWARENESS

Most of us believe that it is easy to know what we feel. We only have to look inside our minds and hearts and discover what is there. If we are honest, if we are sincere, self-awareness is a simple matter.

But love and hate, anger and jealousy, may be more secretive than we would prefer. Our minds are so complex that feelings wear disguises and often appear to be what they are not. Emotions can make us uncomfortable. They can tease us and embarrass us. They can taunt us and fill us with shame. We sometimes turn our backs on them and pretend that they are not there. We sometimes look at them and do not see them. Sincerity is not enough—especially if we are not strong enough to face reality.

Self-awareness needs strength. We need to be strong enough to feel what we do not want to feel. We need to be strong enough to experience what we do not want to experience. We need to be strong enough to remove the masks that shield us from the face of our own desires.

SONG: LAM'TSAPPEEM (No. 56)

AMBIVALENCE

It would be nice if all our feelings got along with each other. It would be so nice if they were friendly to one another, if they worked together to create an internal harmony of mind and heart.

But our emotions are less cooperative than we would prefer. They rub up against each other abrasively. They compete with each other. They fight to seize the energy of our will. Oftentimes we confront the problems of the moment with two opposing feelings. We love and we hate. We want to embrace and we want to reject. We want to reach out and we want to run back. Our emotions pull us in two different directions and make it hard to make decisions. Ambivalence becomes the soul of the human condition.

Being faithful to our feelings is not easy, especially if our feelings give us no clear instruction. Many people are comfortable with this limbo of indecision. They find ambivalence charming. But others find no virtue in waiting. They know that they must master their emotions and choose the direction of their life.

SONG: OUT OF THE NIGHT (No. 76)

BELONGING

When we are born, when we are separated from the womb, we experience a sense of aloneness that never leaves us. As we grow up, as we become more and more aware of our own uniqueness, this feeling of apartness grows stronger and fills our hearts with a need for connecting.

There are many ways to connect. There are many paths to belonging. Men and women find each other and love each other and choose the commitment of marriage. Strangers meet strangers and discover that they can be good friends. Parents have children and nurture them with tender care. Clans and tribes, nations and peoples, embrace their members and give them the security of identity and roots.

Belonging is an experience of transcendence, an experience of being part of something greater than oneself. It starts with the human bonds of family and reaches out to wider horizons. There are times when we feel connected to all the people of the world. There are times when we feel we belong to the universe itself—to the evolutionary drama of life, to the very stars and beyond.

SONG: HINNAY MA TOV (No. 47)

SPIRIT

Some people go through life very carefully. They are afraid of their feelings, afraid of being swept away. They fear all intensity. Caution becomes their byword. Security becomes their dream.

But there are others who are ashamed to be timid. They know that life must be an adventure, that for each of us it happens once and must never be wasted. Boldness and courage discipline their fear. Curiosity and ambition fuel their passion. No tradition can hold them prisoner. No convention can restrain their creative power. They do not seek danger, but they will not avoid it if the moment demands it.

The human spirit is no disembodied soul. It is no quiet and demure thing that finds its home in heavenly bliss. It is the flame of our passions, the fire of our will, the intensity of our commitment to life. When it speaks, it speaks through our striving. It speaks through our deeds. It announces our vision for a better world.

SONG: HAVA NAGEELA (No. 42)

REASON

For many people, reason has a bad reputation. They see it as the subverter of life, the enemy of passion, the foe of feeling. In their eyes, rational people are cold, austere, and distant. Only the devotees of faith and intuition know what to do with their emotions.

But this vision of reason is a dangerous distortion. It sets up straw men only to tear them down. Feelings need reason to make life worthwhile. They need the discipline of common sense to guarantee our survival and dignity. Emotions are like children. They want what they want right away. They want what they want regardless of consequences. Love and anger are blind. They cannot see the future. They cannot even see each other. Sometimes their fires are not the fires of life. They are the fires of death and destruction.

Reason is not a withdrawn logician. It is a concerned parent. It is the defender of our happiness, the protector of our fulfillment. It disciplines our fear. It manages our anger. It restrains our jealousy. It directs our love to wholesome ends.

SONG: SAHAKEE (No. 78)

JEWISHNESS

To be a Jew is to feel many feelings. We feel the security of roots, the pleasure of belonging, the pride of achievement, the warmth of solidarity, the joy of survival. But we also feel the fear of rejection, the anger of victims, the sadness of separation, the loneliness of difference, and the bitterness of remembered wrongs.

Our experience has been no ordinary experience. Our history has been no commonplace adventure. We have been visited by the best and assaulted by the worst that the world can offer. We have achieved the peaks and sunk to the depths of human possibility. Our presence does not arouse indifference. If we have enemies, their hatred is no ordinary hatred. If we have friends, their attachment is no ordinary connection. We have lived too hard and too long to settle for the tamer emotions.

When we sing, our songs have pain and pleasure. When we laugh, our laughter has surrender and defiance. When we hope, our hope has fear and determination.

SONG: HATIKVA (No. 40)

9
EQUALITY

SONG: HAYVAYNOO SHALOM ALAYKHEM (No. 44)

IDEALISM

Equality is a human ideal. It is a humanist ideal and humanistic Jewish ideal.

But what does it mean?

Inequality seems to be so much more natural than equality. Talents are unequal. Intelligence is unequal. Strength is unequal. People are different in so many ways, not only in kind but in degree.

There are many levels of competence. There are superior leaders and mediocre ones. There are inspiring teachers and boring ones. There are exciting performers and dull ones. Some people are quite obviously better than others no matter what they choose to do.

Yet we speak of equality as though it were possible.

And indeed it is.

SONG: HINNAY MA TOV (No. 47)

AUTONOMY

Equality is autonomy. It means freedom for all people to be in charge of their lives.

56   Equality

For most of human history, people were treated as children even when they were adults. Kings, priests, and warrior lords intimidated them not only physically but also mentally. Since authority always came from the top, the masses at the bottom had only one choice—to do what they were told to do. Since the will of God was more important than the will of man, the custodians of God's word chose to command and not to advise. Peasants and workers, women and serfs, saw themselves as rightful subjects of their masters. Freedom meant only one thing—the freedom to obey.

Autonomy rebels against this ancient conformity. It defies this old intimidation. Each of us has the right to choose the people who govern us. Authority comes from the bottom and works its way to the top. Rulers are the servants of the people, not their masters. Women and men, the beautiful and the ugly, the smart and the dumb, the rich and the poor, the talented and the untalented, all are equal in their right to personal freedom.

In human history autonomy is a new idea.

SONG: OUT OF THE NIGHT (No. 76)

INDIVIDUALITY

Equality is individuality. It is the recognition that each of us is unique and, in some special way, incomparable.

Since we live in a world of labels, we tend to think that people are no more than their labels. We tend to imagine that each of us is no more than a collection of familiar measurements. In a world where most of us are strangers to each other we find it necessary to introduce ourselves through impersonal ways. Resumés and transcripts, charts and tests, become our personal portraits. They are designed for a world of competition where comparison is unavoidable.

Individuality is an affirmation of our uniqueness. It is an awareness that each of us can never be fully identical to anyone else. We are more than resumés and transcripts. We are more than charts and tests. Our personalities are too rich and too complex for rough measurements to encompass. In the end, each of us is special even when others make us feel ordinary.

In each personal specialness, no one is superior.

SONG: BAMAKOM (No. 19)

DIGNITY

Equality is dignity. It is the willingness to be responsible for our own behavior.

Many of us love autonomy. We love being in charge of our actions. But we do not enjoy being responsible for them. When it comes to decision making, we insist on being adults. But when it comes to blame-taking, we insist on being children. We want equality only when it is convenient.

Dignity is our demand that we be treated as adults all the time, even when it is inconvenient and even when it is painful. We do not avoid our responsibility. We do not seek the safety of childhood when mistakes happen. We do not run away from the truth when the verdict is "guilty." We refuse to play hide-and-seek with equality. In the face of praise or denunciation, we cling to our dignity.

In a world where success is never guaranteed, we have to work hard to preserve our dignity.

SONG: HATOV O HARA (No. 41)

OPPORTUNITY

Equality is opportunity. It provides that fighting chance to succeed.

The tragedy of human history is wasted talent. The privilege of birth, race, sex, and money has often rewarded the wrong people. The nasty and the mediocre receive the opportunity to develop talents. The loving and the skillful never get a chance to become what they could become. The starting lines are too far apart. Some good runners have to run too far to win.

Opportunity is the chance to win. It is fair competition. Smart people should not be penalized because they are women. Strong people should not be ignored because they are black. Exciting people should not be hidden because they are poor. Useful people should not be wasted because no one knows their origin. Some will write. Others will read. Some will be famous. Others will be unknown. That difference is unavoidable. But letting the best win is no more than fairness.

If we believe in equality, we bring the starting lines closer together.

SONG: LAM'TSAPPEEM (No. 56)

MODESTY

Equality is modesty. It is the good sense not to assault others with our success—or our luck.

Some people love to arouse envy. They love to flaunt their wealth. They cannot wait to exhibit their brilliance. They adore dressing up in the symbols of power. Invidious comparison is what they thrive on. They delight in making other people feel like failures.

Modesty is a sensitivity to the feelings of those who may not be as lucky as we are. Nature may distribute her gifts unevenly, but we do not have to dwell on this reality. The rich do not have to behave like princes. Leaders do not have to parade like kings. The wise do not have to disparage those who are less wise. Because our world is getting smaller there is no place for haughty independence. We depend on each other's good will.

Modesty is understatement. In a world of human pride, it is an act of kindness.

SONG: AYFO OREE (No. 14)

MEMORIAL

Equality is giving the past its due.

In a world of continuous change, in a world that believes in progress, the present always seems superior to the past. We tend to patronize the people who came before. We tend to see them as the victims of their own, more primitive times. If we praise them, we do so with the understanding that they will never know as much as we do. Sometimes we feel guilty about this condescension and we praise them for virtues which they never had and which we do not want.

But the people of the past are our equals. While the human race evolves, it evolves very slowly. Our ancestors were like us. Their senses are our senses. Their feelings are our feelings. Their fears are our fears—especially the fear of death. If change has made some of their conclusions obsolete, it will do the same to our own.

Since it is not superior, the past does not deserve our reverence. But, as our equal, it deserves our respect.

SONG: SHEEM'OO (No. 83)

10
ETHICS

SONG: HINNAY MA TOV (No. 47)

MORALITY

If the world were exactly the way we wanted it to be, there would be no ethics. Morality is born of the tension between what is and what ought to be. Values arise because we can perceive something better than that which already exists.

As human beings, our power to change the universe is very limited. We cannot abolish the law of gravity. We cannot reverse the course of the earth around the sun. We cannot rescue a dying star. Most of nature is indifferent to our evaluations. It simply does what it does, whether we like it or not.

A practical ethics does not concern itself with what we do not control. It focuses on what we do control, on what we have the power to change. It directs its attention to our social behavior, to our human relations. In the perspective of the universe, the deeds of men and women on this little planet may seem very insignificant. But, in our eyes, they are all-important. They define the agony of human decision.

SONG: HATOV O HARA (No. 41)

CONSEQUENCES

Right and *wrong* are familiar words. We use them all the time to praise and condemn. They are the everyday vocabulary of our moral commitment.

For many people the standard of *right* and *wrong* is to be found in tradition, in the voice of the past: The commands of their parents, the decisions of their ancestors, the decrees of their God are the sources of true morality. As dutiful children, they believe that they have the obligation to listen to the dictates of the past and to obey it. Nothing in the present can equal the wisdom and authority of long ago.

But for we who are uncomfortable with naïve faith, the test of *right* and *wrong* is to be found in the present, in what we can directly observe. No old authority, however famous, can make a commandment ethical. No revered prophet, however sainted, can make a law moral. No god, however powerful, can issue rules that we must obey.

In the end, *right* behavior produces good consequences that we can see. *Wrong* behavior has bad results that we can observe. The demands of the past must always yield to the facts of the present.

SONG: MAASEEM TOVEEM (No. 61)

HUMANISM

Throughout human history, in many places, the wishes of the dead have been more important than the needs of the living. People are required to fit themselves to the laws of tradition, but the laws of tradition are not required to adapt themselves to people. Rules and regulations become all-important while the desires and aspirations of human beings take second place.

If we are humanists, if we are committed to the significance of human striving, this kind of thinking is unacceptable. The purpose of life is not to obey arbitrary commandments. The purpose of life is to satisfy our basic human needs.

As human beings we strive for many things. We struggle for survival. We yearn for pleasure. We need the dignity of strength and self-reliance. These needs and desires define our human nature and give a sense of urgency to daily living.

The meaning of life does not fall from heaven. It arises from the heart of the human spirit. In the humanist perspective, morality is not embarrassed by human happiness here on earth. Indeed, it seeks to achieve it.

SONG: SAHAKEE (No. 78)

DIGNITY

If all human needs were compatible, one with the other, making ethical decisions would be easy. But our wants and desires are often abrasive. They challenge each other. Sometimes we cannot satisfy one need without sacrificing its opponent.

If we pursue too much pleasure, we risk our survival. If we are too concerned about our safety and security, we risk our dignity. Life is a series of hard choices. We cannot have everything we want and need. We cannot have our cake and eat it too!

An intelligent morality gives us a priority list. It tells us what to choose when choosing is necessary. It may value pleasure. But it may value personal survival more. It may value safety and security. But it may see them as less important than human dignity, less important than the power to be free, independent, and generous.

Humanist heroes prefer their dignity above all. But they are fully aware of the price they have to pay for it.

SONG: EEM AYN (No. 28)

RULES

No society can live without rules and regulations. Laws make the world predictable and manageable. Chaos is the mother of terror.

But intelligent rules are never absolute. They never insist on their own way, regardless of consequences. They know that they are only guides to behavior, imperfect summaries of past experience and old wisdom. No commandment is so infallible that it produces good results in every situation. Every useful rule has its exceptions.

Insensitive people insist on applying rules no matter what. If they tell the truth, they tell the dying that there is no hope. If they are full of love, they love the people who abuse and harm them. If they do not kill, they offer no resistance to those who are planning to kill them.

Sensitive people follow the rules most of the time. But they do not allow the good advice of the past to blind them to the consequences of the present. They insist on human dignity.

SONG: AL SH'LOSHA D'VAREEM II (No. 8)

RESPONSIBILITY

Ethics is possible only if human beings are free enough to take the blame. If what we choose to do is only the result of causes and events over which we have no control, then asking us to change what we cannot freely change is a waste of time. Our behavior cannot be wrong if we do not have the power to make it right.

Many people live with excuses. They always see themselves as innocent and blameless, no matter what they do. They always view themselves as victims of circumstances, pawns of fate and fortune. Genetic inheritance, childhood environment, social intimidation, and unfair rewards relieve them of any responsibility for their actions. Others have made them what they are. Others should take the blame.

An ethics of dignity resists this self-pity. While it accepts the power of the past, it does not deny the freedom of the present. We always have options. We always have the option of not doing what we know to be wrong. If we are people of dignity, we refuse the excuse of helplessness. We know that, in the end, we consent to whatever we choose to do.

SONG: AYFO OREE (No. 14)

MEMORIAL

Some people can never learn from the past. Because they worship it they cannot see it as it really was. The facts are less important than the fantasy they need. In their imaginary world, ancestors become saints, leaders become gods, and good books turn into sacred literature. Since the people of the past seem more than human, they remain distant ideals to admire but never to understand.

Yet learning from the past is so important. It is important to remember what worked and what did not work, what actions promoted human dignity and what actions took it away. The people of the past were, in many ways, just like us. They had our needs and desires. They had our fears and anxieties. They were the authors of our best excuses. If they are important to us, it is because they too were human and because their struggle for fulfillment was our struggle too.

SONG: SHEEM'OO (No. 83)

11
FAMILY

SONG: MA TOVOO (No. 64)

NATURE

The sun burns. The earth turns. Time moves. A lonely planet floats in space. On its surface travels the chemical wonder of life. Some imagine that life is a unique accident, present nowhere else in the universe.

Others see it as a common thing, replicated among all the stars and distant galaxies out of our world.

Life is a marvel. Within all its forms there move little compulsive units, obsessed with the need to duplicate themselves. Despite their size, they are relentless. They are determined to reproduce, to repeat themselves endlessly in time. As long as nature allows, they will pursue their task. No argument can reach them. They are driven by their own inner mechanism.

The nature of life is repetition. The basic forms seek immortality and cannot stop their game. Evolution may create more complex shapes, more intimate associations of all these forms. Evolution may invent bigger, more vulnerable beings, vast collections of all these little parts. But, in the end, they will prevail. Like persistent individuals they may give up their cell. They will never surrender their being.

We, as living creatures, as the children of nature's evolution, are not single beings. We are the marriage of countless vital units, each seeking eternal life. We often see them as the servants of our will, obedient to our intention. But, indeed, we are often the unknowing instruments of their will, driven to guarantee their survival.

SONG: EEM AYN (No. 28)

64   Family

EVOLUTION

The past lives in our present. Each of our genes is much older than we are. Each has traveled through thousands of years, dozens of places and countless biographies. Genes are bossy things, controlling our shape and behavior while arrogantly doing the same for other members of our family. Parents look into the faces of their children and see themselves. Brothers and sisters watch each other and discover that they are more alike than they would prefer.

Just as our bodies are communities of cooperating cells, so are we, as individuals, part of societies greater than ourselves. We are all bound together by mutual dependence and shared roots.

The evolution of life is reflected in the evolutionary story of each of us. We begin as single cells and travel through embryo time as fishy forms and reptile shapes. Our human style emerges last and tends to hide what we were before. But our behavior betrays our connection. Desires and drives that reason finds uncomfortable display themselves shamelessly or lurk in the shadows of our fears and dreams. Attachments that therapeutic planners find annoying refuse to go away and complicate our lives by their persistence. Mother and father, sister and brother, are more than social conveniences. They are actors in a drama that began many millions of years ago. We are part of that play too.

SONG: KAMIEYEEM (No. 51)

CHILDHOOD

Childhood is a powerful time. We never transcend it. If it is good, we will never lose its benefits. If it is bad, we will never recover from its traumas.

The problem is our brain. It is too big for the womb it grows in. We emerge too soon, helpless blobs of infancy, totally dependent on our mother and father. It takes so long to become independent that we never really do. We spend so much time being children that we never cease to be, even when we no longer need to be. There is a part of us that adores infancy, craves parents, and prefers play to work. There is a part of us that never forgets the love we received as children, never dismisses the hurt inflicted by those we needed.

We both receive and give. As children we are connected to our parents with a bond that neither space nor time can sever. We are their creations. As parents we are joined to our children by a double need—their need and our need. They need our care and recognition. We need to give care and to offer recognition.

Nurturing is a human necessity. It is also a human satisfaction. We like to do what we need to do. Loving children is no arbitrary imposition. It is a creative act, a source of fulfillment. The little genes of our immortality make mutual friends out of survival and pleasure.

SONG: HINNAY MA TOV (No. 47)

LEARNING

Parents start out as children. Children become parents. They are familiar roles. We often play them both at the same time. The family is a human drama, with special parts for all its members. The historic script is clear: The parent is strong, decisive, and loving. The child is deferent, obedient, and respectful. New variations on this drama abound. Some parents are less demanding, less decisive, and more open. Some children are more assertive, less obedient, and more independent. But successful families never reverse the roles. When parents insist on being children and when children choose to be parents, the play collapses.

In all groups designed for survival and mutual support we need to know the role we play. Good parents never abdicate their responsibility. They never hide behind democratic clichés to avoid making decisions. They never deny the value of their wisdom and experience. They never confuse guidance with agreement. They never indulge the fear of failure, nor reward selfishness. Good parents know that they need to be stronger than their children.

Sensitive children never reject their responsibility either. They never assume that strength comes without training. They never imagine that the past has no advice to offer their future. They never reject useful work and necessary skills. Sensitive children know that growing up is a process, not a gift. Good parents need sensitive children. Sensitive children need good parents.

SONG: MAASEEM TOVEEM (No. 61)

ALTRUISM

Selfishness is not the rule of life. If individual plants and animals lived for themselves alone, all life would perish. The individual gene seeks to preserve its form, not its body. The individual cell quietly dies for the sake of the rest. In the realm of higher beasts, the privileges of the young transcend the rights of the old. Parents risk their lives to feed their offspring. Leaders confront certain death to defend their troops. Nature thrives on sacrifice. The old yield to the new. The strong yield to the weak. The creator dies for his creation. To the cry of familiars, we have always responded with love.

Generosity among intimates is never an effort. It is eminently human and flows gracefully from our very nature. Meanness requires self-discipline and arises from living in a world of strangers. When we are natural, parents seek to help their children. Children seek to help their parents. In quiet times, this generosity overflows and creates the bond of community. The danger lies in the possibility of reversal. Our city world of strangers aggravates our meanness and encourages it to move into the realm of the family. We begin to relate to familiars in the same way we relate to strangers. We exalt ruthlessness and make it seem natural. But the truth remains. We are here today because others reached out beyond their own survival to guarantee ours.

CONGREGATION

Listen now, you lovers of love.
Hear this, you seekers of happiness.
There is no happiness without love.

SONG: SHEEM'OO (No. 83)

FRIENDSHIP

There are two families to which we belong. The family of inheritance is the family of mother and father, sister and brother, daughter and son. They mold our childhood and echo our evolutionary past. The family of choice is the family of friends. They are the comfort of our adult years and reflect the needs of our present. The two families do not include each other. Parents and children, brothers and sisters, can become our friends, just as friends can become our first allegiance. Where the family of inheritance may be only the beginning chapter of our life story, the family of friends takes on new power.

If we are good friends, we are as loyal to those whom we love as if they were our own flesh. We enjoy their health and prosperity. We help them in their sickness and poverty. We thrive on their pleasure. We suffer from their pain. We need them as they need us. We give each other gifts of care and recognition.

If we want good friends, we demand the same behavior of ourselves as we do of them. The family of choice is not as old as the family of inheritance. It is very fragile. It needs constant tending. To preserve friendship requires a special effort of will. Friends are our equals, not our parents or our children. We cannot assign them inappropriate roles and then condemn them for their failure. The skill of equality is a new behavior we have to learn. In friendship we can be neither patrons nor infants. We must see our own dignity reflected in the dignity of those we choose to love.

SONG: AYFO OREE (No. 14)

MEMORIAL

Families are more than those who live in the present. They extend back into the past to encompass thousands. Some of these people we remember with the vividness of personal experience. They are imprinted on the powerful memories of our childhood. Others we know through written records and old photographs. They are dimmer figures our imagination plays with. Still others are but names on a list, rumors in a memory. They provide the fragrance of roots and a sense of immortality.

We remember them gratefully because families do not abruptly begin and abruptly end. They flow through time, merging and expanding and contracting. Although our ancestors are shadowy persons we either romanticize or ignore, their sense of community is a clear and warm emotion we share with them. They viewed their forebears with the special awe that generosity breeds. We see them with an equal reverence. In time, our descendants will extend to us an equal tribute.

SONG: ZAYKHER (No. 103)

12
FEMINISM

SONG: HINNAY MA TOV (No. 47)

RESISTANCE

The struggle for human dignity is not easy. Many people who have achieved their own dignity do not wish to share it with others. And many people who have been denied their self-esteem do not imagine that they are entitled to more than destiny has given them. It is convenient for oppressors to persuade themselves that they are worthy of special privilege—and to persuade the oppressed that they deserve subjection.

Throughout the centuries of human history, many groups have been deprived of their dignity. Jews, blacks, and religious dissenters suffered humiliation and insult from the cruelty of self-righteous masters. But their worst degradation was their own passive acceptance of what they experienced. They came to believe in the justice of their own suffering.

Women, especially, were persuaded to accept the rule of men. Religion and politics conspired to keep them weak in both body and mind. The greatest asset of male domination was the consent of women themselves.

Feminism is the refusal to give that consent anymore. It is the awakening of women to the reality of their own power and to the justice of asserting their own dignity.

SONG: HANAAVA (No. 36)

DIGNITY

Female dignity is not different from male dignity. Dignity is the right of all people to be the masters of their own lives and the servants of no one. It is the right of all individuals to choose their unique lifestyles and to aspire to whatever honors their talents allow. No single script fits all men. No single script fits all women.

If we have dignity, we recognize our uniqueness. Before we are men, before we are women, we are humans of power and potential. Our role in the drama of life cannot be justly determined by the biology of sex alone. It needs to be fashioned by our own free will and desire. It needs to be modeled by our own awareness of what we can do well.

Feminism is the refusal to be treated as a sexual label. It is the insistence that, first and above all, we be regarded as persons and individuals.

SONG: SAHAKEE (No. 78)

EQUALITY

Every society has leaders. In a complex world of planning and cooperation, leaders are unavoidable. For most of human history, in most places, all leaders were men. All women were given the task of following and obeying. Many male leaders were incompetent. Many women followers would have made extraordinary leaders. But social convention was too powerful to allow talent to prevail.

A just society gives leadership to people who can lead. It does not confuse strength with brawn and violence. It does not imagine that women can only be what men have trained them to be. Where blacks are more competent than whites, they should lead. Where Jews are stronger than Gentiles, they should lead. Where women are more able than men, they should lead.

Feminism is a plea for good rulers. It prefers facts to stereotypes. It prefers talent to labels.

SONG: LAM'TSAPPEEM (No. 56)

UNIQUENESS

Denying reality is a waste of time. Denying facts is a useless exercise. In the end we must come to terms with what we cannot easily change.

Some people have responded to the silliness of the past with an equal silliness. If the past overemphasized the differences between men and women, they deny that there are any. If the past exaggerated the power of biology, they ignore biology. If the past underestimated the importance of environment, they make it all-important. They became partners in extremism—mirror images on the opposite side.

Biology is real. No anger or resentment can make it disappear. No political slogans can hide it. There *are* differences between men and women. Men do not bear children. Men create war. Men respond to stress more harmfully than women. Sexual differences are part of the story of evolution, and evolution is millions of years old.

A true feminism is not foolish. It does not negate what women do naturally. It simply adds many more options.

SONG: MEE HAHAM (No. 65)

NEW MAN

Feminism is not only the liberation of women. It is also the liberation of men. When women are free from the tyranny of old customs, so will men be.

The old society imprisoned men too. It confined them to a single style and to a single script. If men were not fierce, warlike, protective, and controlled, others saw them as less than men. If they were gentle, emotional, and aesthetic, others condemned them for being like women. The options for men were as limited as the choices for women.

Dignity for women also means dignity for men. When women are free to be leaders, men will be free to be followers. When women are free to be scientists, men will be free to be artists. When women are free to be assertive, men will be free to be gentle.

If women find their liberty, so will men.

SONG: BASHANA HABAA (No. 21)

OPTIONS

The future of women will be more interesting than their past. The world has awakened to the power of the female potential. The past has cruelly wasted some of its greatest human resources. The future will be wiser and more considerate.

Women will continue to be wives and mothers. But they will also be more. They will join a sisterhood of self-respecting people who will be able to share leadership and social decisions with men.

Equality and dignity are human rights. They are the rights of Jews. They are the rights of women.

SONG: AYFO OREE (No. 14)

MEMORIAL

Historians have often been unfair. They weave the story of the past out of the tales of heroes and famous people, most of them men. They ignore the work of women because women had little chance to become famous. Like slaves whose toils gave reality to the power of their masters, women nurtured and sustained the men of fame.

When we remember the past, when we remember the forces that gave us hope and strength, we are not naïve. We pay tribute to our heroes, to those who managed to take the center stage of history. But we also pay tribute to all the unknown people, women and men, who nurtured, worked, and sustained life without the reward of recognition. Some of them would have been heroes had their times been freer. Although we do not know their names, we are grateful for their gifts.

SONG: ZAYKHER (No. 103)

13
FREEDOM

AFFIRMATION

Freedom is power.
The power to know oneself.
The power to understand others.
The power to control fear.
The power to pursue life.

SONG: V'SHOOV ITKHEM (No. 95)

SELF-INSIGHT

Freedom is a magical word. Most people like the sound of the word. Most people say they want to be free.
Can people be free if they are prisoners?
Can a prisoner of ignorance be free?
Can a prisoner of fear be free?
Can a prisoner of other people's opinions be free?
Can a person without power be free?

Freedom is the power to know ourselves. Without self-insight there is no liberty. To be out of contact with our inner feelings and thoughts is to live in the jail of our own ignorance. People cannot be free if they are the puppets of needs and desires they cannot control. Liberty is an illusion when people do not know why they are driven to do what they do. Lust, hate, and envy are human and normal. But they love to hide behind respectable excuses. Freedom is the power to know them intimately, so that they become our servants—and not our masters.

SONG: MEE HAHAM (No. 65)

INTEGRITY

Freedom is the power to understand others. We live in a world of spoken goodwill. Parents, friends, teachers and public leaders—all inform us that our welfare is their special concern, our happiness their special desire. If we are naïve, we become the victims of propaganda. We become the prisoners of speech. Genuine goodwill can be easily distinguished from false affection. It passes from the tongue to the hands and feet. It becomes action and behavior. Freedom is the ability to tell the difference between those who really care and those who pretend to. Liberty is the power to see the hate through the loving words, the wisdom to see the love shining through dark anger.

SONG: MAASEEM TOVEEM (No. 61)

SELF-CONTROL

Freedom is the power to control fear. When our fears and anxieties overwhelm us, they paralyze our will. We cannot choose between alternatives. We cannot make decisions. As weak and dependent children we seek the protection of a strong father who will assume the burden of our will, who will tell us what to do. Many people crave obedience and slavery. It makes everything more secure, more predictable. Gods and dictators may indeed be overwhelming. They may be pushy and oppressive. But they love to take responsibility.

Rational fear is the fear of losing control. Irrational fear is the fear of being in control. People who refuse their own power cannot be free.

SONG: OUT OF THE NIGHT (No. 76)

COURAGE

Freedom is the power to love ourselves when others do not. As little children we need the approval of our community—we crave the acceptance of our parents and teachers. As little children we need to please—in order to survive—in order to achieve our self-respect. We cannot love ourselves unless other people love us first.

Many men and women are physical adults. But they remain spiritual children. They possess an insatiable need to please—a fearful desire to win the approval of others—an eternal wish to conform to the expectations of their peers and superiors. They are prisoners of their childhood. Hostility and disapproval terrorize them. Public opinion fills them with dread. Self-respect eludes them. They become the perennial followers—who never create—who never resist. In their drive to win the love of others, they come to hate themselves. They despise their weakness and bear contempt for their continuing surrender. No laws and no police restrict their activity. But they are not free.

Genuine liberty is the careful strength to say *no* when others say *yes*—and to say *yes* when others say *no*.

SONG: HATOV O HARA (No. 41)

MEMORIAL

Freedom is the power to release the past. It is the good humor to give up what cannot be altered—the easiness to surrender what cannot be changed.

Countless men and women live in the prison of their past. They are the tortured victims of their memories. They are the martyred slaves of their regrets. The present and the future hold no special challenge to them. They are merely opportune moments to reflect on old pleasure and on old pain. *What might have been* is an obsession. *What could be* is scarcely a thought.

Free people learn from the past. But they do not live there. They do not seek to recapture old pain. They work to achieve new pleasure. They do not need to survive on the faded memories of faded happiness. They strive to create new joy. They use the past to fashion a more interesting future.

SONG: AYFO OREE (No. 14)

AFFIRMATION

Freedom is power.
The power to know oneself.
The power to understand others.
The power to control fear.
The power to pursue life.

14
FRIENDSHIP

AFFIRMATION

Just as the face of one person mirrors the face of another,
So does the heart of one person reflect the heart of another.

SONG: KAMIEYEEM (No. 51)

PERSONHOOD

Friendship is like the air we breathe. We cannot live without it. We are not designed for loneliness. We thrive on the opportunity of human response. If we need to receive the love of others, we also need to give love. If we need to feel the concern of others, we also need to give our care. To cry alone, to laugh alone, to think without the challenge of other minds and other voices is to cease to be human. In a world without familiar people, no man or woman can become a person.

SONG: KEE V'SIMHA (No. 54)

HONESTY

Sometimes we are more afraid of ourselves than we are of others. We are often afraid of our thoughts, of our feelings, and of our desires. We cannot listen to others in friendship because we refuse to listen to ourselves. We cannot reveal ourselves in honest confrontation because we do not know what we are and what we want. A wall of fear and apprehension shuts us off from our inner self and separates us from our reality. Before we can ever be truthful to others, we must first be truthful to ourselves. Honesty without the effort of self-insight is only pretense.

SONG: HAEMET YOTSAYT (No. 32)

ACCEPTANCE

To be a friend is never to be a judge. We will not reveal ourselves to others if we know that we are on trial. We will not understand others if we devote our time to counting virtues and faults. From the moment of our birth, society makes us a defendant, a continual victim of moral prosecution and conviction. From the moment of our birth, the power of conformity condemns our individual uniqueness and makes us suspicious of our personal difference.

We find it hard to hear ourselves because we are always thinking about the social verdict. We find it hard to hear others because, in painful imitation of those who judge us, we are much too eager to condemn our neighbor. How wonderful it would be to live in a world where human relations would not be trials but invitations to friendly understanding. How exciting it would be to find a place where people could truly be free, where they could explore thoughts and feelings in the peace of mutual acceptance. When difference is dangerous, when a person desires power more than knowledge, friendship is not possible.

SONG: B'AYLE HAYADIEYIM (No. 22)

COMMUNICATION

Is real communication possible? Are we strong enough to open our hearts and our minds to others? Are we able to disclose our fears, our anger, and our love? Or do we believe that these revelations will make us vulnerable, the victims of adverse criticism and rejection? The risk of friendship is the risk of trust. To have no faith in the gentleness of other people is to cut oneself off from the world. It is to turn conversation into a game of disguise and to make every human involvement an act of manipulation.

Loneliness is more than the absence of other people. Where mutual trust does not exist, whether in the intimacy of the family or in the closeness of a crowded room, we are alone. If peace and friendship are to be real in our world, then we must give each other the benefit of the doubt. Perhaps when we express our faith in others, they respond by being faithful. Perhaps when others are genuine with us, we discover the pleasure of our own sincerity.

SONG: AYFO OREE (No. 14)

MEMORIAL

Friendship is possible when we know how to trust, when we know that others can be faithful and honest. In the earliest experiences of our childhood, in the first awakening of our infant mind, we discover the security of love. Families may scold and complain. Parents may lecture and cry. But their deeds are always sweeter than their words. In the hour of need, they do not judge. They help.

When parents die, they leave us more than memory. They leave us the well-being of acceptance, the possibility of trust, and the reassurance of unconditional love. Without their gifts we would stand alone in fear. We would not be able to reach out to other people in friendship.

SONG: Y'HEE SHALOM (No. 98)

AFFIRMATION

Just as the face of one person mirrors the face of another,
So does the heart of one person reflect the heart of another.

15
HAPPINESS

SONG: SHALOM L'YISRAEL (No. 82)

REFLECTION

Quiet reflection is essential. Through meditation we resist petty detail and view the vistas of our life. In the rush of our daily pursuits, we feel the pressure of our passions and strive to fulfill them. There seems to be no time to discern the special quality of each experience and to discover the unique value of every moment. Yet the grace of living is never a matter of quantity. It is always the presence of quality. It is the rhythm of refinement that enables all of us to dance to the music of our everyday surroundings and to see the color and splendor of ordinary things.

SONG: HAOLAM MALAY YOFEE (No. 38)

REALISM

All people desire happiness. It is the supreme value of life. We search for the formula to fulfillment. We seek the way to salvation. To many of us, happiness is a state of bliss, a time when all wants are satisfied, all frustrations resolved. Heaven is the hope of life without problems. Pain and suffering seem endurable if they will give way to endless pleasure. The tedium of hard work seems bearable if it is the prelude to leisurely joy. Millions of people have withstood the cruelty of the present because they believed in the kindness of the future. Millions more have accepted the horrors of revolution because they imagined that utopia would follow.

But reality is a sober teacher. It refuses to meet the rules we set for it and to conform to our expectations. Only a child believes that discontent is curable and that living happily ever after is more than the fantasy of legends. Life is a relentless succession of problems, one dilemma hanging onto the tail of another. Each desire satisfied breeds a dozen others. Each new pleasure achieved finds that excitement yields inevitably to boredom. The rich are lonely, the educated puzzled, and the irresponsible are devoured by their leisure. As age advances, the hour of bliss recedes from view. Even thoughts of heaven bore us with the fantasy of eternal retirement. Indeed, when happiness is divorced from the present and assigned to some idyllic future, it never comes. It lingers in unfulfilled dreams and the betrayal of time.

SONG: KAN AL P'NAY ADAMA (No. 52)

SENSITIVITY

Sensitivity makes pain more painful and pleasure more pleasurable. It is the basic ingredient of true wisdom. In the arts we cultivate the immediacy of color and sound: Their value is intrinsic to the moment, not determined by an endless chain of consequences we can neither see nor calculate. Yet we lovers of life are less perceptive in the art we practice. Of necessity, we are bound to search for the usefulness of things and see their goodness in the results they bring. Eating is good for health, love is good for security, study is good for wisdom. And then, in turn, health, security, and wisdom are good for other more distant goals. Present experience seems to be a means to some future end. But the future end never arrives. It simply turns into another useful present, without the dignity of inner value.

If we are wise we see that the moment of "now" is as important as the moment of "later." We know that happiness is expressed in a faculty of perception, a judgment of the senses, that joyfully views the meaning of life in the very act of living. If we relax, if we transcend our obsession with the future, if we respond to our present with the full power of reason and feeling, we too can be wise; we too can be happy. Today will suddenly become more real than tomorrow, this hour more important than the future we dream of.

SONG: B'AYLE HAYADIEYIM (No. 22)

CLIMBING

We cannot escape the tyranny of time. We are the products of our past and the creators of our future. The elusive present makes us apprehensive and teases us with the prospect of fulfillment. To foolish people, problems are burdens, curses of the present to be dismissed by the future. They believe that work and exercise are painful prices they pay to stay alive.

To wise people, problems are opportunities, challenges to the future that give meaning to their present. We know that we do not solve problems in order to live. Rather, we live in order to solve problems. Our addiction to games profoundly reveals our nature. We love to create challenge for the sake of challenge. The fools may find the secret to mountain climbing in the love of mountain tops. But the wise are never so naïve. They know that the value of the climbing is always in the climbing, and the value of the game is in the game.

SONG: LAM'TSAPPEEM (No. 56)

MEANING

The most provocative and dangerous of all questions is the word "why." We sometimes ask it to good purpose. "Why does the sun rise in the east?" "Why do living things require water?" But sometimes it is used blindly and to no purpose. Anguished saints cry out, "Why should we be compassionate to others?" "Why should we be honest with friends?" They ask the question as though the value of the deed described depended on the words of some past authority or the consequences of some future event, as though compassion and friendship derived their meaning from a feeling more important.

But people who are alive to the present know differently. They never ask "why" when "why" is irrelevant. What is intrinsically valuable is just, ultimately worthwhile, and exists for its own sake. Being kind to others needs no justification. It exudes its own pleasure and fulfillment. Honest friendship requires neither the endorsement of the past nor the testimony of the future to give it meaning. If it lives in the present, it needs no explaining. It does not create fulfillment. It is fulfillment.

The meaning of life is happiness. Yet happiness is no distant event which we strive to achieve, some future bliss we suffer to enjoy. It is the sensitive awareness of what is intrinsically valuable in the here and now. It is the special pleasure of helping others, the beauty of friendship, the thrill of running, the excitement of learning, the exaltation in simple striving. Happiness is not, in reality, the goal of life at all. It is the gift of present experience.

SONG: SHEEM'OO (No. 83)

VARIETY

The luster of life is dulled by the too familiar. Eternal life is appalling if it means doing the same thing forever and ever. Variety is indeed the flavor of life. Without it, the most exquisite pleasures degenerate, through repetition, into unendurable pain.

The good life has a unique rhythm; its beat is both fast and slow. Its pitch is both high and low. It is never a flat plain marked by sameness in every square. It is a vista of mountains and valleys that complement each other by their sharp difference. Human happiness is a harmony of contrasts, a delicate balance that defines fulfillment.

SONG: HAVA NAGEELA (No. 42)

MEMORIAL

Death makes us angry. It seems to cheat us of what we worked so hard to secure. Many of our loved ones spent their years in struggle. They knew poverty, disease, and deprivation in the battle for survival. They dreamed of so much for themselves and their families and lived to taste so little of their vision. How painfully aware we are of our limits and how fearfully conscious that, in a moment, the blind hand of circumstance can also steal our future. But anger and fear are inappropriate. No person, however young, is fully denied the opportunities of the good life. If in the worry of the present we cannot find the intrinsic beauties of life, we will never find them. Indeed, death can never deny us and those we love what life bestows in every moment.

SONG: B'ROOKHEEM HAHIEYEEM (No. 25)

16
HONESTY

AFFIRMATION

Who are the wise?
People who can distinguish between their words and their behavior.
Who are the strong?
People who have the power to see themselves as others see them.
Who are the noble?
People who seek to rule their own lives instead of the lives of others.

SONG: MEE HAHAM (No. 65)

LIBERATION

Wise people are honest people. They tell the truth about themselves. They know that honesty is a form of freedom, that genuine self-insight is the beginning of liberation.

Self-deception is a kind of slavery. Our fantasies imprison us and terrify us with the threat of exposure. When we lie to ourselves about what we are and what we do, we become the victims of our lies. They paralyze us with flattery and prevent us from changing what needs to be changed.

Most dishonesty is not practiced on others. It is practiced on ourselves. All of us are self-deceivers. We deny what we really desire. We refuse to confront our hate, our anger, and our fear. We refuse to accept what we truly feel and believe. The world around us invites our curiosity and objective study. But the world inside us arouses our hostility and resistance to knowledge. When we do not wish to know the truth about ourselves we call the soul an enigma, the mind a mystery. We pretend that our thoughts and feelings are beyond our understanding and that it is futile to pursue them, or we list the respectable virtues of our society and claim them to be ours. We fight reality with all our might and are exhausted by the struggle.

SONG: EMET L'YISRAEL (No. 29)

ACTION

Honesty begins with behavior. What we really think and feel is reflected in what we do. Too often we imagine that we know what we want and believe. We check our conscious mind and encounter numberless ideas and convictions which claim to be the essence of our being. But they are obvious frauds. Our tongue speaks love, but our hands speak hate. Our mouth exudes serenity, but our eyes exude fear. Our lips utter friendship, but our whole body screams anger. We feel sincere, and so we imagine that we are sincere. We feel honest, and so we imagine that we are honest.

If we listen to our hearts we shall never discover the truth. It is only when we coldly watch our own behavior that we confront reality. Our deepest convictions about ourselves and others can never really be hidden. They boldly proclaim themselves through our actions. While our mouths spin tales of fantasy, our bodies speak with honesty. When we plead that we cannot act on our beliefs we are self-deceived. We *always* act on what we believe. When we run away from what we say we love, then our love is an illusion. And when we passionately embrace what we say we hate, then our hatred is unreal. We simply are what we do. From the awareness of this truth all self-insight proceeds.

SONG: HAEMET YOTSAYT (No. 32)

EMPATHY

Some of our behavior is private. Most of our behavior is public. We observe others and they observe us. Although we cannot see the thoughts and feelings of our friends, we can see their actions. And because we are not burdened by all their conscious fantasies, by all the illusions they have created to defend themselves against reality, we can often know them better than they can know themselves.

And so it is with us. Others can see us in a way that we are not able to see ourselves, for our friends and the strangers we encounter do not have to hurdle the barrier of our self-image. They view us simply and directly. They see our gestures and our deeds. Often, through empathy, they are conscious of our deepest feelings before we are.

Human encounter can be a path to honesty. When we talk about each other to each other we can share the truth. If we can have the strength to see ourselves as others see us, then our own understanding of what we are will become more sensitive and more realistic.

Good friends help us understand ourselves in the same way that we help them confront their reality. We use each other's eyes to see together what each of us cannot see alone.

SONG: HINNAY MA TOV (No. 47)

SELF-AWARENESS

Ignorance is darkness. Knowledge is light. To live without an awareness of one's true being is to linger in darkness. To live with an acceptance of one's real feelings and desires is to bask in the light. Some people walk in the sunshine and remain prisoners of their own internal night. Others walk in the night and are illumined by the light of their self-understanding.

Truth is an act of cooperation. It is the gift of our friends to us. It is also our gift to our friends. Genuine solidarity does not depend on lies and guileful flattery. That is the unity of weak people. It thrives on openness and directness, and seeks to make people strong.

SONG: AYFO OREE (No. 14)

MEMORIAL

The people we love do not win our love by what they want to do. They earn our loyalty by what they do. Meaning to be kind is no substitute for being kind. Intending to give is no alternative to generosity. We cannot remember what we do not experience. The gift of the past is never the pious intention. It is always the loving act.

SONG: SHEEM'OO (No. 83)

AFFIRMATION

Who are the wise?
People who can distinguish between their words and their behavior.

Who are the strong?
People who have the power to see themselves as others see them.
Who are the noble?
People who seek to rule their own lives instead of the lives of others.

17
HOPE

AFFIRMATION

Without hope even the day is like night.
And with hope even the darkness becomes light.

SONG: V'SHOOV ITKHEM (No. 95)

SELF-RESPECT

We live through hope. Where there is darkness we wait for the light. Where there is pain we anticipate pleasure. Where there is boredom we yearn for the arrival of new excitement.

Living without hope is like dying. It is a denial of everything vital. It is an abject surrender to evil. It is a humiliating affirmation of the darkness, the pain, and the dullness of human experience. If the future holds no promise of better things to come, then the present weighs down like an intolerable burden.

Persons of self-respect, people who esteem their own power, do not welcome despair. In the darkest hour they resist the self-pity that paralyzes action. Where the pessimist sees only the risk of failure, they see the risk of success. Where the skeptic condemns courage, they condemn the cowardice of cautious men and women. Even when the night seems more than eternal, they plead for the morning.

SONG: HAOR SHEL HAYOFEE (No. 39)

ACTION

Our ancestors lived through hope. Many saw their hope in prayer. They prayed and prayed and waited patiently for their dreams to be realized. Even when nothing happened they continued to pray and found comfort in waiting.

Others knew that their hope did not lie in words. It lay in action. It lay in the power that all of them possessed together to create their own future and to determine their own destiny. Talent without courage is useless. But skill with bravery is the mother of the impossible deed, the author of the incredible event. Jewish freedom is the product of no passive waiting. It is as bold as Mendelssohn, as daring as Herzl.

SONG: HALBEESHEENEE (No. 35)

ZIONISM

Not so long ago our Jewish ancestors lived in a continual darkness. In the ghettos of Europe they were condemned to a prison of hatred and envy. No ray of brotherly love ever penetrated to warm the night. No light of compassion ever broke through to relieve the blackness. The pain seemed endless. The humiliation touched forever.

Some of our forefathers responded with despair. They turned their anger inward and cursed themselves instead of the darkness. Convinced that to be Jewish was to be guilty, they listed their sins with diligence and announced that they were worthy of suffering. Drawn to hopelessness, they justified it.

Others among our ancestors replied with hope. They peered through the blackness and saw the possibility of light. They resisted the night and waited for the morning. They dreamed of their homeland and believed that they would return some day to live in peace and dignity. Their vision gave them the will to work and the determination to strive for better things. They called this vision *HATIKVA*.

SONG: HATIKVA (No. 40)

STRENGTH

Despair is a style of coping with life. It is the other side of self-denial. It is the affirmation of helplessness. It is an invitation to pity. When we are afraid of our own strength, when we are terrified by our own power, we deny them. We play the child. We cry for help. We know that style. It is the earliest and most familiar role we learn to play.

Hope is also a way of coping with life. It is the other side of self-esteem. It is the affirmation of competence. It is an invitation to respect. When we take pleasure in our own strength, when we enjoy our own power, we release their possibilities. We play the adult. We take responsibility. We choose that style. It is the only role which rescues us from infancy, which gives us our dignity.

SONG: BASHANA HABAA (No. 21)

FUTURE

Many of us find the meaning of our life in the past. We search for our roots and we revel in every famous ancestor. The dead fill our memories, granting us the pleasure of approval with the terror of guilt. Wisdom from the past grows wiser with age and takes on the mystery of holiness. Old teachers become more profound than new ones. Old rituals become more important than our own inventions. If there is a golden age, it happened a long time ago. We see the world getting worse and worse.

Many of us find the meaning of our life in the future. Visions of new worlds fill our thoughts, granting us the expectation of success. Wisdom from the present displays its youth and prefers good humor to reverence. New teachers often seem as profound as old ones. New rituals become the friends of our creativity. If there is a golden age, it is yet to come. Because we live with hope, we will make the world better and better.

SONG: MAHAR (No. 63)

MEMORIAL

After every spring comes the fullness of summer. After every summer comes the color of autumn. Beyond every autumn lies the serenity of winter. And beyond every winter reappears the freshness of spring.

So it is with all people. Death is sweetened by hope. The old person always yields to the child. The old life is forever the prelude to the new.

SONG: ZAYKHER (No. 103)

AFFIRMATION

Without hope even the day is like night.
And with hope even the darkness becomes light.

HUTSPA

Fanatics are always dangerous. Even when they claim to be humanistic Jews, neither their enthusiasm nor their intensity can redeem them. Fanatics are insufferable because they are humorless. They laugh—but never at themselves. They challenge—but never their own creations. They encourage defiance—but never of their own authority. Fanatics are addicted to holiness. They love to worship. They cannot abide imperfection. They prefer gods to heroes, sacred books to useful information, absolute truth to experimental science. They are willing to smash other people's idols but stand in awkward humility before their own.

The opposite of fanaticism is *hutspa*. *Hutspa* is an untranslatable Hebrew word—a unique Yiddish gift to every language. *Hutspa* is the essential ingredient of the humanist temperament, the ultimate skill for humanist survival. *Hutspa* respects, but never worships—believes, but never eternally—loves, but never unconditionally—changes, but never for the last time. *Hutspa* refuses all idols. Neither Moses nor Marx can intimidate it. Neither the past nor the chic can arouse its reverence. *Hutspa* enjoys without having to stand in awe. *Hutspa* laughs—because, after all, there are always alternatives.

SONG: HAVA NAGEELA (No. 42)

MEMORIAL

Death hovers over all our deeds, over every action we perform. For some of us death is an obsession, destroying our pleasure and filling our souls with anxious fear. For others death is a challenge, prompting us to enjoy life while we live and urging us to taste our talents while we can. If we are people of dignity, we respond to death with courage and to life with zest.

SONG: Y'HEE SHALOM (No. 98)

19
HUMANITY

SONG: V'AHAVTA (No. 93)

IDENTITY

We have many identities. We have a personal identity that defines our uniqueness and makes each of us an individual unlike any other. We have a family identity that gives recognition to our childhood and to those who nurtured us. We have a Jewish identity that gives us roots, a place in history, and a wider brotherhood. We also have a human identity. It defines our place in the chain of life and gives us connection to all other men and women.

Our human identity is primary. In the end, our differences are fewer than our similarities. We share with all other people a common form and a common nature. Our bodies may vary in details. But against the other forms of nature we appear the same. Our desires may differ in intense degrees. But from the vantage point of some imaginary observer, our behavior is the expression of certain universal needs. We are less individual than we imagine. We are more alike than we want to be.

SONG: AHEE ADAM (No. 4)

SCIENCE

Universal communication is very difficult. The human race is divided by so many things. We speak different languages. We wear different costumes. We eat different foods. We pay tribute to different ancestors. We even fear difference itself. It is hard to see the familiar because we are always looking for the strange. It is difficult to experience what we have in common because we confuse the appearance with the substance. Although the traditional teachers of religion speak of human unity, they are unable to bring it about. Each of them is confined to his own system of truth and to his own sacred texts. In the end, there is no procedure for resolving disagreement. There is only the cliché of tolerance and mutual respect.

The teachers of science have done far better than the sages of religion. They have penetrated boundaries with the power of technology. They have transformed a planet of mysterious strangers into a global village. If their inventions have been used for war and cruelty, they have also been directed to peace and to healing. Their greatest triumph is the method by which they pursue the truth. Reason is a universal discipline which owes no debt to national culture and revered ancestors. It is no prisoner of family guilt and local patriotism. It expresses the common sense which is present in every tribe and every nation. It is the servant of the evidence of the senses. It is the tester of consequences. It is the reformer of prejudices. Unlike dead ancestors, it can change its mind and admit mistakes gracefully. Reason crosses the frontiers that tradition builds and lets us speak one to the other.

SONG: RAYSHEET HOKHMA (No. 77)

ACTION

Many cultures have invented stories about the origins of the human race. Some saw themselves as fallen gods. Others imagined that they were manufactured from the elements of the earth. Still others believed that they were visitors from some distant world. But no story equals the drama of the truth. The evolution of life is an epic tale in which life and death struggle with each other in an unending battle. Living forms struggle to survive. Their enemies are legion. Against the overwhelming hostility of circumstances, most perish. A few survive. The wastebasket of evolution is very large. Only the most skillful manage to elude the grim reaper of natural selection. Who will live and who will die? As the saga unwinds, that question defines the suspense.

We are the survivors of two billion years of vital evolution. We are not miniature gods; we are not manufactured puppets; we are not visitors from outer space. We are the proud culmination of an epic struggle. The earth is our home. We know it intimately. Its plants and animals are our cousins. Like them we have tasted both the kindness and cruelty of nature. Our brutal setting has made us strong. We have many talents for survival. Our brain, our limbs, and our senses cooperate to make us hardy fighters for life. We are not the heirs of the passive and the resigned. We are the children of action. We are the offspring of the will to live.

CONGREGATION

For the expectant is the glory.
The future is theirs.
Whoever stands against the mountain without recoil
Shall ascend its summit.

SONG: LAM'TSAPPEEM (No. 56)

HAPPINESS

Happiness is not a need but a consequence. When our basic needs are satisfied, we feel the pleasure of fulfillment. Knowing our needs is very important. Without that understanding we may pursue what we do not really want. But it is so easy to be deceived! When one desire finds no satisfaction, it seizes the center stage of our attention and pretends to be the most important one of all. When we are hungry, food is an obsession. When we enjoy no sensual pleasure, sexual desire becomes an inner beast. When we receive no love or recognition, loneliness and indifference make all other problems seem trivial. We imagine that what we urgently want is our first and most fundamental need.

The truth is otherwise. We humans share a host of inner demands. Some are more important than others, but none is primary. People will even forego food and sex to obtain other more compelling ends. Wise people do not narrow human nature. They do not restrict happiness to what their culture either allows or forbids. They do not confine fulfillment to what their experience makes scarce. Rather, true happiness rests on the harmony of many satisfactions. Love, recognition, and usefulness are universal needs which transcend any particular culture. They are our needs. They are a bond we share with all other people. If we know this truth, no local obsession, no private compulsion, can deceive us.

SONG: B'AYLE HAYADIEYIM (No. 22)

NOBILITY

The spiritual option is not confined to those who spend their time with imaginary spirits. It has nothing at all to do with people who avoid sensual pleasure and who turn their mind to meditation. The spiritual condition is the special radiance we perceive in noble people.

Nobility starts with the strength of reason. It grows with self-reliance and sensitive awareness of the human condition. It expands the human spirit and allows it to cross the barriers of ethnic pride and parochial vision to encompass humanity. The noble person avoids indiscriminate tolerance and patronizing niceness. He is humane because he allows himself to feel the common fate we all share. He knows that, in some fundamental way, the stranger is a member of his own family.

True nobility rests on no social gift. Neither pedigree nor wealth can guarantee it. Neither humiliation nor poverty can prevent it. The noble person is the member of no special class or race. He is an aristocrat of the spirit whose style is an enormous compassion and whose wisdom is an extraordinary empathy. His generosity and openness make him radiant. He shines with the special power that kindness brings when it can flow freely. The spiritual option is our option. Let those who wish to meddle with mysterious spirits do so. We shall train the spirit of our own humanity.

SONG: AYZE HOO GIBBOR (No. 18)

HUMANISM

We are humanists. We believe in the power and beauty of the human potential. We believe in the necessity of human reason. We believe in the human right to satisfy human needs. We believe in the human ideal of human unity. Cynics may mock our commitment. They will give examples of human weakness and ugliness. They will testify to the irrational decisions of countless men and women. They will decry the pettiness of so much human desire. They will point triumphantly to the scourge of hate and war. But they will not prevail. They confuse our present limitation with our future possibility.

We do not praise what we are. We praise what it is possible for us to become. If human history has featured the base, it has also presented the noble. If the human saga has revealed the terror of irrational destruction, it has also delivered the marvel of rational survival. If human nature has chosen its movements of petty selfishness, it has also found its seasons of grand compassion. If nations have killed and slaughtered, they have also made peace. They have exchanged ideas and useful work. They have fostered a new world society where no great nation is any longer independent and where no little people is unknown.

For many timid spirits cynicism is more comfortable than hope. It justifies inaction. But we will not be seduced by this fatal reward. We shall strive to be what we believe we can become. To do less is to betray our potential and to become the victims of our own fear.

SONG: AYFO OREE (No. 14)

MEMORIAL

Nations and empires have spawned an abundance of different styles for different people. They pay tribute to the strong attachment that we all have to our ethnic roots and ancestral pride. Judaism is an expression of this need to preserve old communities. But, like all good religions, it does best what it was created for. It allows Jews to enjoy their Jewish connection.

The human connection needs its own celebration too. Humanism is the way we, as human beings, affirm our membership in the human community. It does not replace old family ties. It supplements them and makes them more humane. It reminds us that we have other attachments too.

We resolve to enrich our Jewish loyalty with our human awareness. All that we are and do must be judged by standards more universal than the patriotism the past demanded. We know that strangers are no longer distant beings. They share our streets, our schools, and our cities. If we see them still as strangers, if we run away from them to rebuild old barriers, we will condemn ourselves to the prison of anxiety. We cannot run away from the world we helped to create. We cannot build fences to exclude people whose labor and goodwill we need. We cannot deny what is undeniable. In the end, these people share our human fate. They do not deserve our hostility. They do not deserve our pious exclusion. They deserve our warm attachment. They share our human memories.

SONG: Y'HEE SHALOM (No. 98)

20
HUMOR

SONG: V'SHOOV ITKHEM (No. 95)

LAUGHTER

Religion and humor do not usually go together. For most religious people, the world is a very serious place to live in with very serious things to do. Laughter does not sit well with piety and reverence. While religious ceremonies often encourage people to cry, they rarely encourage them to laugh.

Laughter is dangerous to most religion. While worship makes human things seem divine, humor makes so-called divine things seem human. There is a challenging edge to laughter. It refuses all pretense and loves to put the pin into the balloon of illusion. While pious people believe in the emperor's clothing, good-humored people can see that the emperor is quite naked.

SONG: ZEMER LAKH (No. 104)

ABSURDITY

Humor needs a sense of dignity.

The world is a little bit crazy most of the time, and we need to be a little bit crazy in order to deal with it.

For pious people, the order of the universe needs to be perfect. There must be a perfect God who rules the world with perfect justice. If life seems to be unfair, if the good seem to be punished and the wicked rewarded, our perception is only an illusion. After all, the human vision is very limited.

For good-humored people, the universe could use better management. The administration of the world, if any exists, could use a lot more justice, a lot more attention to our hopes and aspirations, a lot more awareness of our moral concerns. If tornadoes vanished, if famine went away, if holocausts were abolished, we would hardly miss them.

Just when we think that everything is all right, a new surprise shakes our confidence in the meaning of it all. In an unpredictable, crazy world, we can either despair or laugh. Laughter is healthier.

SONG: TUM BALALAIKA (No. 92)

HUTSPA

Humor needs "hutspa" to give it strength.

Hutspa is that indefinable Hebrew and Yiddish word which points to more than gall and less than disrespect. If you have *hutspa,* you are not afraid to tread on sacred territory. You are not intimidated by sacred authorities. Even before you go to heaven, you are checking on the living conditions.

Pious people do not like to challenge the holy side of their lives. Holy things are never funny. Tradition is never silly. Ancestors are never ordinary. Gods are never incompetent. Laughing at any one of them is nothing more than blasphemy.

Good-humored people know that most of the world is a comic stage on which the actors perform their roles much too seriously. They know that doctors make mistakes. They know that clergy are not saints. They know that professors can be dumb. When faced with the pretense of the world, they turn their embarrassing questions into jokes.

SONG: ZOOM GALEE (No. 106)

SKEPTICISM

Humor needs a lot of skepticism to keep it healthy.

True believers like to divide the world in two. On the one side are the "good guys"; on the other side are the "bad guys." On the one side are those who love the "right"; on the other side are those who love the "wrong." The enemy is fair game for mocking, but your own group is too pure for jokes.

100 *Humor*

True believers like to divide beliefs in two. On the one hand are the true ideas; on the other hand, the false teaching. On the one hand are those who preach the word of truth; on the other hand are those who teach terror and lead people astray. Laughing at the message of the enemy goes without saying. But your own message is never very funny.

Good-humored people resist this simple division. They laugh as easily at themselves as they laugh at others. If they notice inconsistency in others, they also notice it in themselves. If they observe the stupidity of others, they also observe it in themselves. Self-righteousness makes them uncomfortable. Eternal truth annoys them. When they look at their neighbors through a comic eye, they also stand in front of the mirror to include their own funny face.

SONG: KAMIEYEEM (No. 51)

SURPRISE

Humor needs surprise to make us laugh.

Nothing is really funny when all is predictable. Punch lines would die an early death if we could figure them out at the beginning of the joke.

Some people suddenly slip on a banana peel. Some people get their noses caught in the door. Other people forget their speech in the middle. Other people show up in the wrong costume for the wrong event. There are millions of ways to make people laugh. And all of them have some element of surprise.

The joke is a reflection of the human condition and how we try to cope with it. We plan and we plan, we strive and we strive—and, at the last minute, something happens to turn our dream into frustration. If we want to, we can scream and shout, we can weep and wail—but none of that pitiable activity will reverse the past. If we want to, we can do what Zorba did when everything came tumbling down the mountain. We can throw our heads back—and roar with laughter—and dance—and start all over again.

SONG: HAVA NAGEELA (No. 42)

KINDNESS

Humor needs kindness to make it behave.

Smiling and laughing did not start out as a kindly behavior. Showing your teeth to another is not, by history, a friendly act. Teeth bite and so can humor.

The evolution of laughter began with hostility and confrontation. It began with defiance and mockery. We taunted our enemies with our strength and their weakness. As time went on, we learned to bite less and to laugh more, but the biting edge remains.

Good-humored people know that laughter can be both cruel and kind. And they choose to be kind—at least, most of the time. They understand the pain of mockery. They understand the difference between laughing at and laughing with.

Some humor should never be indulged. Some jokes should never be told. Poking fun can only be fun when other people are not hurt.

SONG: AYFO OREE (No. 14)

MEMORIAL

What would the Jewish personality be like without humor? It simply would not be Jewish.

Jewish humor is the legacy of the Jewish experience. It did not arise from the Bible and the Talmud. It did not come down from priests, prophets, and rabbis. It did not emerge from famous texts and famous writers. Jewish humor is the response of ordinary Jewish people to the extraordinary horrors of Jewish history. In the face of an uncaring and unjust world, we Jews learned to laugh rather than to surrender and die.

Sometimes our laughter mocked our enemies. Sometimes our laughter demeaned ourselves. But most of the time it was a healthy combination of resignation and defiance. We laughed at the things we could not change. And we laughed at the absurdity which governed our fate.

When we pay tribute to our past, we pay tribute to the people who affirmed life, not only through their tears, but especially through their laughter.

SONG: B'ROOKHEEM HAHIEYEEM (No. 25)

21
IDEALISM

AFFIRMATION

The world is neither good nor bad.
The world is neither beautiful nor ugly.
The world is neither positive nor negative.
People are.

SONG: HATOV O HARA (No. 41)

ACTIVISM

Some of us are always waiting. We wait for God to tell us what to do. We wait for destiny to declare our fate. We wait for complete understanding before we act out of ignorance. We wait for the right mood before we act out of despair. We wait for the guarantees of happiness before we dare risk failure. We even wait to find ourselves, though we are not sure that there is anything to find. We wait and wait and wait.

Endless waiting is depressing. It is a sickness of the will, a disease of the ego. Waiting breeds waiting. As a lifestyle it is more than caution. It is inefficient self-destruction.

Life is action. It is doing more than thinking. It is loving more than being in love. It is trying more than worrying about trying.

Active people are patient. But they are never passive.

SONG: MAASEEM TOVEEM (No. 61)

DECISIVENESS

Some of us hate to make decisions. Decisions are so risky. They may lead to failure. They may sponsor embarrassment. They may expose our fantasies. Decisions burden us with responsibility. They make us confront our freedom to choose. They make us shoulder the blame. They make us apologize for our mistakes.

Avoiding responsibility may be unattractive, but it seems so much safer than the risk of being wrong. It seems so much safer to find respectable ways to be irresponsible. Our genes, our social conditioning, our helplessness, are comfortable excuses. Gods, dictators, and bossy bosses are convenient blame takers even though we choose to forget that we consent to our own obedience.

Our lifestyle is defined by the way we make decisions. Some of us prefer to be pitiable, always pleading our innocence and dependency. Some of us prefer to be attractive, taking responsibility for our actions and confronting other people with the dignity of our self-esteem.

SONG: LAM'TSAPPEEM (No. 56)

CREATIVITY

Old rituals are comforting because they are familiar and predictable. They are safe and secure. They relieve us of the pain of continuous surprise. They reflect the mood of stability and eternity. Old rituals help us relax because they require no more exertion than the effort of repetition.

Life without imagination is dull. People without imagination are boring. Imitation and conformity are necessary for survival, but they need to be challenged if life is to go beyond survival, if life is to yield the excitement of happiness.

Creative people are vital people. They refuse to accept the world as fixed. They refuse to believe that life offers only one script for living. They see old things and imagine new ways of putting them together. They see new things and fancy old settings which they will transform. They gaze at one scene and envision a hundred ways to describe it. They experience one life and imagine a thousand ways to live it.

SONG: HAKH PATEESH (No. 34)

GENEROSITY

Some of us are always giving, but we are never generous. Some of us are always extending ourselves to others, but we are not joyous. We feel inadequate. We feel insecure. We see ourselves deprived of the very things we need and want. We see ourselves as small in a world of big enemies. We believe that we are the victims of unjust fates, that destiny has handed us less than we deserve. If we give to others, we give because we feel guilty or because we are afraid not to give or because we need to please. When we give, our hand is eager but our spirit is reluctant. Giving to others is sacrifice. Helping others is diminishing ourselves. Extending ourselves to others is giving up part of our identity.

Generous people are vital people. They know that martyrdom is neither beautiful nor noble. They know that self-pity is neither interesting nor necessary. They are wise enough to affirm that personal identity is no external possession. It is an inner self-assurance which can be neither yielded nor stolen. If they give, they give because giving is an expression of their personal power. When they help, they help because they are generous. They feel full and overflowing.

SONG: EEM AYN (No. 28)

OPTIMISM

Living is hard. Living is always solving problems. Living is frustration and unfulfilled desire. Living is loneliness, aging, and the awareness of death. Living is failure, despair, and undeserved hatred.

Living is wanting. We want to know more than we know. We want to have more than we own. We want to be more than we are.

The negative side of the world is enormous. We have a right to be cynical—we have a right to be pessimistic—if we choose to be.

Living is also joyous. Living is solving difficult problems. Living is fulfillment and satisfied desire. Living is friendship, pleasure, and the awareness of beauty. Living is growing. We know more than we need to know. We do more than we used to do. We ARE more than we used to be.

The positive side of life is immense. We have a right to be idealistic—we have a right to be optimistic—if we choose to be. The world is neither positive nor negative. People are.

SONG: MAHAR (No. 63)

MEMORIAL

As human beings, we are unique. We know that we are going to die. We know that our span of life is limited. We know that our story must have an end. Death frightens us and has the power to become our chief concern. Death fills us with dread and threatens us with nothingness.

Successful people do not deny unpleasant realities. They do not run away from them. They do not pretend that they do not exist. They accept their presence. They do not exhaust themselves trying to change what cannot be changed. Good humor and common sense become their friends. Joyous living becomes their companion. If the story has to have an ending, it might as well be exciting while it lasts.

SONG: Y'HEE SHALOM (No. 98)

AFFIRMATION

The world is neither good nor bad.
The world is neither beautiful nor ugly.
The world is neither positive nor negative.
People are.

22
INDIVIDUALISM

AFFIRMATION

We are free.
We are free to choose.
We are free to choose our own life.
We cannot avoid choosing.
We are condemned to be free.

SONG: MEE HAHAM (No. 65)

RESPONSIBILITY

Each of us tastes the loneliness of the human condition. To be an individual is to stand apart and sense the separation that makes every person unique. In a soul where instinct has yielded to the challenge of free choice, decision is personal. Neither the tyranny of the species nor the oppression of society can dictate our will without our moment of consent. Birds and flowers conform to their inner plan and offer no resistance. But men and women are plagued by the unpredictable freedom of their conscious mind. We are each of us distinct and different, defined by the path of our own behavior.

Within the limits of our possibility we can become what we will to become. Within the boundaries of our talents we can achieve what we choose to achieve. The open possibility of our future is a frightening excitement. We can withdraw in fear and seek to hide from its reality. Or we can boldly assume its challenge and bravely confront our destiny with the courage of free people.

SONG: BAMAKOM (No. 19)

ACTION

The world often appears the victim of disorder. Event follows event without apparent uniformity of pattern and arouses the fear of chaos. In our hearts we understandably resist this reality. We prefer to believe that the universe is not spontaneous, that it is guided in every cube of space by certain unchanging laws. The comfort of the predictable always reduces anxiety.

But the wise person knows that his wisdom not only perceives the outer order but also helps to mold it by its direction. The immortal words of great teachers are more than passive. They tell us more than how the world molds us. They are impetuously active: they invite us to mold the world.

SONG: TOV LEEH'YOT (No. 90)

COURAGE

The moment of personal decision exposes our inner reality. Within ourselves we sense the turmoil of feeling and drive. Contrary desires and hopes fight each other in endless struggle and strive to claim the energy of our action. The mystery of our psyche puzzles our waking moments and taunts us with its secrets. From time to time hidden wants expose themselves and make us cringe with the shame of recognition. It is hard to be honest because honesty is painful to our pride. It is easier to take our fears and lusts and transfer them to convenient strangers. Prejudice spares us the pain of coping with ourselves.

Each person's most vicious deceit is rarely practiced on others. It is reserved for himself. We lie to ourselves in the futile effort to avoid the truth. We deny the value of inner searching and shield ourselves behind this wall of skepticism. Yet no person can meet life who runs away from himself. The strength to face the world outside arises out of no sudden burst of faith. It feeds on the courage to know the reality within. A person who is not afraid of himself will not be afraid of others.

SONG: ASHRAY HAGAFROOR (No. 13)

AUTONOMY

We crave the assurance of an outer security. We look upon the world and demand its love. We gaze on infinity and cry out for its attention. The silence of a universe without purpose terrifies us and makes us the authors of mythology. If only the fates would declare our destiny and assure us that our future is in the will of some knowing providence! Hate is less painful to endure than the taunt of indifference.

To affirm that the vastness beyond does not care whether we live or die is to burden each of us with the lonely challenge of responsibility. If indeed the world has no mission to use us for its own purpose, then the world itself is a lifeless clay that awaits the determination of human molding. If we are not planned fixtures designed to serve the need of eternity, then eternity is an endless jungle of events that invites the discipline of human desire. Each of us, through the passion of our own goals, creates values and imposes them on a silent reality. We become the authors of our own fate.

SONG: OUT OF THE NIGHT (No. 76)

FREEDOM

We are condemned to be free. We cannot escape our liberty. We cannot run away from the trauma of decision. If we want to live, then we must face the daily dilemma of choice. If we want to live well, then we must accept the truth of our human condition. We and we alone are responsible for the direction of our fate. Neither instinct, nor heredity, nor the power of nature's mechanism can assume this burden. The brave person knows the risk of his decision and revels in the opportunity of creating his future. The courage of commitment is the price of happiness.

SONG: AYFO OREE (No. 14)

MEMORIAL

Memory is a precious possession. It captures the past and trains it to our need. The harshness of events is softened by vagueness, and the pleasure of happy moments is sharpened by vivid imagination. Loved ones linger on in the glory of their individual uniqueness. In life they willed to live and hewed the path of their personal difference. In death they transcend decay and find their niche in fond remembrance. No person is defined by the sameness of another. If it were so, memory would die from generalities. In the particular grace of every man and woman lies their immortality.

SONG: ZAYKHER (No. 103)

AFFIRMATION

We are free.
We are free to choose.
We are free to choose our own life.
We cannot avoid choosing.
We are condemned to be free.

23
JUSTICE

SONG: SHALOM L'YISRAEL (No. 82)

JUSTICE

Life is unfair. The fates do not give us what we really deserve. The good die young. The wicked prosper. Aging and death confront us at the very time that we are best able to enjoy the fruits of our labor.

Life is unfair. Destiny is less generous than it ought to be. The summer is too short. The winter is too long. Floods, drought, and disease arrive as uninvited guests. When we think that we are finally in control of our lives, some unwelcome surprise reminds us that we are not.

Life is unfair. The righteous often look so plain, and the wicked seem so attractive. Healthy discipline is hard, and harmful pleasure is seductive. Appearances are deceiving.

So the message is clear. Since life is unfair, since the fates are unjust, we have to make up for it. We have to bring some order into this moral chaos. In defiance of an uncaring destiny, we shall strive to be fair. In the face of an indifferent universe, we shall work to be just.

SONG: EEM AYN (No. 28)

INDIFFERENCE

Justice is responsibility.

Responsibility is growing up. Children rarely want to take the blame. Parents and teachers are such handy scapegoats; unpleasant circumstances are such convenient blametakers. Complaining and apologizing become our best skills. They help us avoid adulthood. Since the world is unfair, we might as well be too.

Growing up is wanting to do better than resigning ourselves to destiny. It is wanting to be the masters of our own lives. It is finding complaining and apologizing uncomfortable and humiliating. It is the refusal to turn the other victims of our personal drama into the sole directors of the play.

Becoming an adult is never automatic. Some children who look like children start very early taking responsibility for their actions. Some children who look like adults never give up the familiar skills. Surrender and resignation can be made to look so mature that others will never know that we are still children.

Justice is hard work.

SONG: KAN AL P'NAY ADAMA (No. 52)

FAIRNESS

Justice is fairness.

Fairness is equality. We offer equal rewards for equal acts. Women do not receive less because they are not men. The weak do not receive less because they are not powerful. Strangers do not receive less because they are not friends.

Fairness is generosity. We want others to enjoy the dignity that we enjoy. We want others to experience the self-esteem that we experience. We want others to know that good work leads to good rewards.

Fairness is discipline. It is not instinctive to yield to women as much as one yields to men. It is not instinctive to yield to the weak what one gives to the strong. It is not instinctive to reward strangers in the same way as one rewards friends.

Justice is hard work.

SONG: HATOV O HARA (No. 41)

MERIT

Justice is merit.

Some people believe that pedigree is the issue. They believe in the privilege of birth and family connection. They believe in the claims of caste and inherited status. For them, justice guarantees the power and wealth their parents enjoyed. For them, privilege is a gift of destiny. It does not need to be earned.

Some people maintain that being human is the issue. They believe in the privilege of mere existence. They affirm the claims of need and deprivation. For them, justice insures equal rewards to all. For them, privilege is the gift of being born. It also does not have to be earned.

Some of us believe that merit is the issue. We applaud the privilege that comes from useful talent and useful work. We affirm the claims of commitment and successful labor. For us, justice rewards those who seek to help themselves and to help others. Privilege is the gift of personal effort and personal skill.

Justice is hard work.

SONG: MEE HAHAM (No. 65)

LIMITATIONS

When we pursue justice, when we try to be fair, we have to be good-humored and recognize our limitations.

It is sometimes difficult to resist the claims of pedigree. Our children, our family, our friends are very important to us. Even when they abuse us, even when they are undeserving, we are reluctant to deny them our support. So much of our motivation for working comes from their existence that when they misbehave we are willing to overlook their actions. We temper justice with forgiveness and loving indulgence.

It is sometimes difficult to resist the claims of human need. Poverty may be unavoidable even for those who want to work hard. Education may be unavailable even for those who want to learn. Even the lazy and the indifferent may look needy enough to arouse our pity. We temper justice with compassion and generosity.

It is even sometimes difficult to enforce the claims of merit. Talents are so unequal that the casual genius may receive far more than he needs, and the hard-working drone may receive far less than survival will allow. We temper justice with a concession to effort.

In the face of all these limitations, justice is hard work.

SONG: BAMAKOM (No. 19)

MOTIVATION

Justice is more than an idea. It is more than an ideal. It is action and behavior. It needs motivation.

Why, then, should we be just? Why should we be fair? In what way will an unjust world serve us worse than a world in which fairness prevails?

Sometimes sharing rewards with those who deserve them leaves us with less than we want and need. Sometimes asking for more than we truly merit makes life easier and more comfortable.

The reward of justice is neither guaranteed pleasure nor guaranteed survival. It is personal dignity.

Dignity is respect. And respect comes from neither pity nor compassion. It arises from the realization that others regard us as competent human beings, as useful citizens. It emerges from the awareness that we see others in the same way.

Justice is hard work. And so is mutual respect.

SONG: AYFO OREE (No. 14)

MEMORIAL

We have two kinds of memories.

We have memories of people who always demanded and never gave, who complained and never achieved, who chose to be known by who they were and not by what they did, who preferred pity to respect.

We also have memories of people who trained their talents and shared them, who took the blame and worked to change the world, who presented their

Physical strength, like physical health, is always welcome. But it is never enough. A toughness of the inner self is required. The spirit, as well as the body, needs to be strong.

If we are good leaders, we are strong enough to be careful. We do not yield to every demand. We make a distinction between what is important and what is unimportant. We do not waste our energies.

If we are good leaders, we are strong enough to be hated. If we try to please everybody, we will please nobody. If we try to stand for everything, we will stand for nothing. If we are afraid of hostility, we will never be able to earn love and devotion.

If we are good leaders, we are strong enough to compromise. Weak people are afraid to yield. They are afraid that if they give up one thing, they will give up all. Strong people do not turn every idea into a principle. They realize that people are not the servants of ideals, but that ideals are the servants of people.

Good leaders need a special kind of strength.

SONG: LAM'TSAPPEEM (No. 56)

WISDOM

Good leaders need wisdom.

Wise people are more than smart people. Photographic memories and analytic skills are important assets, but they do not guarantee wisdom.

Wise people are sensitive people. They understand their own needs and the needs of others. They understand their own feelings and the feelings of others. They know what it means to be human.

Bad leaders always make impossible demands. They expect people to be what they cannot be. They expect people to do what they are unable to do.

If we are good leaders, we listen to others. We listen to their worries, their fears, and their problems. We listen to their hopes, their dreams, and their ambitions. We do not mold their needs to our vision. We mold our vision to their needs.

SONG: MEE HAHAM (No. 65)

RESPONSIBILITY

Good leaders take responsibility for their actions.

Responsibility separates leaders from followers. Children—and adults who prefer to be children—love to plead their innocence. They love to see themselves as victims of forces over which they have no control. They hate to take responsibility.

If we are good leaders, we pay for our privileges. Power and status are not free gifts without price. They bring with them risks which are sometimes frightening, especially the risk of being wrong.

If we are good leaders, we are strong enough to admit our mistakes. We do not search for scapegoats. We do not pretend that what is imperfect is perfect. We do not plead infallibility or self-righteousness. We let our humanity show. We become greater by admitting that we are smaller.

If we were always right, we would be intolerable.

SONG: HATOV O HARA (No. 41)

OPTIMISM

Good leaders are optimists.

A realistic optimism is not a Pollyanna view of the world. It is no maudlin denial of ugliness and disaster. Realistic optimism is the refusal to surrender to despair, even when despair comes easy.

If we are good leaders, we do not cultivate dread. We do not make our expectations an excuse for doing nothing. Some people always expect to lose, always anticipate defeat. Some people always see catastrophe, always prepare for doom. But they cannot lead.

If we are good leaders, we notice our strength more than our weakness. We see our opportunities more than our limitations. We yearn for the positive more than the negative.

Realistic optimists do not imagine that all will be well. They are simply willing to take action without guarantees.

SONG: BASHANA HABAA (No. 21)

INSPIRATION

Good leaders inspire the people they lead.

All men and women need strong motivation to go beyond their private needs to serve the needs of others. All men and women need compelling reasons to risk their lives and fortunes for the sake of distant strangers and future goals.

If we are good leaders, we are experts at motivation. We inspire people to do what is good for them and what is good for others.

If we are good parents, our children seek to help their family. If we are good teachers, our students are eager to learn. If we are good bosses, our workers are willing to cooperate. If we are good presidents, our citizens are prepared to share.

Transmitting the excitement of desires and ideals is not always easy. But good leaders have mastered the skill.

SONG: AYFO OREE (No. 14)

MEMORIAL

Good leaders teach by example.

So many people ask others to do what they are not prepared to do themselves. Their demands and their behavior never seem to meet. They are comfortable with hypocrisy and are puzzled by the fact that so very few really listen to their advice.

The leaders of the past whom we admired—the parents, the teachers, the people of authority who inspired our respect—did not earn their tribute by their words. They won it through their deeds. They lived with integrity.

When we remember them, we remember not only their words of love but especially their acts of love. If they left a legacy, it lies in our willingness to follow their example.

SONG: SHEEM'OO (No. 83)

25
LIGHT

SONG: V'SHOOV ITKHEM (No. 95)

WINTER

Winter is the season of darkness. The sun spends less time with us and is reluctant to show its face. The night grows longer, a freezing blackness hovers over the landscape, and we long for the light of summer.

In the summer the sun is too available to be precious. We take it for granted, using its heat and its light shamelessly. But in the winter the sun is our longed-for and valued friend. When it emerges, even for a short while, it fills us with wonder and with joy. And we fear its departure.

If absence makes the heart grow fonder, then winter is the season of sunlight.

SONG: BAROOKH HAOR (No. 20)

LIFE

In the winter nature sleeps. In a world of cold and darkness, life withdraws for a while and waits for more congenial times. Like winter, life and heat are part of life and make it possible.

Our early ancestors started out in a tropical land of eternal summer. Our naked bodies are made for warm places. Winter was not part of our origins.

Today we live in cold places. We may dread the winter, we may fear the chill—but we have learned to live with it. Human ingenuity has invented its own heat. We can make summer even in the winter.

SONG: HAOR SHEL HAYOFEE (No. 39)

LIGHT

Vision is very human. It is our strongest sense. We see better than most of our animal cousins. Even our face brings our eyes together so that depth and distance become real for us. When we cannot see, we are terrified and disoriented.

But vision needs light. It needs the energy of the sun. It needs the parade of photons that illumine the world and make it a place for human habitation.

Darkness is our enemy. We cannot live with it unless we sleep. We are destined for the light. And when the winter takes away the brightness of the sun and gives us too much darkness, we strive to make our own light.

SONG: NAE HAOR (No. 70)

FIRE

Fire was our foe until we tamed it. It burned and killed. It maimed and destroyed. It drove us from the shelter of our trees.

But fire became our friend. When we seized it and held it captive, the winter could not push us away. Like a miniature sun, it gave us light and heat. Like a small star, it brightened the darkness. In time we learned to make our own fire. We learned to make our own light. We learned to make cold places warm.

Flames of fire arouse our deepest memories. They remind us of security and protection. They remind us of survival and safety. They remind us of family and food. In an age of science and technology, there must be some overwhelming reason why we still contrive to sit in front of the fire.

SONG: ASHRAY HAGAFROOR (No. 13)

HOPE

Fire continues to be a symbol of hope and survival. Our past lives in our present and gives our culture a sense of continuity.

All nations, all tribes, have ceremonies of fire that reach back to dim antiquity. Altar flames, eternal lights, holiday candles and bright menorahs—these are testimony to our age-old romance with fire. We fear it, and yet we know that we cannot live without it.

In wintertime ceremonies of fire are especially strong. The cold and the darkness remind us of our dependence and of our ancient struggles with nature. We seek out the fire as a sign of our past success and as an expression of our will to live.

In wintertime flames of light and heat give us hope.

SONG: LOO Y'HEE (No. 59)

MENORAH

In the darkness of the Jerusalem Temple, our ancestors erected a stand of fire and light. Its seven lights mirrored the fires of the seven stars—the sun, the moon, and the five visible planets. Tribal law insisted that these lights burn eternally, that they never be extinguished. Tribal law insisted that there was some mysterious connection between the fire and national survival.

The Menorah was only a new form of an old flame. Its light was a reflection of the first light our ancestors ever captured. It was a reminder of the power of the sun in human hands.

This Menorah became the first symbol of the Jewish people. It still speaks to us of survival and hope.

SONG: AYFO OREE (No. 14)

MEMORIAL

Fire created the hearth and the home. Around the fire, families sat together and shared their food. Around the fire, they huddled and shared their warmth. Around the fire, they told stories and sang songs and invented culture.

Culture began with fire. It began with the struggle for life. Like a continuing flame, its light is fed by the parents of one generation for the children of the next.

Before the winter fires, we remember the fires of the past. We remember the stories and signs of the past. We remember the loving gifts of the past. We remember our roots.

SONG: Y'HEE SHALOM (No. 98)

26
LOVE

AFFIRMATION

Listen now, you lovers of love,
Hear this, you seekers of happiness,
There is no happiness without love.

SONG: SHEEM'OO (No. 83)

REFLECTION

The night is a good time for reflection. Darkness covers all distraction and frees us from the bother of noticeable change. Our vision turns inward and confronts the reality of our desire and worry. In the evening our dreams become more vivid and our fears more real. In the night our hopes become more intense and our dread more awesome. We sense the promise of life in the warmth of our bodies. We feel the menace of death in the cold of the night air. Present wisdom is a fragile help. It seems much too meager for comfort. The secrets of life still plague us. The way to fulfillment eludes our constant search.

Yet within our hearts we know that life is worthy of the struggle and that happiness is possible. Within our minds we strive to find the way to victory.

SONG: EREV SHEL SHOSHANNEEM (No. 30)

INDIVIDUALITY

Each of us is condemned to be an individual. From the moment of birth, from the moment we are separated from the womb of our mother, we become distinct and conscious of our difference. A sense of privacy is uniquely ours. It defines the human condition. We stand alone with our feelings and thoughts and know that they are too personal to be fully shared. Even in the crowd we feel the physical closeness of others and sense the mental distance that separates soul from soul and heart from heart. We want to reach out and touch the lives of others. We want to communicate. We want to reveal our innermost fears and doubts and to share their burden with someone who really understands.

The threat of loneliness is eternal. It never ceases to assault the soul of man. For we are like stars in a cold heaven signaling to each other our desire in the darkness. Out of the pain of separation we strive for union with others and we discover love.

SONG: HINNAY MA TOV (No. 47)

GIVING

To receive or to give; that is the ultimate question of love. To many who love, involvement is never an action, a state of doing. It is always a passion, a state of being. For these people, the problem of life is to find someone who admires them, cares for them, and makes their welfare his ultimate concern. How nice it is to be loved and to revel in the devotion of another human being! How ecstatic it is to receive the special reverence of friends and to sense that in their eyes we are supremely important! How delightful—and how fragile! If our happiness rests on feelings and deeds we do not control, our life leans on risky support. If our test of inner joy is in what others do for us and in what others think of us, then love is a cruel torture which aggravates our loneliness by the threat of withdrawal. When the fickle behavior of others can deprive us of our security and make us beggars for attention and gratitude, then love is nothing more than the prelude to hate. In our rejection by those we love the pain is unbearable and we defend ourselves by blaming them.

If, then, the deepest pleasures of our life depend on what we receive, we shall search for happiness and never find it.

SONG: EEM AYN (No. 28)

MATURITY

Mature love is an art, a skill of the soul. It is more than an instinctive rage of feeling. It is more than a biological cry for erotic pleasure. Love is something to be learned.

Newborn infants come into the world in helpless dependency, knowing only how to receive. As they grow up, as they cease to be children, they sense a new power—not the power to demand love, but the power to express love. To sense that we not only need to be helped but also need to help, to steadily feel that we not only require the care of others but also are able to give care, is the beginning of inner security. We do not transcend our loneliness by only finding others to love us. We transcend our sense of separation by finding others to love. In the act of being useful, in the work of fulfilling the desires and needs of other human beings, we feel our creative power and discover our strength.

True love is an ironic deed. It binds us closer to other people while it awakens within us the thrill of independence. The more we help, the stronger we feel. The stronger we feel, the more secure we become.

Love is the developed art of expressing our human power through the act of giving to others. It overwhelms our fears and gives us hope through the promise of our strength.

SONG: V'AHAVTA (No. 93)

WISDOM

Wisdom is power. Through the force of our reasoning mind, we scan the map of the universe and look for truth. Since knowledge of the outer world is never enough for our fulfillment, we must also probe and understand the inner world of will and feeling. To the wise observer the inner search reveals that no person achieves happiness without the act of love. The scholar who has uncovered the deepest mysteries of the universe and who does not know this fact is as helpless in the struggle of life as the newborn child. From the history of all humanity we can learn no greater lesson.

SONG: AYFO OREE (No. 14)

MEMORIAL

Love is never self-sacrifice; it is never the act of giving up what belongs to us. Self-sacrifice is the twin of self-pity. If helping others means diminishing ourselves, then kindness is nothing more than the suicide of martyrdom. People who truly love may suffer, but they do not love in order to suffer. The heroes of our past gave us the best of their devotion and care without demanding our gratitude. They knew that the act of giving is its own compensation. They toiled beyond their energies and worked beyond their strength for the welfare of others. They saw that love is its own reward.

SONG: SHEEM'OO (No. 83)

AFFIRMATION

Listen now, you lovers of love,
Hear this, you seekers of happiness,
There is no happiness without love.

27
LOYALTY

AFFIRMATION

Each of us is more than an individual.
Each of us is part of other people as they are part of us.

SONG: HINNAY MA TOV (No. 47)

COMMUNITY

Human life begins with other people. It grows with other people. It finds its fulfillment in other people. Each of us is more than an individual, more than a unique person independent of society. To be alone, to live alone, to avoid the world of other men and women is to be less than human. From the very moment of our birth we are bound to other people who give us food, and love, and speech, and the reward of usefulness. The human smile may be less radiant than the sun, less awesome than the sea. But the human heart responds to it more quickly than to any other natural wonder.

SONG: KAMIEYEEM (No. 51)

COOPERATION

We are not born to be selfish. If each of us were interested in our personal survival alone, the human species would long since have perished. If most of us were unwilling to subordinate our own welfare to the welfare of our group, neither family nor community would be possible. There is within each of us an instinct for cooperation, a tendency to feel ourselves a part of a social whole greater than ourselves.

Cooperation is more than enlightened self-interest, more than rational selfishness. The gifts of kindness and tenderness are not always good for the giver. Deeds of love and generosity are not always beneficial to the doer. Countless people have sacrificed their lives and fortunes to protect their family and their nation. Others have endured pain and dishonor to serve the cause of humanity. When we transcend ourselves in the pursuit of an ideal greater than our own personal pleasure, loyalty is born.

SONG: EEM AYN (No. 28)

CONFLICT

There are two kinds of moral tension. There is the tension between the group and the individual. How much pleasure, safety, and security must each of us forego in order to satisfy the welfare of our family, our friends, and our people? There is also the tension between group and group. Is my loyalty to my family more important than my obligation to my country? Is my duty to humanity more significant than my commitment to my nation? Whom do I serve first when I cannot serve both?

Each of us is a member of many groups. Sometimes the well-being of one group does not seem compatible with the well-being of another. Sometimes what is best for my family may not be best for my community, and what is best for my community may not be best for humanity as a whole.

Deciding to be unselfish does not solve the problem of morality. When there is no clear order of conflicting loyalties, ethical decisions are impossible. Who is deserving of my first loyalty? That is the ultimate question.

SONG: V'AHAVTA (No. 93)

FRIENDSHIP

There are two kinds of families to which we belong. Each requires our loyalty and our compassion. There is the family of our mother and father, sister and brother, husband and wife, son and daughter. We enter it at birth and we learn through childhood to fear its rejection. For even when it is oppressive, it gives us roots and a sense of continuity.

There is also the family of intimate friends. We enter it by choice and we learn through experience to value its opportunities. Parents and cousins are compulsory gifts whom we respect even when they do not share our own hopes and ideals. But friends are personal discoveries, whom we love and honor because they reflect our deepest feelings. Friends are equals. They complete our being by their unique presence and in turn are fulfilled by our own attachment. To be loyal to a friend is to be loyal to oneself.

SONG: B'AYLE HAYADIEYIM (No. 22)

LOVE

Life is not possible without light—without the light of the sun. Life is not possible without water—without the liquid womb in which evolution began.

If the light of the sun should go out, if the water should vanish, all life would be lost.

Human life is even frailer. It needs more than sun and water. We are not islands unto ourselves. We cannot endure alone. We need the healing power of love. We need the secure strength of loyalty.

SONG: AYFO OREE (No. 14)

MEMORIAL

We live through the loyalty of others, not only the devotion of loving family and friends, but also the loyalty of the past to the future. Our ancestors worked, saved, and renounced their pleasure to provide for generations yet unborn. They pursued distant goals which they knew they would never reach so that their children and their grandchildren could seize them. The mountain of human culture is built out of many layers of human achievement, each generation resting on the work of the one before.

We are here today because the people of the past did not forget us. Our ancestors have planted and we have reaped. Let us also live for more than the present. Let us also work for those who will follow.

SONG: SHEEM'OO (No. 83)

AFFIRMATION

Each of us is more than an individual.
Each of us is part of other people as they are part of us.

28
MATURITY

SONG: SHALOM L'YISRAEL (No. 82)

CYCLE OF LIFE

Life is change. It never stands still.

Life is evolution. Old forms change into new forms. Old patterns turn into new patterns. Creatures are born, grow up, and die.

The human condition is also change. We are born. We grow up. We find work. We get married. We have children. We age. We die.

We cannot avoid changing even if we want to. The flow of time is relentless, and life follows with equal determination. Like the leaves of autumn, nothing is permanent. Everything is temporary.

We hope that along the way, in the midst of all these alterations, we will be able to create our own individual identity and discover maturity.

SONG: HAYAMEEM HOL'FEEM (No. 43)

CHILDHOOD

When we come into the world, we are very dependent. We cannot take care of our needs. We are helpless infants.

But time, nature, and love give us new skills. We learn to walk. We learn to talk. We learn to feed ourselves. We learn to play with other children and to protect ourselves from danger.

As the years pass, we become more independent. We discover that we have more control over our behavior. We find that we can trust our own power.

The awareness of this strength is very important to our self-respect. Good parents encourage us to depend more and more on our own skills. They make us understand that our talents are greater than we imagine.

A good childhood gives us nurturing love. We feel that we are worthwhile even when we make mistakes, even when we do wrong. Loving parents enable us to stand up on our own two feet because we know that they are there when we fall.

SONG: SHEEM'OO (No. 83)

YOUTH

Youth is the time for adventure.

Childhood needs love and security. Childhood needs nurturing and safety. But youth is less timid. Competition intrigues it. Risk gives it pleasure. Curiosity consumes it.

When we are young, we have a need to prove ourselves. We have a need to test our talents. We are driven to discover what we want to do. We are driven to discover what we want to be.

Youth is a time of highs and lows. When we meet our expectations, our enthusiasm is strong and hopeful. But when we fail them, our despair is equally intense. Our desires are so powerful that they do not allow compromise. And our vision is so new that it is hard to see through present frustration.

In youth, everything is fresh. Our loving, our learning, our striving, our giving—all of them are new excitements that repetition has not had the opportunity to dull. Sometimes enthusiasm makes the young naïve, but it is a small price to pay for the opportunity of spring.

SONG: MAHAR (No. 63)

MIDDLE YEARS

Our middle years are the time for achievement.

In childhood we discover our strength. In youth we refine our self-esteem. In the middle years, we express our power and wisdom.

We commit ourselves to work. We choose our partners. We create our families. We train our children. We enrich our friendships. We plan our future. We arrange for our security.

When we are in the middle of our life, we have to be most responsible. Both the young and the old depend on us. Both our family and our workplace make demands on us. We sometimes feel burdened. We sometimes feel torn by conflicting loyalties.

As we become more mature, as the mellowness of our minds begins to correspond to the adulthood of our bodies, we learn to negotiate our inner arguments with grace. We come to understand that we cannot have everything we want. We learn to compromise. We value other points of view. Living with the absurdities of fate strengthens our sense of humor. And we find that we are doing more while expecting less.

SONG: HALBEESHEENEE (No. 35)

LATER YEARS

Our later years are a time for integrity.

We no longer have to prove ourselves. We no longer have to mold a career. We no longer have to meet the demands of family and work. We no longer have to be what others want us to be. Our later years can be a time of extraordinary freedom when we can say and do what we never said and did before.

But many of us, as we grow older, also grow afraid. Our body does not obey us as easily as it did before. Our usefulness to others seems less apparent. Our money dwindles. Our friends depart. Our family does not give us the attention we think we deserve. We come to believe that we are too weak and too vulnerable to do the things we want to do. We are obsessed with security. We cease to be curious. We stop living.

Yet many of us, as we grow older, also grow more interesting. We discover that our mind may be younger than our body. We learn that our wisdom is useful to strangers. We find that we need fewer material things and we can make new friends. We invent new games. We study new subjects. We open our minds to new thoughts. We affirm life.

SONG: TUM BALALAIKA (No. 92)

MATURITY

Maturity takes a long time. It is the special gift of our later years.

Maturity needs the nurturing love of childhood, the brashness of youth, the mellow achievement of our middle years, and the integrity of aging. Each stage of our life rests on the other and needs its foundation.

If we never get enough love, we shall remain the child. If we never test our skills, we shall stay a fearful youth. If we never taste achievement, we shall fall into bitter envy. And if we are too afraid to have integrity, we shall cease to live before we die.

Life is change. Life is growth. Even when our bodies grow weaker, our minds and spirits can grow stronger with wisdom. Our experiences become the roots that nourish us.

The strength of maturity is the most satisfying strength that we can possess.

SONG: AYFO OREE (No. 14)

MEMORIAL

The individual identity of each of us is a string of memories tied together by our will to live. In these memories are many people who gave us the love, support, and recognition we needed to survive. Some of them were physically present—parents, friends, and teachers who taught us to be generous. Others were present in books and stories that gave us inspiration—heroes and role models who were examples to be followed.

Each of us, too, is part of the memories of others. Our lives are intertwined. We receive and give. We honor each other through mutual dependence.

SONG: TS'REEKHEEM (No. 91)

29
PEACE

SONG: SHALOM LARAHOK (No. 81)

PEACE

Peace is more than an ideal. It is an achievement. There is no divine power that will give it to us for nothing. There are no laws of history that will guarantee its arrival.

Peace is hard work. The forces of war and violence are very strong in our world. They hide in the deep unconscious of our mind. They attach themselves to personal greed. They find a friend in the lust for power.

Too often our mouth prefers peace, but our behavior prefers war. We praise love and harmony, but we indulge hate and hostility. We endorse kindness, but we subsidize cruelty.

We have to work for peace in the same way that we work for a living. In the age of nuclear destruction, it may be even more important.

SONG: HEVAY MITTALMEEDAV (No. 46)

RESPECT

Peace begins with respect—not only the respect we bear for our own dignity, but the respect we give to the dignity of others.

As human beings we are all entitled to be the masters of our own lives and the planners of our own destiny. When others seek to take away that right and to impose their vision of the good life on the victims of their power, rebellion and war follow. If we cannot abide a world of human differences, we will never enjoy a world of peace.

So many times we want other people to do what we do so that we will feel more secure about our own decisions. Conformity is reassuring and gives us the illusion of group solidarity. But forcing people to be what we want them to be often makes them reject what they would freely choose if it were freely offered. The struggle for personal dignity becomes the fight to be different.

SONG: NAASE SHALOM (No. 69)

COOPERATION

Peace needs cooperation. If we feel too self-sufficient, if we think of ourselves as too independent, we will easily risk the hostility of others. But if we know that we depend on the goodwill of many people, if we realize that most of what we desire cannot be secured by ourselves alone, we will become more trustworthy and will cultivate friendship.

Nations are like individuals. When they are arrogant enough to believe that they can easily fend for themseles and that they have nothing to fear from other nations, they will take as much power as they can seize.

But in a global village of atomic weapons, independence is an illusion. No one is free of danger. The peril is all-pervasive. We are all vulnerable. The decision of one leader can destroy us all.

Cooperation is a world necessity. If we will not work together, then we will die together.

SONG: V'AHAVTA (No. 93)

TRUST

Peace needs trust. If we are to lower our guard, if we are to reduce our defenses, then we must believe that others will not take advantage of our new weakness. When our competitor is unreliable, we will yield nothing.

It is dangerous to be too self-righteous. If we divide the world into good and evil, if we ascribe all noble sentiments and moral behavior to our own team, and all wicked thoughts and criminal action to our opponents, we will widen the gulf of distrust.

But if we are willing to see our own faults, if we are able to admit that the fear of war is universal, if we can restrain our need to humiliate our enemies, then the breach will grow smaller and bridges of cautious faith can be built.

Trust begins with the danger of not trusting. We take risks because we have no alternative.

SONG: TAYN SHABBAT (No. 86)

HOPE

Peace needs hope. If we are too impatient with the performance of others, if we expect people to change too quickly, we will despair before we need to.

Utopian fantasies are dangerous. A world in which all hatred and jealousy vanish is not likely. A society in which the danger of war disappears is improbable. A revolution that will abolish all human hostility is a foolish dream. If we expect the impossible, then we will always live with disappointment.

But some dreams are not foolish. They depend for their fulfillment on a patient realism. Armies can be made smaller. Weapons can be reduced in number. Disputes can be resolved through talking. It is possible to make war less warlike and peace more peaceful.

Hope needs perspective and the willingness to settle for undramatic victories. We need to climb our steps one by one.

SONG: LOO Y'HEE (No. 59)

COMPROMISE

Peace needs compromise. It needs a willingness to tolerate a world that is less perfect than we want. If we insist on having our way all the time, we shall make fighting inevitable.

For some people, life is all or nothing. Justice is getting what you deserve, and integrity is never settling for less than you dream of.

For others, life is give and take, a balancing act of not so good and not too bad, an endless negotiation among incompatible needs and desires.

People who want the world perfect make revolution and wars. Peaceful people settle for less—and guarantee the future.

SONG: AYFO OREE (No. 14)

MEMORIAL

Death is a reminder of human frailty. We are very vulnerable creatures, and we have so many natural enemies. Floods and earthquakes, disease and famine, heat and cold take their toll and thin our ranks. Even in this time of scientific wonders, ancient enemies of aging and decay still creep upon us uninvited and make us mortal.

In a world of peace, there is still a war to be fought—not a war of people against people, but a war against death and all its friends. If we must fight, let us fight poverty. If we must battle, let us battle with disease. If we must assault the enemy, let us assault the poisons of our environment. There are many real foes to face.

Let our tribute to the dead be our struggle against death.

SONG: SHEEM'OO (No. 83)

30
PEOPLE

SONG: V'SHOOV ITKHEM (No. 95)

HUMANITY

We have many identities. We are Jews. We are Americans. But first and above all, we are human beings.

Human identity is so obvious and so ordinary that we sometimes forget about it. We strive so hard to be unique and different that we fail to remember how much alike we all are. Old hatreds and old hostilities prevent us from seeing through our artificial barriers and noticing that our enemies share with us the same fears and the same needs.

When we feel our humanness first, our hearts and minds open up. We no longer seek to exclude others. We seek to welcome them, to embrace them. We become aware of the larger family to which we belong. The human race becomes our race, and all men and women become our brothers and sisters.

SONG: AHEE ADAM (No. 4)

SOLIDARITY

There are times when it is important to feel separate, distinct, unique, and individual. Our sense of personal identity is a very important part of our self-esteem.

But there are also times when it is important to feel our connection with other people. Without the stimulus of family, friends, and even strangers, our individuality would not be very rich and our personalities would not be very interesting.

We are most ourselves when others evoke the best from us. The reason we can be truly individual is that we are truly human. Our human connection enables us to reach out to others and enables others to reach out to us. In this connection, we discover that we are not alone with all our fears and hopes. Others share our anxieties and give us the strength to cope with them. Others share our visions and help us to make them real.

Without human solidarity, all of us would be too frightened and too lonely to notice who we are and what we can do.

SONG: HINNAY MA TOV (No. 47)

OPENNESS

In the story of the human race, almost every nation imagined that its culture was the best of all possible cultures and that its customs were the best of all possible customs. Some even imagined that, without them, there would be no true religion and no true morality in the world.

Egyptians and Persians, Greeks and Romans, shared this arrogance. Even we Jews were no exception. Many of our own sages maintained that the Jewish people were the custodians of the one eternal truth and that no useful wisdom could be found in the writings of other nations.

But common sense resists this narrowness. The concern for human dignity is to be found among all cultures and is as universal as the lust for tyranny. Every people features both the good and the bad, the moral and the immoral. The noble sentiments of the human heart have been articulated by great men and women in all places.

Modesty makes us better Jews and opens our hearts and minds to the wisdom of the world.

SONG: MAHAR (No. 63)

PEACE

The story of humanity has often been the story of peace. Families live side by side. Tribes share space. Nations trade goods. Empires embrace many cultures.

140 *People*

But too often the story of humanity has been the story of war. Family assaults family. Tribe invades tribe. Nation exterminates nation. Empires seek to conquer the world.

Our biology tells us that people are more alike than they are different. But our memories tell us that the human race is divided into "insiders" and "outsiders," natives and strangers.

Our biology tells us that humanity can be one family. But our memories tell us that nations must hate nations, that hostility is normal.

In an age when the weapons of war have the power to destroy all the people of the world, our memories are very dangerous. We must resist them.

SONG: NAASE SHALOM (No. 69)

WORLD CITIZENSHIP

Reality often begins with dreams. People are inspired by the vision of some great ideal and strive to achieve it. The power of their dream changes the world.

Throughout the centuries of human conflict and war-inspired hate, many dreamers in many lands dreamed of a new world where war would disappear and where all nations would become one nation. Every person in every place would belong to a single family and would share a single allegiance.

That vision has not yet come true. Brutal reality defies it and mocks its hopes. But the attachment to that dream is so strong that it never seems to die.

For us, the dreamers, the future lives in our present. Perhaps, if we insist that we are citizens of the world, our opponents who resist us now will ultimately come to realize that they are world citizens too.

SONG: BASHANA HABAA (No. 21)

ADAM

In the minds of many people, peace and human harmony are inevitable. No matter what human beings do, God will make it all right in the end. The Messiah will arrive and everybody will live happily ever after.

This vision of the future is a dangerous vision. One world is no more inevitable than is human self-destruction. But both are possibilities. Only human decision will determine which alternative will turn into reality.

Adam is a Hebrew word which means "person." It is a symbol of people-power and people-responsibility. In the end, the future of humanity is up to us, to all the people of the world. We can raise bigger walls of separation, fight bigger wars, and make bigger weapons. Or we can tear down the barriers between nations, seek conciliation and compromise, and use our ingenuity for peace.

There are no guarantees. The choice is ours.

SONG: AYFO OREE (No. 14)

MEMORIAL

Each of us is an heir, an heir to the wisdom and achievements of the past. Our inheritance comes from many places—from our family, from our community, from our nation, and from all the nations of the world.

While there are many races and many cultures, they are all interconnected, giving and taking from each other. In a sense, there is a universal culture into which all nations have poured their contribution. As science shrinks our world by its inventions, our new closeness to all people expands our sharing.

When we remember the heroes of our past, we remember that they are not confined to our own family, our own race, our own nation. They come from many places and many lands and their creations grace the lives of many people they never knew—all over the world.

SONG: Y'HEE SHALOM (No. 98)

31
PHILOSOPHY

SONG: HINNAY MA TOV (No. 47)

BELIEFS

Everybody has a philosophy of life.

Humanists have a philosophy of life.

Humanistic Jews have a philosophy of life.

A philosophy of life is that set of personal beliefs about the world which determines the way we make important decisions. For most people these beliefs are unconscious, guiding their behavior without ever being noticed. For some people these convictions are conscious, directing their actions with the full power of awareness.

Uncovering our beliefs helps us to understand them, to evaluate them, and to apply them more consistently. We can reaffirm our commitments. We can distinguish between the important and the unimportant. We can change what is no longer satisfactory.

A conscious philosophy of life makes us the masters of our own decisions and the captains of our own behavior.

SONG: AYZE HOO GIBBOR (No. 18)

TRUTH

Every philosophy of life recommends a path to truth.

We all have many ways to discover the truth. Sometimes we rely on the testimony of old books and tradition. Sometimes we yield to the inner summons of instinct and intuition. Sometimes we test our ideas on the scale of reason and pursue the facts.

Faith, intuition, and common sense are part of everybody's search for truth. But for us, for humanists, they are not of equal value. Trust in old authority is convenient at times. But it is dangerous as a lifetime habit. Inner conviction is valuable in crisis. But the certainty of one day is often the falsehood of the next.

Reason is our most trusted guide. It is not afraid of the facts. It does not run away from unpleasant reality. It loves to change its mind in the face of new evidence. It puts emotion in the right place, keeping us away from convenient answers. It is even willing to wait for a while, preferring honest uncertainty to desperate belief.

Reason is our path to truth.

SONG: EMET L'YISRAEL (No. 29)

REALITY

Every philosophy of life distinguishes between what is reality and what is illusion.

It is sometimes hard to make that distinction. Our needs get in the way of our better judgment. There are certain painful truths that we try to avoid. There are certain facts that make us uncomfortable. There are certain desires that make us feel guilty. The world is not always the way we want it to be. Death, injustice, and change are not always the most popular alternatives. Illusion is very tempting.

Supernatural worlds in particular are seductive. They avoid death. They always reward the just. They resist change. They are full of the power we feel we lack. When we are feeling vulnerable, they are easy to believe in.

To accept nature—its beautiful side and its ugly side, its useful side and its harmful side—is not easy. To accept the universe—with all its aloof grandeur and with all its vast indifference to our personal fate—is more than difficult. But it makes us strong. And it makes us see that we need to rely more on ourselves and on other people.

As humanists, we are never fully satisfied with nature. But we learn to live with it honestly.

SONG: OUT OF THE NIGHT (No. 76)

ETHICS

Every philosophy of life tells us the difference between right and wrong.

For some people, morality is a set of divine rules which never change. Old authority makes them credible. Tradition is their justification. Ethical commands are absolute. Ethical living is obedience.

For other people, morality is an arbitrary decision. No single authority claims the direction of human behavior. No objective standard governs human behavior. Each person chooses the path his conscience dictates. Each person refrains from judging the commitment of others.

For humanists, for people like us, consequences are more important than tradition. Results are more compelling than mere freedom. We do not exist to serve rules. Rules exist to serve our basic needs. We do not live in order to be free. We use freedom so that we can live with dignity.

The right way is never absolute, nor is it ever absolutely free. It tests every human decision with the compelling goal of human dignity. A good rule elevates human self-esteem. A moral conscience protects the dignity of all.

As humanists, we may disagree about the means, but we strive for common ends. Freedom with dignity, for ourselves and for others, is our shared goal.

SONG: HATOV O HARA (No. 41)

POLITICS

Every philosophy of life is more than personal. It recognizes that we are social beings, that we live in intimate contact with other people, that the fate of each of us is woven into the fate of humanity.

Politics is a branch of ethics. It deals with power and the sharing of power. Every group of people has to deal with the issue of power. Parents and children argue about power. Friends and neighbors argue about power. Nations and empires struggle for power.

Some people believe that power should be divided unevenly. They affirm that the wise, the strong, and the talented have the right to rule the masses, who are less fortunate. Others believe that power should be divided equally. They dream of a world where there are neither leaders nor followers, neither masters nor servants.

Most humanists stand somewhere in between. Neither the elitist Right nor the egalitarian Left captures their loyalty. They prefer the middle ground, choosing the best from either side.

As humanists we are wary of dogmatic answers. We are wary of authoritarian leaders. We are wary of pretentious followers. We avoid easy labels. We defend human dignity.

SONG: AL SH'LOSHA D'VAREEM II (No. 8)

COMMITMENT

Every philosophy of life is only as good as the commitment it inspires.

It is easy to be a spectator. It is easy to be an armchair philosopher, never making a decision, always postponing judgment.

It is harder to have conviction. It is harder to risk commitment, seeking to act on what we say we believe.

Many humanists are spectators, always pleading confusion as the excuse for their passivity. Many of us strive to be humanists of conviction, making decisions without absolute guarantees, acting on beliefs without absolute certainty.

Commitment is our dignity. It makes us confront our real philosophy. It helps us understand that study is only the prelude to living.

SONG: AYFO OREE (No. 14)

MEMORIAL

When we think of philosophy, we tend to think of words and spoken ideas. We tend to think of articulate men and women who write profoundly about the human condition.

Philosophy

But philosophy is not confined to those who can talk about it. It is also the intimate possession of those who live it.

Most of the people who have touched our lives in a positive way cannot fully explain their vision of truth, reality, and moral virtue. But they speak through their deeds and grant us the gifts of integrity.

We honor all people of conviction who have made their humanism an act of living, who have turned their feelings and ideas into visible commitment.

SONG: ZAYKHER (No. 103)

32
REALISM

AFFIRMATION

Sometimes we see—but are blind.
Sometimes we stand firm—but continue to run.
Sometimes we are honest—but never tell the truth.

SONG: SHALOM LARAHOK (No. 81)

REALITY

Many of us are running—even though we think that we are standing still. We are not running with our arms and our legs. We are running with our fears and anxieties. Our race is a mental race. It is a mental flight—a flight from the reality of ourselves and the reality of others.

Reality is often hard to accept, and so we block it out, pretend that it doesn't exist, refuse to confront it. We substitute fantasies. We invent excuses. We describe pain as pleasure and suffering as happiness. We rage against blindness even though we do not wish to see. We rage against deafness even though we do not wish to hear.

We do not want to accept what seems to be unacceptable. We are running away from reality.

SONG: LEER'DOF BAEMET (No. 57)

FEELINGS

The risk of being human is always real. To be human is always real. To be human is to feel all the feelings the heart can provide. To be human is to hope all the hopes the mind can imagine. We are more than love and kindness. We are more than goodness and tender care. We are also hate and anger, contempt and envy.

Many of us are ashamed to hate, or to be angry, or to feel contempt, or to be jealous. Since we are human and cannot avoid feeling what we feel, since we are human and cannot escape our natural emotions, we deny what we feel. We spend our time refusing what has no need to be refused. We give our precious hours to defending what has no need to be defended. We feel compelled to prove to ourselves and to others that only love fills our hearts and that we seek only to help and never to harm. We are running away from the fullness of our being.

There are moments in life when it is all right to hate, it is good to be angry, it is appropriate to feel contempt. To love all the time is less than human.

SONG: V'RAK ANAKNOO (No. 94)

DECISIVENESS

The risk of failure is always real. It is the other face to the opportunity of success. The present offers no guarantees for the future. Every new job, every new marriage, every new friendship, every new trip may succeed and fill our lives with the pleasure of fulfillment. It may also fail and envelop our days with the pain of frustration. If only we could know for sure! If only we could be positive that all will be well.

Some people can never make a decision. They hang in the agonizing limbo of yes and no. They are paralyzed by the fear of risk. The possibility of failure terrifies them and renders them impotent.

Every firm decision is a potential victim of the future. An unpredictable universe sponsors many surprises, and the uncertainty of things is unavoidable.

Postponing decisions is a way of running away from reality. It adds no guarantees, takes away our peace of mind, and prevents us from living.

SONG: MAASEEM TOVEEM (No. 61)

ACTION

The risk of having eyes is that we can see our own behavior. Behavior never lies. It never confuses. Its message is always clear, direct, and honest. What we really believe, what we really value, what we really desire, is always revealed in what we do. If we say that we are intellectual but never read a book; if we say that we are compassionate but never help a neighbor; if we claim to love life but proceed to destroy ourselves, then we are not what we think we are. Behavior always exposes our fantasies. We cannot be what we are unwilling to do.

Many of us run away from our behavior. We prefer to build imaginary worlds within our minds. We think that we believe what we do not really believe. We think that we feel what we do not really feel.

We are self-deceived and we call it honesty. Watching behavior is the best way to confront reality. It dispels all illusions. It rescues us from phony sincerity. It restores our vision, the only vision that really counts, the vision of truth.

SONG: HAEMET YOTSAYT (No. 32)

LIBERATION

To face the truth is sometimes hard because it denies us the protection of our fantasy walls. It is also liberating. It frees us from having to hide—from having to run away. It fills us with new pride—the pride of strength—the pride of honesty. It fills us with good humor—the laughter of humanness—the ease of accepting oneself. It fills us with goodwill—the goodwill of shared feelings—the goodwill of not having to pretend.

May we, in friendship, always support each other in our quest for truth. May we help each other face the light of truth by simply admitting that we can face it together.

SONG: AYFO OREE (No. 14)

MEMORIAL

We often run away from life. We think of death and are obsessed by it. The threat of aging fills us with dread and casts a shadow over all our youthful pleasures. The end of our story ruins the middle and sours the taste of our

150   *Realism*

happiness. Why bother to pursue what must pass away? Why bother to value what must cease to be?

To love life is to dismiss death. It is to risk every possible joy, every chance for vitality, every invitation to beauty.

It is to affirm the dignity of the human struggle and the victory of human survival. Death is real and inevitable. But we do not have to prepare for it. It will happen all by itself.

SONG: Y'HEE SHALOM (No. 98)

AFFIRMATION

Sometimes we see—but are blind.
Sometimes we stand firm—but continue to run.
Sometimes we are honest—but never tell the truth.

33
REASON

SONG: MA TOVOO (No. 64)

LIGHT

The mood of darkness is the mood of mystery. In the blackness of night our minds conjure a world of fantasy to fill the silent void. All that is obscure and vague in life, all that resists definition and boundary, finds its temperamental home in unlit spaces. The romantic imagination thrives on this absence of clarity and dances freely among the dim outlines of dark reality.

Daylight is a sober experience. It harshly exposes the definite lines of our horizon and checks the flights of fancy with the plain testimony of our senses. The sun burns out a purity of form that even the power of our dreams cannot defy. The world, in its pedestrian truth, loves the light that illusion resists. We need the warmth of the sun's rays. We also need the bright clearness it sheds upon the world. To see the universe in all its glory is to invite bold reason to be our guide to truth.

SONG: NAE HAOR (No. 70)

OPTIONS

Bewilderment is a very human state of mind. All of us struggle with the complexities of daily planning. Decision is never difficult if we really understand the goal to be achieved. But facts have an annoying dumbness about them. They persist in describing what is, without the graciousness to indicate what ought to be. They insist on neutrality and leave us to our own moral devices.

When we search for the ultimate purpose of life, we discover many attractive destinations. Their variety puzzles us. We are overwhelmed by options. Which path is our road to fulfillment? And which procedure is our guarantee for blissful happiness? Which commitment will produce the utopia of no anxiety? And which ecstasy will justify the daily struggle? If only simplicity were a human virtue! Then reasoning would be the childish game we dream of. Life resists our wish and makes us more profound than we desire. Each of us is a complex mechanism that defies the easy intuition of the amateur scholar. The orderly chaos of human behavior challenges our sanity and drives us to find protection in each others' confusion. From such muddled beginnings does brotherhood arise.

SONG: KAMIEYEEM (No. 51)

COURAGE

We view our blunders one by one. They march as guilty children before our judgment seat and plead the defense of our ignorance. Clarity of goal is a rare human virtue. When we weigh alternative actions, we need a list of priorities. Effective decision is only possible if the relative importance of each value is clearly discerned. Ordering our desires may seem a bit contrived, but it is indispensible to intelligence.

Many of us resist probing our values. The haze of haphazard thinking shields us from the risk of exposing foolish commitments and revealing the idiocy of trivial goals. There is a vegetative comfort in steering our moral boat through placid waters. Why rock the ship with waves of challenge when the dullness of everyday living is tolerable? Why test the vessel with a storm of protests when the repetition of blunders is inevitable? It takes more than dry courage to pick our settled goals apart and to expose them to the painful scrutiny of the reasoning mind.

SONG: MEE HAHAM (No. 65)

WISDOM

Life needs wisdom. To pursue the truth without the guide of reason is to endure the pain of searching without the pleasure of real discovery. Many of our mistakes are the sins of method. We perceive our ends with mature sensitivity, and then we proceed to botch the achievement with childish attachments. Intuitions and the prejudice of feelings become our favorite indulgence.

They are comfortable to use since they stand beyond the annoying challenge of evidence. We seek to secure what is hard in the easy way. The bitter taste of failure is our reward.

We possess the ability to be more than our dearest desire can envision. Only one requirement defines this potential. It is the willingness to look at the world realistically and to accept its truth without denial. It is the determination to follow the facts wherever they lead and never to allow the protest of fear to check our advance. The heat of passion is more than welcome after the calm of sober research has delivered the truth. When we solve our problems in the world of our own fantasy, we demean our courage. We need to be strong enough to be rational.

SONG: AYTS HIEYEEM (No. 17)

VISION

We always stand on the threshhold of greatness. Only the hand of tested truth can open the door of mature happiness. Our mistakes are often both sad and ludicrous because they are feeble blunders in the pursuit of pettiness. To envision the possible magnificence of man triumphant and to stumble in the hot chase of this ideal is to endure failure heroically. But no figure is more pathetic than the nearsighted prophet who stands appalled before his own possibility.

The flavor of life is determined by the breadth of its objectives. Cheap ends cheapen people and make them the victims of narrow vision. So many of us tremble before the demands of our talents and adjust our horizon to meet our fears. Human glory is never attained through success in the pursuit of trivia. It is often bestowed by failure in the search for nobility. Amos and Hosea walked the precipice of destruction and fell. But one moment of their zest was worth a thousand of their dull competitors. Our greatness lies in reaching out to what is unattainable and then discovering that it can be ours.

CONGREGATION

For the expectant is the glory
The future is theirs.
Whoever stands against the mountain without recoil
Shall ascend its summit.

SONG: LAMTSAPPEEM (No. 56)

REALISM

To be fully human we must merge our sober reason with the dreamy excitement of visionary causes. We must build the inner fortress of our mind and soul so that we can admit the cold wind of genuine fact and resist the fiery assault of petty emotion. We must see the richness of our being and strive with all our might to give it expression. Life can be a drama of vitality that carries each of us from act to act with increasing skill. The reality of our talents goes beyond our expectation. The hope of life transcends the ordinary.

SONG: AYFO OREE (No. 14)

MEMORIAL

Our lives are painfully judged by the standards of great men and women. Jeremiah and Hillel, in all their glory, expose the poverty of our own courage. Newton and Einstein, with all their wisdom, give our minds the stature of children. The heroes of virtue and intellect are daring reminders of our present mediocrity. Yet, by their extraordinary power, they are symbols of the human potential.

The memory of noble people we knew and loved gives us equal inspiration. By the special grace of their lives they reached our hearts and transformed them. In their strength and perception they confounded our weakness, as we leaned on them shamelessly. Their absence calls us to a frightening independence which needs the courage and wisdom of their example.

SONG: SHEEM'OO (No. 83)

34
SCIENCE

SONG: V'SHOOV ITKHEM (No. 95)

REVOLUTION

We live in the age of science, but very few people really know what science is all about.

For some people, science is machines, the glistening technology of automobiles and computers. For others, science is the mysterious formula, the strange equation which only experts can understand. For still others, science is power, the newly found ability of humans to do what even the gods never dreamed of doing.

But science is really much more and much less than that. It is not machines, even though machines come from it. It is not equations, even though mathematics may be its faithful assistant. It is not power, even though power may come to those who use it well.

Science is a revolutionary new way of looking at the world.

SONG: MEE HAHAM (No. 65)

AUTHORITY

In the past, people looked at the world through the eyes of tradition and faith. They consulted holy books and sacred scrolls. They trusted the words of their ancestors. They revered old insights and expected them to be true.

In the world of faith, beliefs are an inheritance from the past. They are an expression of our loyalty to family and nation. They unite us with teachers and sages who came before.

But science is different. It does not reject tradition or faith, but it asks for more. No ancestor, no sacred book, however famous, can guarantee the truth. No reverence, however pure and intense, can determine the nature of reality.

Facts are facts. They are enormously discourteous. They do not revere old books. They do not stand in awe before old beliefs. They do not bow before famous ancestors. They are simply the stuff out of which reality is made and the final judge of truth.

SONG: EMET L'YISRAEL (No. 29)

REALISM

Science demands discipline. It asks for the most difficult self-control we are capable of. It insists that we face the truth, no matter how unpleasant.

Unpleasant reality intrudes in so many ways. Sometimes it appears as a danger we do not wish to face. Sometimes it marches in to deflate our ego and makes us feel less important than we would want to be.

There are many ways to deal with unpleasant truth. We can pretend that it is not there. We can imagine fantasy alternatives and claim that they are real. We can push awareness of the truth deep down in our mind so that we never have to confront it except in our dreams. We can even persecute the people who dare to point it out and make them suffer for what we cannot bear to face.

The hardest thing to do, but certainly the most noble, is to let reality be reality. We cannot use our power well unless we understand its limits.

SONG: OUT OF THE NIGHT (No. 76)

CHANGE

Some people like the truth to be eternal. They want their beliefs to be guaranteed forever and ever. They hate change.

For most of human history, religion accommodated them. The proclamations of priests and rabbis resisted temporary endorsements. Only the stamp of eternal truth would do, and so dogma was born.

Science resists this game. It knows that no description of the world, no matter how insightful, no matter how profound, can be true forever. Every tomorrow brings the possibility of some new fact, some new piece of evidence, which may render the truth of today obsolete.

In the world of science, human energy is not wasted in defending old proclamations. It is invested in new and better ways to describe reality.

Human insights always need improvement. And the willingness to live with change is the heart of the scientific temperament.

SONG: RAYSHEET HOKHMA (No. 77)

COURAGE

Science needs courage, the courage to live with uncertainty.

Over the past few centuries, we have learned so much about the world. We have so much more information than we ever had before. We have so much more power than we ever thought possible.

But the universe is vast. Most of its events are still unknown to us. Many important questions still remain unanswered.

It would be so nice to understand the origins of the universe. It would be so helpful to see clearly the origins of life. But the evidence is still too stingy for definite answers. All we can honestly say is, "We do not know."

Admitting that we do not know when we do not know takes courage, especially when we want so much to know. It is too easy to grab at answers simply because we cannot bear the uncertainty of not knowing.

"I do not know" is a brave and dignified answer, especially when it is true.

SONG: SAHAKEE (No. 78)

BENEVOLENCE

The truth is morally neutral. It simply describes reality. It does not tell us what to do with it.

Science is neutral. It discloses to us the nature of our own power. It tells us about the limits of our power. But it cannot tell us what to do with that power.

This revolutionary way of looking at the world has given us a revolutionary new control of the events of the world. We can alter old forms of life. We can create new forms of life. We can move mountains. We can postpone death. We can make weapons so deadly that they can destroy humanity.

Science has given us the power of the gods, the power to do both good and evil.

Only we, through our own benevolence, can defend human dignity and human freedom. Science is our servant, not our master.

SONG: AYFO OREE (No. 14)

MEMORIAL

When we look at the past, we often do not deal with it honestly. We want to use it for our own purposes more than we want to see it as it really was.

We want our ancestors to endorse our opinions, even when they didn't. We want our childhood to be romantic, even when it wasn't. We want our roots to be extraordinary, even when they are less than our pride may require.

Loved ones, too, suffer from our need to make them what they weren't. In their death they deserve their dignity. They deserve their right to be seen as they chose to be.

Our honesty is our greatest tribute.

SONG: SHEEM'OO (No. 83)

35
SECULARISM

SONG: HINNAY MA TOV (No. 47)

THISWORLDLINESS

Loving this world is not always easy. There is poverty, disease, and natural disaster. There is frustration, death, and disappointed dreams. Our universe does not give us everything we want, and often it gives us less than we deserve.

Many people who find this world less than perfect dream of other worlds. They dream of places where there is no poverty, no disease, no natural disaster. They dream of lands where there is no frustration, no death, and no disappointment. In this haven beyond our present experience, we get everything we need. We receive everything we deserve.

Many people who find this world less than perfect dream of making it a better world. They find no need for other worlds and other places. They find no need to see the bad and ignore the good. They take pride in their power to live with reality. They take pride in their own willingness to resist evil and to improve the human condition. They value the good they see, the opportunities for love and happiness in this world and in this life.

The supernatural world holds no special fascination for them. They find their home in the secular world of everyday experience.

SONG: KAN AL P'NAY ADAMA (No. 52)

SECULARISM

Some people love mystery. They love holy places and sacred things. Stories of miraculous events and deathless people fascinate them. Priests and prophets, the voices of the supernatural, are their heroes. The religious dimension of life makes everything else seem unimportant and trivial.

Some of us find the extraordinary in the ordinary. We are impressed by the sun rising every morning, the snow-topped mountains, the autumn leaves turning color. We are impressed by growing children, loving parents, and good friends. We are overwhelmed by the power of skillful farmers, careful carpenters, and inspired musicians. The heroes of our existence are the millions of unnamed workers and creators who make existence possible.

The profane world of ordinary life is an extraordinary place.

SONG: HALBEESHEENEE (No. 35)

NATURALISM

Many philosophers of the past disliked nature. They disliked the fact that it was always changing. They disliked the fact that it was too messy for precise descriptions and forever-and-ever statements. They preferred a more perfect world without these deficiencies.

But many philosophers fell in love with nature. They loved the profane world of change and surprise. They loved to probe, to explore ordinary places and to find extraordinary things. They studied bugs and plants, trees and flowers. They studied wind and water, animals and people. Amid all the change, they found law and order. They found laws of nature. Without knowing it, they became the forerunners of scientists.

True science is more than a description. It is a searching adventure. It is a love affair with nature.

SONG: LAM'TSAPPEEM (No. 56)

HUMANISM

Self-esteem is no easy achievement. There are so many reasons why we should feel weak and inadequate. Our childhood is so long that we never really stop believing that we are still children. The skills for survival are so difficult that we never fully master them. Our expectations of life are so great that we often feel that we are failures.

When we have no confidence in our own power, we demean ourselves. We think ourselves unworthy of pleasure and happiness. We invite suffering. We notice our failures, but never our successes. We do not take credit for what we do well. We are afraid of responsibility. We plead helplessness. We start believing that strength and power come from elsewhere.

Self-esteem begins with a recognition that we have more power than we imagine, more strength than we feel, more endurance than we experience, more ingenuity than we want to accept.

Inside this world, inside ourselves, lies the source of self-respect.

SONG: HAKH PATEESH (No. 34)

MORALITY

Questions of right and wrong plague us all the time. We have to make decisions. We have to choose.

For some of us, morality is obedience. We are the servants of outside powers who claim authority over our lives. Like good parents, they promise us safety and security if we comply. They promise us approval if we conform. Like good parents, they assume responsibility for the purpose of our lives. We do not have to worry about what the rules are. We only have to worry about our ability to obey them.

For many of us, morality is common sense. We are the servants of reason and testing. We are wary of outside powers who claim to be the rulers of our lives. We are skeptical of the voices of people who claim to be the voices of God. We know that right and wrong are not heavenly rules. They are human attempts to satisfy human needs.

Human survival, human happiness, and human dignity are human aspirations. Making them real is the task of human existence. In the world of everyday existence, they come before the rules and give them meaning.

SONG: SAHAKEE (No. 78)

CHANGING

Change is often threatening. Routine provides the comfort of the predictable. Familiar pain is, for many of us, more desirable than unfamiliar pleasures.

But life is change. Every day makes us different. No matter how hard we hang on to summer, autumn overtakes us. No matter how hard we cling to youth, aging captures us. No matter how hard we try to lose ourselves in the past, the present confronts us. Nothing stands still; everything is motion.

If we do not accept change, we resist reality. We turn the moment into eternity. We freeze our talents. We never grow. We never learn.

If we accept change, we embrace reality. We turn the present moment into an opportunity for the future. We unleash our talents. We grow with grace. We are always learning.

In the never-never land of our fantasies, nothing changes. But in the natural world of our day-to-day living, change is the stuff of existence. Making it useful is the test of our strength.

SONG: AYFO OREE (No. 14)

MEMORIAL

Death is real. In the world of changing nature, it is inevitable. It may be postponed, but it cannot be avoided.

Loved ones do not pass away. They die. They do not escape the rhythm of life.

But they leave their gifts. We still bask in their love. We still use their instruction. We are still inspired by their deeds. We still linger on the memories of their style.

Immortality is very intimate. It is part of our mind. It is as close as our power to remember.

In the real world, death is part of the drama of life. So is the loving tribute of remembrance.

SONG: SHEEM'OO (No. 83)

36
SELF-RESPECT

AFFIRMATION

To understand others is to be wise.
But to understand ourselves is to be enlightened.
People who overcome others are strong.
But people who control themselves are mighty.

SONG: MEE HAHAM (No. 65)

HAPPINESS

Every person wants to feel worthwhile. Every person seeks self-esteem. Individuals who believe in themselves and in their power to do good are the strongest of people. Individuals who despise themselves and condemn their own talent are the weakest of human creatures. No physical prowess can redeem them. No outer praise can rescue them.

Without self-respect there is no happiness. If we hate ourselves, neither money nor fame will give us comfort. If we esteem ourselves, neither poverty nor namelessness will destroy our pleasure. In the end, we become what we think we are. If we think ourselves worthy of life we will live. If we think ourselves worthy of death we will destroy ourselves.

Self-esteem is as necessary for man as food and sex. It is the fulfillment of his ultimate need.

SONG: OUT OF THE NIGHT (No. 76)

POWER

Self-respect is never a gift. It is always an achievement. Neither the flattery of friends nor the reassurance of family will give us the feeling of self-worth. Neither the counseling of therapists nor the comforts of religion will elevate our dignity. Self-esteem is the child of competence. It is the offspring of personal skill. If we think that we are unable to help ourselves or to help others, we cannot respect ourselves.

If we like ourselves, we believe that we have power. We believe that we have the power to determine the course of our own lives. We believe that we have the competence to be useful to others. We believe that we have the strength to make decisions even when the consequences of these decisions cannot easily be predicted. We know that when we give to others we do not threaten our own welfare, for our security lies in no possession. It resides in our own creative skill.

SONG: LAM'TSAPPEEM (No. 56)

COMMUNITY

A congregation needs self-respect. A community requires self-worth. The test of its dignity is not to be found in words, in pretty formulas nicely phrased. The test of its self-esteem is revealed in action, in the ability to turn beautiful speech into beautiful deeds. To extol love, but never to love; to adore compassion, but never to help; to admire courage, but never to risk public rejection; to praise the open mind, but never to change an opinion—is the well-traveled road to pretension and self-contempt.

A community must earn its self-respect. It must love more than it talks of love. It must be brave more than it speaks of bravery. It must be open more than it praises openness. A community is not what it says. A community is what it does.

SONG: AYFO OREE (No. 14)

MEMORIAL

The past is unchangeable. What happened yesterday is beyond our control. We can cry and shout. We can scream and complain. But the events of just a moment ago are as far from our reach as the furthest star.

Fools never forgive the past. They devote every present moment to worrying about it, scolding it, and wishing it were different.

Wise people release the past. They do not need to assault what cannot be taken. They do not need to forgive what cannot be altered. They simply accept what they are not able to change. Since the future is open to human decision they turn their energy forward and choose to create rather than to regret.

People of self-respect do not dwell on helplessness. Since death is irreversible, they accept it and turn to the living.

SONG: ZAYKHER (No. 103)

AFFIRMATION

To understand others is to be wise.
But to understand ourselves is to be enlightened.
People who overcome others are strong.
But people who control themselves are mighty.

37
STRENGTH

SONG: AYFO OREE (No. 14)

LIGHT

Where is my light? My light is in me.

Each of us is two people. Each of us is two realities. We are what we do. We are also what we *could* do. If we are weak now, we have the possibility of being strong. If we are lonely now, we have the power to reach out to others in friendship. If we are bored, we have the imagination to create new excitement.

The light that dispels the darkness is not only external, it is also internal. There is an inner sun which shines, even though we often deny its radiance. There is an inner fire which burns, even though we often resist its power.

Life can be more than regret and resignation. If we can confront the light of our own potential, life can be the path to fulfillment.

SONG: ASHRAY HAGAFROOR (No. 13)

HOPE

Where is my hope? My hope is in me.

Many of us find the meaning of our life in the past. We search for our roots and we revel in every famous ancestor. The dead fill our memories, granting us the pleasure of approval with the terror of guilt. Wisdom from the past grows wiser with age and takes on the mystery of holiness. Old teachers become more profound than new ones. Old rituals become more important than our own inventions. If there is a golden age, it happened a long time ago. The world seems to be getting worse and worse.

Many of us find the meaning of our life in the future. We search for our needs and we revel in every thrust to satisfaction. Visions of new worlds fill our thoughts, granting us the expectation of success without the fear of failure. Wisdom from the present displays its youth and prefers good humor to reverence. New teachers often seem as profound as old ones. New rituals become the friends of our creativity. If there is a golden age, it is yet to come. Because we live with hope, we will make the world better and better.

SONG: BASHANA HABAA (No. 21)

STRENGTH

Where is my strength? My strength is in me.

Our lifestyle is determined by the way we see our strength. If we see ourselves as weak and powerless, if we feel ourselves empty of will and wisdom, we will choose the style of self-pity. When we are committed to self-pity we know how to appease. We are experts in humility. We cry with charm and confess our ills apologetically. We never provoke the strong, and we strike back at those we sincerely believe are weaker than we are. Since we are afraid, we thank the fates for our misery and stand in awe of what we do not know.

Our lifestyle is determined by the way we see our strength. If we see ourselves as strong and powerful, if we feel ourselves full of will and knowledge, we will choose the style of self-esteem. When we are committed to self-esteem we enjoy integrity. We do not avoid hostility in the defense of our dignity. We do not revere authority, but we respect it when it is competent. We do not deny our limitations, but we prefer to think about our power. The greatest humiliation is the surrender to fear. Even when we are afraid, we listen to new ideas. Even when we are afraid, we try new adventures. We neither bully nor worship. We are willing to be bold.

SONG: HAZAK (No. 45)

GOOD HUMOR

Where is my strength? My strength is in me. And in you.

Humorless people think that they are self-sufficient. Humorless people think that they are gods. If they feel in need of other people, if they feel lonely and cold, if they crave the presence of good friends, they view their desires as temporary. Self-discipline will yield them the pleasure of needing nobody.

Good-humored people know that they are strong but never strong enough. They know that neither nature nor introspection is a substitute for people. They understand that neither meditation nor self-insight is as delicious as a good friend.

If we are good-natured, we know that we grow by growing with others. We can only really laugh by laughing with others. We can only truly live by living with others. Intimacy is when my own inner radiance is discovered in the face of my friend.

SONG: AYFO OREE (No. 14)

38
UNIVERSALISM

SONG: HINNAY MA TOV (No. 47)

UNIVERSALISM

We live in a world of many differences. But we also live in a world where people are very much alike. Since the differences are easier to notice than the similarities, we tend to exaggerate what separates us from others and to give too little attention to what binds us together.

When we are parochial, we look for differences. We point out how strange and bizarre the behavior of other people is. We stress our personal uniqueness or the uniqueness of our own group.

When we are universal, we allow ourselves to notice the similarities. We allow ourselves to see how much we share with others. We allow ourselves to pay tribute to our human condition.

SONG: KAMIEYEEM (No. 51)

HUMANITY

It is easy to be diverted by differences. There are so many races, so many colors, so many sizes, so many shapes. We sometimes forget that we are all part of one species, that we are all part of one humanity.

Before we are Jewish or American, male or female, we are human. There are human needs we all have. There are human drives we all feel. There are human emotions we all express. Under the costumes of different cultures lie identical desires.

Wherever we are in the world, we are all struggling for survival, for safety, for love, for dignity. We are all intimidated by pain and frightened by death. We are all encouraged by pleasure and eager for recognition.

Behind the labels, behind the ostentatious differences of culture and language, we are all human.

SONG: AHEE ADAM (No. 4)

OPENNESS

Groups provide security. They also provide boundaries that keep other people out. When we are fearful of the world beyond, we often become pretentious. We imagine that our culture is the best of all possible cultures and that our wisdom is wiser than all the rest. We make ourselves believe that our tradition contains all useful knowledge and that everything we need for life is there.

But truly wise people know that cultural arrogance is dangerous. It keeps us from seeing the beauty of other traditions. It keeps us from tasting the good fruit of other ethnic trees.

Our loyalty to our own group is not diminished by our openness to others. Open minds and open hearts allow the fresh winds of other cultures to blow away self-righteousness and to invite new ideas and new perspectives to enrich what we already have.

SONG: B'AYLE HAYADIEYIM (No. 22)

COMMUNICATION

Communication is more than words. It is more than exchanging ideas. Our whole body communicates. Our eyes and muscles bring messages of feeling and thought which cannot easily be hidden. Our touching and laughing express deep attachments which cannot easily be ignored.

Love and respect are not mere verbal courtesies. If they are genuine, they proceed from the very heart of being and direct all our behavior. They determine the way we listen, the way we share, the way we reach out to others.

Too often we give double messages to strangers. Our mouth speaks love, but our body speaks indifference or even hostility. Getting closer to other people requires more than verbal commitments. It needs a sensitive awareness of our own behavior.

SONG: HAEMET YOTSAYT (No. 32)

GENEROSITY

Love is not the child of any one nation. Wisdom is not the offspring of any one people. Kindness was not invented by only one culture. Nor is truthfulness an ideal that began in any one place.

The noble life had its origins in many lands and in many countries. In every nation, a small band of men and women discerned the truth that peace and generosity are better than war and rejection. Some were peasants. Others were prophets. Some were bold. Others were timid. But they spoke that message through their deeds.

We Jews have our teachers of love. So do many other peoples. We have also had our preachers of hate, and so have many other nations.

No group is entitled to be self-righteous. True love is more generous.

SONG: V'AHAVTA (No. 93)

SHARING

The world is getting smaller. Modern inventions have turned our planet into a global village. Nations have become neighbors and have had to learn to share space.

But sharing space is not easy. We want our own ground, our own place which belongs to us and to no one else. If there are strangers among us, we resent their closeness and wish they would go away.

But they do not go away. In a world of wandering peoples and dispersed nations, there are few places where strangers are absent. There are few lands where only one group is present. Either we learn to share our space with strangers or we shall destroy each other in hateful struggle.

Living with difference is not just being nice. It is a matter of survival.

SONG: AYFO OREE (No. 14)

MEMORIAL

We are the children of the past. We are the parents of the future. If we dwell too much on the past, we shall neglect the future. But if we only look forward and never backward, we shall forget the lessons that history provides.

History can be a good teacher. It can teach us that arrogance is dangerous, the arrogance that prefers labels to people, propaganda to life. War and destruction thrive where humanness is less important than the glory of the nation, where visions of victory replace the will to survive. Too many slogans can kill us.

When we plan for our future, we remember our past. We are not here because of prideful hate. We are here because our parents loved us and nurtured us, just as parents love and nurture their children all over the world.

SONG: SHEEM'OO (No. 83)

39
WONDER

AFFIRMATION

The fool knows all the answers.
The wise person continues to ask.

SONG: V'SHOOV ITKHEM (No. 95)

TIME AND SPACE

The world we live in is ageless. It has no beginning and no end. It has no author and no conclusion. It may explode and contract. It may expand and shrink. But it never dies. It is simply there—with its infinite variety and its never-ending change.

The world we live in is ageless. Even time is unreliable. The lights of a million stars travel a million years before they bless the earth with their splendor. The distant past of another galaxy shines in our heaven as an immediate present. Once upon a time becomes today and yesterday becomes tomorrow.

SONG: ZEMER LAKH (No. 104)

MEANING

People give meaning to the universe. If we call to the stars and say, "Tell us the purpose of life," the stars are silent. If we caress the earth and ask, "What shall we do," the earth gives no reply. If we pursue the wind and plead, "Let us know the path we must follow," the wind has no answer. The universe, with all its complexity, is dumb. It can neither be born nor die.

Wonder

People give meaning to the universe. The commands of the gods are only the echoes of our own striving. Although we are part of the world, we are different from all other worldly things. We can hear and speak. We can love and hate. We can choose and deny. Out of our needs arises desire. And out of desire arises our passion for life. We are not told to be happy. We simply want to be.

SONG: HAVA NAGEELA (No. 42)

COURAGE

The age of science is the age of uncertainty. No more eternal answers console the human heart. No more changeless doctrines pacify the human mind. Religious dogma has been replaced by the humility of testing. Mythical fantasy has yielded to the stingy help of public experiences.

The age of science is the age of courage. Bravery is not possible when all is predictable. Only the danger of surprise gives us the dignity of true freedom. The heroes of modern times are not fanatic believers. They are the people of patience who are strong enough to live with uncertainty. They are the people of integrity who are honest enough to wait for reasonable answers. They are the people of good humor who can value what they cannot totally explain.

SONG: LAM'TSAPPEEM (No. 56)

EXPERIENCE

Love is no less lovely because we do not yet know the chemistry of feeling. Beauty is no less beautiful because we do not yet understand the physics of thought. Even the wonders of nature are no less wondrous because they have not yet revealed to us the secret of their evolution. If the experience of these mysteries fulfills us, what more is required?

SONG: AYFO OREE (No. 14)

MEMORIAL

The glories of our universe are never eternal. They shine for a while and are then consumed by the darkness. All things change. All life yields to death.

If the beauties of nature endured forever, they would not be precious. We cannot love what we do not fear to lose.

SONG: Y'HEE SHALOM (No. 98)

AFFIRMATION

The fool knows all the answers.
The wise person continues to ask.

PART II
JUDAISM

Judaism has always been more than a religion. Membership in the Jewish people is determined by birth, not by any creedal test or ceremony of initiation. Even without circumcision a Jew is always a Jew.

The word "Judaism" is not parallel to the word "Christianity." It is, rather, parallel to the word "Hellenism." Just as Hellenism is the culture of the Greek people, so is Judaism the culture of the Jewish people. A culture is much more than a religion. It embraces all the customs and creativity of an ethnic community.

The Jewish people began as a nation three thousand years ago. From the very beginning that nation embraced great diversity. Polytheists and monotheists, monarchists and theocrats, chauvinists and universalists were all part of the people. No ideological or theological test was ever imposed to determine Jewish identity. Before the time of Ezra foreigners were welcomed. After the time of Ezra (450 B.C.), a racial, non-theological criterion determined membership in the Jewish people.

Today the Jewish nation has become a world people. While part of this people has reconstituted itself a territorial nation in the land of Israel, the overwhelming majority still live in the Diaspora, primarily by choice. While the majority of Jews still give nominal assent to the rabbinic tradition, a large minority have rejected the premises and practices of this tradition. Many of these dissidents remain fervently Jewish in a secular way. The Zionist movement and Yiddish nationalism, with their strong emphasis on the ethnic and national character of Jewish culture, were created by these secularists.

If, in the twentieth century, religious tests were applied to determine Jewishness, a high percentage of people who identify as Jews would be excluded from membership in the Jewish people. The implication is quite clear. Theological beliefs have nothing to do with Jewish identity. The Jewish people encompass theists and atheists, Zionists and anti-Zionists, capitalists and communists. The Lubavitcher Rebbe and Isaac Asimov are both Jews. But they share no ideological agenda.

Judaism, as the culture of the Jewish people, is as comfortable with Yiddish

178   Judaism

jokes as with the psalms. It is as interested in folk customs as in rabbinic laws. It is as fascinated with the secular present as with the religious past.

In the contemporary world the culture of Judaism continues to thrive. Its most dramatic triumph was the Hebrew revival, the resurrection of the Hebrew language as the secular speech of four million Jews. Zionist creativity has become the primary stimulus to Jewish cultural development.

The celebration of Judaism pays tribute to *all* of Jewish culture. A humanistic celebration of Judaism acknowledges the humanistic elements in Jewish culture, especially the skills for survival which were responses to the overwhelming assaults of persecution and repression.

THEMES

The Jewish themes which follow are designed to deal with the unique perspective of humanistic Judaism on Jewish history and Jewish survival. They can be comfortably integrated into a Shabbat celebration or into any occasion where the themes seem appropriate.

1
ANTI-SEMITISM

SONG: SHALOM L'YISRAEL (No. 82)

ANTI-SEMITISM

Being Jewish has both advantages and disadvantages. The positive side is membership in a historic international family distinguished by its achievements and pride. The negative side is the hatred and hostility which have followed our footsteps for the past two thousand years and will not turn back.

Our enemies are to be found everywhere. They wear a thousand masks. Some of them are rich and powerful, others are poor and weak. Some of them are intellectuals and molders of public opinion, others are inarticulate and ignorant. Some prefer their home in the political parties of the right, others mobilize the political movements of the left. Some hate us because of our religious beliefs and practices. Others detest our imagined success and power. Still others condemn our birth and race.

In the century of the Holocaust, hatred of the Jews is no trivial matter. It is the father of pogroms, the mother of genocide. Even when we think that it has faded away, it suddenly reappears to terrify us with its fury.

SONG: V'RAK ANAKNOO (No. 94)

ORIGINS

Where did this hostility to the Jews come from? Why did it ever arise?

We Jews imagine that we are lovable, that what we do is good for other people and the world. We have shared with humanity so many good ideas, so many new inventions, so many earnest achievements. We have tried so hard to be responsible workers, model citizens, and social reformers. We find it difficult to understand why others see our virtues as vices, turn our good into evil.

But, then, like most people, we are naïve. We fail to remember that a long time ago we chose to be different and that difference arouses fear and suspicion. We forget to notice that success and hard work do not always elicit admiration and respect; they often breed envy and resentment, the twin emotions of violence. We are unable to see that when people are uncertain about themselves and cannot admit their discomfort, they project their own self-hate onto innocent victims who are too weak to resist. The Jew becomes the mirror image of what the anti-Semite cannot bear in himself.

If we choose to remain an ambitious international people with urban skills, we shall continue to do good for the world. But we shall also have enemies.

SONG: L'MAAN TSEEYON LO EHESHE (No. 58)

REALISM

The experience of our people through the centuries of constant assault tells us something about ourselves and others.

In modern times a view of human nature arose which challenged the pessimism of the past and kindled the revolutionary passion of young imperialists. Many philosophers announced it. Many reformers proclaimed it. They declared that human beings were basically good, that love and cooperation were the essence of human emotional temperament, that cruelty and barbarism were simply due to ignorance and faulty training. With enough education, with enough material plenty for everyone, social evil would vanish. Utopia would follow.

The horrors of this century have rescued us from this naïveté. Human cruelty is not a passing effect of a passing condition. Genocide is not an expression of ignorance and imperfect social conditions. There are deeper roots, and they live in the very depths of the human soul.

We are divided beings, ambivalent creatures. Part of us wants to love and nurture; part of us wants to hurt and destroy. Ending war and bigotry is not easy, because the fury is not only outside of us, but chiefly within us.

We must be realistic about our enemies. We must also be realistic about ourselves.

SONG: AYIT (No. 15)

TRANSFORMATION

Jew-hatred is an instrument of evil. It has consumed millions of victims. It has extinguished billions of dreams. The martyrs of racism died a tragic death. They are bold reminders that the Fates are less than just.

Yet, strangely enough, with no real help from destiny or from our enemies, some good did emerge from all that suffering. The tragedy remained just as tragic as before, but the survivor learned new skills for survival.

The Jews were transformed by anti-Semitism. Their mind and their spirit were changed. Some became more timid. They were obsessed with guilt and imagined that the evil was their own fault, the result of their own sins. They accepted their fate as just and devoted their life to repentance. Some became more pitiable. They were filled with fear and doubted their power to resist. They prepared the posture of appeasement and were always afraid of provoking their enemy.

Others chose another path. They were too proud to surrender and too life-loving to commit the suicide of active rebellion. They learned courage, cultivated subtle defiance, and worked on the skills of group solidarity.

Because of them, a new Jewish spirit was born.

SONG: SHAALOO SH'LOM Y'ROOSHALIEYIM (No. 80)

SURVIVAL

Human nature is sometimes perverse. The negative brings forth the positive. The determination of our enemies to destroy us makes us want to live all the more.

Anger can be the parent of both good and evil. In the hearts of our foes, it gave birth to terror and extermination. But in the hearts of the Jews who survived the assault, it became the mother of defiance. Since our enemies desired the destruction of our people so very much, we would never give them the satisfaction of realizing their dream. The more they sought to destroy us, the more we fought to live.

There has always been a Jewish resistance, a refusal to accommodate the wishes of our haters. Sometimes it was quiet, a silent resolution to go on living when living seemed impossible. Sometimes it was dramatic, the passion of a Masada, the Warsaw Ghetto, the Zionist dream.

Anti-Semites gave an urgency to Jewish survival. They inadvertently reinforced our will to live.

SONG: ZOG NIT KAYNMOL (No. 105)

SELF-RELIANCE

Our history is our teacher. It gives us lessons all the time. Sometimes wise leaders write them down in books and they become part of our national literature. Sometimes the people themselves receive the message, record it in their hearts and minds, and use it as a guide to living.

The message of our suffering is clear. In the end, we cannot rely on the kindness of God nor on the kindness of strangers. We must rely on our own strength and determination.

Self-reliance is one of the themes of the Jewish experience. We cannot sit passively by and wait to be rescued. We must train ourselves to be strong. We must be strong enough to accept adversity, strong enough to be useful to others, strong enough to move on when resistance is futile. Our flexibility is our strength. If we cannot be farmers, we shall be merchants. If we cannot own land, we shall own talent. If we cannot live here, we shall live there.

Our enemies forced us, against our will, to become adaptable. Inadvertently, they made us strong.

SONG: AYFO OREE (No. 14)

MEMORIAL

Danger is the author of human solidarity. The more we feel the hatred of our foes, the closer we huddle together to find our safety and to increase our strength.

Jewish togetherness emerges out of the trauma of persecution. Our family became a haven against a hostile world. Our community became a refuge for help and mutual support. Our people became a center for roots and the pride of self-esteem. While the enemy raged, we created our own security.

Our ancestors are part of a human chain of solidarity which was strengthened by persecution and by the awareness that we depended so much on each other. Our loved ones, who are no longer with us, were also part of this passionate commitment. They deserve our tribute.

SONG: SHEEM'OO (No. 83)

2 JEWISH HISTORY

SONG: HINNAY MA TOV (No. 47)

ROOTS

The Jewish people is an old people, older than most nations. We began so long ago that it is very hard to know when the Jewish adventure really started. In some dim antiquity, obscured by myth and legend, our Hebrew ancestors made their debut and stepped up onto the stage of history.

Our national drama has featured many achievements. Famous books were written. Famous battles were won. Famous ideas were shared. It has also provided many frustrations. Too many enemies assaulted us. Too many martyrs died. Too many hopes were dashed.

Jewish history is four thousand years of this Jewish experience. It is the sum total of all the pleasure and pain, triumphs and defeats, fulfilled dreams and disappointments which have entered into our memories through centuries of struggle and striving.

We are the children of that Jewish experience.

CONGREGATION

We are the children of the Jewish experience.

SONG: AM YISRAEL HIE (No. 9)

PEOPLEHOOD

The Jewish experience is a national experience.

We Jews did not begin as a religious denomination. We did not start out as a theological fraternity. We began our adventure as a nation, as a federation of clans and tribes. Language, lifestyle, the ties of family loyalty, and the sentimental memories of shared ancestors bound us together.

No single set of religious ideas defined our character. No single system of ethical commitments embraced our personal ambitions. From the very beginning Jewish identity was a matter of birth and not a matter of belief. More important than theological convictions were the mothers and fathers, the matriarchs and patriarchs, who gave us entry into the Jewish nation.

To be a Jew is to feel our national roots, to affirm our ancestral past, to experience our family connections. We have many opinions. But destiny has made us one people.

CONGREGATION

We are one people. We feel our national roots. We feel our ancestral past. We experience our family connections.

SONG: HATIKVA (No. 40)

DIASPORA

The Jewish experience is an international experience.

Two thousand years ago our ancestors left the land of Israel. There were many reasons for leaving. The land was too crowded. Foreign conquerors were oppressive. Hostile invaders settled down.

The dispersion posed a threat to Jewish survival. A homeland without a Diaspora was normal. But a Diaspora without a homeland seemed a historical impossibility—like limbs without a body, like trees without their roots. Was it possible for a nation without a country of its own to remain a nation? Was it possible to cut out the ancient heart of a people and to keep it alive?

In the Galut, we Jews achieved a new self-image. We became an international people. While we still loved our native land, we also grew attached to the places where we lived. As members of a world family, no land could fully claim us. We carried our holidays, our memories, our language with us wherever we went. Hebrew was still Hebrew, even in Minsk.

CONGREGATION

We are a universal family. We are an international people. Israel is our homeland. But the world is our home.

SONG: NAASE SHALOM (No. 69)

CHANGE

The Jewish experience is the experience of change.

The power of people is the power of change. Circumstances never stay the same. People never stay the same. Culture never stays the same.

Judaism did not fall from heaven. It was not invented by a divine spokesman. It was created by the Jewish people. It was molded by Jewish experience. It was flavored by Jewish sadness and Jewish joy.

Holidays are responses to human events. Ceremonies are celebrations of human development. Music and literature are the expressions of human needs.

Life is an evolution, a continuous flow of transformation. And so is culture. When circumstances change, people change. When people change, their laws and customs change.

A healthy people welcomes change. It understands its history. It knows its own power. It leads the past into the future.

CONGREGATION

We welcome change. We understand our history. We know our power. We seek to lead the past into the future.

SONG: BASHANA HABAA (No. 21)

REASON

The Jewish experience is an experience of human ingenuity.

Blind faith is often so dramatic and so noisy that it diverts our attention from the quiet power of practical day-to-day decisions. Most people live by common sense. They test the truth of ideas by their consequences. The ordinary people who learn to grow food, to build houses, to make friends, to fight disaster may easily be forgotten. But their undramatic efforts have more to do with human survival than priestly proclamations.

Jewish survival has a similar origin. We are sometimes so obsessed with the literature of prophets and rabbis that we often ignore the unrecorded heroes of Jewish life—the people who, day by day, solved their problems and improved their world by adapting old advice to new situations. Peasants and merchants, workers and bankers, doctors and engineers—all of these are heroes of the unacknowledged tradition of Jewish reason.

When, two hundred years ago, the Enlightenment officially came to Jewish life, it was not entirely new. Science is only the refinement of the practical common sense of centuries of survivors.

CONGREGATION

We pay our tribute to the unknown heroes of Jewish ingenuity.

SONG: SAHAKEE (No. 78)

VULNERABILITY

The Jewish experience is the experience of danger.

Jewish identity is no casual connection. It is no matter-of-fact involvement. In a world of Jew-hatred it is often dangerous to be Jewish.

We Jews have had many enemies. Some of them despised our religious ideas. Some of them coveted our possessions. Some of them envied our skills. Some of them were threatened by our success. But all of them made our humiliation an important part of their lives.

Coping with hostility is never easy. A vulnerable minority cannot fall back on the strength of numbers, nor can it claim for itself the privileges of the native born. It has to be much more inventive.

188   Jewish History

In the face of hatred our ancestors learned many new skills. They learned to be cautious. They learned to be protective of one another. They learned to be ambitious, striving for the security of money and power. They learned to be strong, doing much and expecting little. They even learned to laugh at the absurdity of their own suffering.

Out of this confrontation emerged the Jewish personality, a figure too proud to surrender, too wise to rely on the promises of enemies, too determined to give up hope.

CONGREGATION

We are too proud to surrender, too wise to rely on the promises of enemies, too determined to give up hope.

SONG: ZOG NIT KAYNMOL (No. 105)

HUMANISM

The Jewish experience is the experience of humanism.

Through the eyes of tradition, through the vision of priests, prophets, and rabbis, Jewish history is a testimony to the power and justice of a loving God. The Jewish people is a chosen people, chosen for special duties, special suffering, and special rewards. All that happens to the Jewish nation is part of a noble divine plan, even though we humans, like poor Job, have difficulty understanding its nobility.

But the real history of the Jews has a meaning different from that which the authors of its tradition—the priests, prophets, and rabbis—wanted it to be. No historic belief sytem can hide the undeserved suffering of the Jewish past. No age-old ideology can hide the cruelty of the Fates. In the century of the Holocaust the illusions of the past insult the memories of our martyrs.

If Jewish history has any message, it is the demand for human self-reliance. In an indifferent universe there is no help from destiny. Either we assume responsibility for our fate or no one will. A world without divine guarantees and divine justice is a little bit frightening. But it is also the source of human freedom and human dignity.

We stand alone, and yet together, to create the world we want.

SONG: AYFO OREE (No. 14)

MEMORIAL

Jewish history is Jewish survival. Our story is over three thousand years old.

For many Jews the endurance of our people is a supernatural event. Nothing our ancestors did is responsible for our preservation. Nothing that human effort provided made us more lasting. If we had relied on our talents alone we would not be here today. Only destiny, divine protection, and the devotion of heaven have made our survival possible.

For others, the endurance of our people is a human event. In the face of an indifferent universe, in defiance of all the relentless cruelty that hate can conjure up, in confrontation with all the absurdities of the human condition, our ancestors marshalled their talents, their determination and their courage—and persevered. No divine plan made us invulnerable. Jewish ingenuity and Jewish imagination gave us the power to live and the skill to transcend the most difficult of circumstances.

We have no thank-you for destiny. We pay our tribute to the memory of the people of the past who made our present possible.

SONG: SHEEM'OO (No. 83)

3
JEWISH HUMANISM

SONG: HAYVAYNOO SHALOM ALAYKHEM (No. 44)

HUMANISM

We are humanists.

We believe in a world of change and evolution. We believe in the power of science and reason. We believe in the ultimate importance of human dignity and human autonomy. The secular world of human achievement wins our admiration and devotion.

But we are also Jewish humanists.

We believe in the value of Jewish identity. We applaud the survival of the Jewish people. We participate in the heritage of Jewish culture.

Our humanism and our Jewish identity are intimately connected.

SONG: SAHAKEE (No. 78)

JEWISH HUMANISM

Humanism is universal. It can be practiced by people of all nations, all cultures, and all ethnic backgrounds. It has been created by teachers and philosophers from many diverse countries. No single group can claim it as its very own private creation.

Humanism is not uniquely Jewish. It may be espoused by Jews, loved by Jews, and defended by Jews. But it may be loved, espoused, and defended by people of many backgrounds.

Jewish humanism is humanism-plus. It is humanism with an attachment to Jewish identity. It is humanism with the pleasure of Jewish holidays. It is humanism with the sound of Jewish words. It is humanism with the memories of Jewish roots.

SONG: EEM AYN (No. 28)

OPTIONS

Jewish identity has its ups and down.

Some people see it negatively. They view it as a social liability, a curse of fate. They experience it as a burden, a surrender to separation. While they are humanists who happen to be Jewish, they are not Jewish humanists.

Some Jews treat it with indifference. They neither like it nor dislike it. They neither praise it nor condemn it. If it survives, it will give them no greater pleasure than if it vanishes.

Many of us like our Jewish identity. We enjoy it as part of our lives. While we recognize the painful side of the Jewish experience, while we refuse to deny the horror stories of the Jewish past, we find much to love in our Jewish connection. We are Jewish humanists.

SONG: AM YISRAEL HIE (No. 9)

JEWISH IDENTITY

Jewish identity gives Jewish humanists a lot to do.

It gives us holidays to celebrate, ceremonies to share, languages to speak, songs to sing, and dances to dance. It gives us heroes to admire, victories to imitate, wisdom to live by, and stories to enjoy. It gives us roots to rest on, ancestors to investigate, families to love, and communities to live with.

It also makes our humanism stronger. Our culture, our history—even our vulnerability—make a humanistic difference.

SONG: Y'ROOSHALIEYIM (No. 100)

JEWISH HISTORY

Jewish history improves our humanism. It make us more reasonable.

Jewish history never fit the categories that priests, prophets, and rabbis wanted to squeeze it into. It never accommodated itself to religious dogma. The good never seemed to receive the rewards they deserved. The wicked never seemed to endure the punishments they earned. Contrary to official teaching, the universe appeared to be either mean or incompetent. Or perhaps indifferent.

A sense of absurdity pervades the Jewish experience. It makes us more skeptical than pietists like. It makes us less grateful than worshippers want. It makes us laugh more than serious believers prefer. After all, in the face of craziness, a sense of humor is more rational than faith.

We dare not forget our history. If we look at it straight, we will become instant secular humanists.

SONG: AYIT (No. 15)

ANTI-SEMITISM

Living with anti-Semitism improves our humanism. It increases our self-awareness.

The modern anti-Semite ignores the Jewish religion. He is bored by Jewish theological beliefs. He sees the Jew as a moral threat, a secular violation of the secular order. He fears cities—and the Jew is a city person. He fears education—and the Jew is a devotee of university training. He fears mobility—and the Jew is the embodiment of the wandering people. He fears money—and money is the symbol of freedom of choice.

A free and open secular society frightens the anti-Semite. He wants no part of it. He wants to run away from it. He holds the Jew responsible for it. In his mind, secular humanism is an invention of the Jewish people.

Jews and secular humanists share a common fate. The anti-Semite hates them both for the same reason.

SONG: MEE YITT'NAYNEE OF (No. 66)

DANGERS AND OPPORTUNITIES

Jewish humanism is both a danger and an opportunity.

If our Jewish identity becomes an obsession, if it shuts us off from other people and other wisdom, if it closes the door to human communication, then our humanism will fade away.

If our Jewish identity is only a nod, if it takes neither time nor effort, if it only dwells on residual guilt, if it never demands any concrete action, then Jewishness too will vanish.

But if Jewish identity makes a difference in our lives—if it leads us to explore our culture—if it deepens our roots—if it sharpens our awareness of the Jewish condition—and if it does all this without diminishing the power of our individual uniqueness and our humanity—then Jewish humanism will be something good in our lives, a healthy harmony, a wholesome commitment.

SONG: AYFO OREE (No. 14)

MEMORIAL

Our past is a guide to our future. It is no sacred temple requiring reverence. It is no sacred book with immutable decrees. It is no sacred song with only one melody. It is a treasury of memories from which we can draw. Our past is a storehouse of wisdom from which we can borrow. It is a drama of creativity which we can choose to imitate.

We are always the bridge between the past and the future. We are always the continuity between the old and the new. We do not betray the future by ignoring our needs. We pay tribute to both. We use the past to dream of our future.

SONG: Y'HEE SHALOM (No. 98)

4
JEWISH SURVIVAL

SONG: SHALOM LARAHOK (No. 81)

SURVIVAL

The Jewish people is our people. It is also an ancient people, older than most other nations.

When the Egyptians built their empire along the Nile, the Jews were there. When the Greeks sailed the waters of the Mediterranean, the Jews were there. When the Romans united the nations of the Western world under their military might, the Jews were there. When the Arabs burst out of their desert home to conquer their conquerors, the Jews were there. In almost every century of recorded history, the people of Israel were part of the human drama. Sometimes we were spectators of the grand events. Sometimes we were actors. Sometimes we were victims.

There have been many trials and traumas throughout our history. There have been many dangers and threats to our existence. There have been many individuals destroyed by ruthless foes. But we, as a people, continue to survive.

The Jewish people lives.

SONG: AM YISRAEL HIE (No. 9)

DISPERSION

We Jews have been tested by circumstance. When new problems arose, we developed new skills. Even when the problems seemed insurmountable, we managed to surmount them.

Our first great test was the departure of Jews from Israel to other lands. We call it the Great Dispersion, and it took our ancestors to the four corners of the earth.

There were many reasons for leaving. The land was too crowded. Economic opportunity was limited. Foreign conquerors were oppressive. Other places seemed more interesting. Whatever the reason, the challenge remained the same. Was it possible to remain a Jew when one no longer lived in a Jewish land and no longer spoke a Jewish language?

In the Diaspora, the Jews developed a new self-image. Not only were they a territorial nation, they also became an international people. While they still loved their native land, they also loved the place where they now lived. This double loyalty filled their lives with a creative tension. As members of a world family, no land could fully claim them. They carried their holidays and ceremonies with them wherever they went. The Shabbat was still Shabbat, even in Timbuktu.

SONG: SAHAKEE (No. 78)

DESTRUCTION

Our second great test was the loss of our homeland. Foreign enemies occupied our land, ravaged our cities, tore down our Temple, drove out our people.

Dispersed to the four corners of the earth, the Jews were confronted with the pain of separation—separation from their land, separation from their roots. Could a people live, cut off from the country of its birth? Could a culture survive, with no special place for its language and lifestyle? Could a nation endure when it was merely an alien part of other nations?

Many other nations were defeated by the challenge of dispersion, but the Jews remained undaunted. If they could not have the Temple in Jerusalem, they would make synagogues. If they could not have kings and high priests, they would train rabbis. If they could not live in Zion, they would dream of it.

The homeland became a fantasy. But Jewish survival was real.

SONG: HATIKVA (No. 40)

ANTI-SEMITISM

We Jews have had many enemies. Some of them simply want our possessions. Some of them hate us for what they think we do. Some of them hate us for what they think we are.

In the century of the Holocaust, anti-Semitism is no trivial disease. It is a terrifying social force which, once unleashed, aims at nothing less then the destruction of our people.

Coping with hostility is never easy. A vulnerable minority cannot fall back on the strength of numbers. Nor can it claim for itself the privileges of the native born. It has to be much more inventive.

In the face of dreadful anti-Semitism, our ancestors learned to do many things. They learned to stay on the alert. They learned to be economically indispensable. They learned to be ambitious, striving to please and to be useful. They learned to be skeptical, suspicious of what destiny might offer. They even learned to laugh at the absurdity of their own suffering.

Out of this struggle emerged the Jewish personality, a figure too proud to surrender, too wise to rely on the kindness of others, too determined to give up hope.

SONG: ZOG NIT KAYNMOL (No. 105)

FREEDOM

Some challenges to Jewish survival are frightening. They threaten death and destruction. But some challenges are pleasantly seductive. They offer attractive alternatives. In modern times personal freedom is one of these seductive challenges.

In a free society, the individual takes precedence over any group to which he belongs. He is imprisoned by no ancestral scripts. He is bound by no ancient tribal code. He is free to be what he chooses to be.

In a free society, the Jew enjoys many options he never enjoyed before. He can be Jewish in the way his forefathers were. He can be Jewish in his own way, picking and choosing what is important to him. He can decide not to be Jewish at all.

Freedom is both friend and foe to Jewish survival, but it is morally irresistible. Enforced conformity may make groups more cohesive, but it also undermines personal integrity and individual dignity.

A Jewish world needs greater diversity. It may be harder to handle, but it is ethically more satisfying.

SONG: BASHANA HABAA (No. 21)

PURPOSE

Is there any purpose to Jewish survival? Is there any reason why Jews should bother to save the Jewish people as a people?

For traditional Jews, there is no reason to bother. The Jewish future is guaranteed by divine promise. What will be, will be. Individual Jews choose to be good or bad Jews, but the ultimate triumph of the Jewish people is guaranteed.

For humanistic Jews, their Jewish identity reinforces their humanism. If there is one lesson to be drawn from the drama of Jewish history, it is that people cannot rely on the kindness of destiny. In the face of an indifferent universe, they must assume responsibility for their own fate and their own destiny.

The message of Jewish history is the message of humanism.

SONG: AYFO OREE (No. 14)

MEMORIAL

The Jewish people lives.

It lives not because the forces of history have chosen to be kind and supportive. It lives because brave and creative people refused to surrender to the cruelty of destiny. It lives because the human spirit confronted adversity with dignity and defiance. It lives because the hostility of the outer world was softened by the inner world of loving family and friends.

Some people view it very narrowly, only seeing its religious side. Others perceive it broadly, emphasizing its ethical outreach.

But Judaism is more than theology and moral rules. It is more than parochial faith and universal sentiments. It is the living culture of a living people.

Judaism is family, love, and nurturing. Judaism is memory, roots, and pride. Judaism is music, dance, and humor. Everything that Jewish people, throughout the ages, did and yearned to do, is Judaism.

SONG: ZEMER LAKH (No. 104)

PEOPLE

We did not begin as a religious denomination. We began as a nation. We began as a collection of families, clans, and tribes. We began as an ethnic group, with our own language, on our own territory.

We became a dispersed nation. We left our land. We traveled the surface of our globe. We lived among many nations. We learned many languages.

We changed into a world people. We became the citizens of many states. We recovered our homeland. It became our new center.

Each of us is part of an extended international family. Family is no trivial connection. It is our first connection. It gives us life and identity.

SONG: AM YISRAEL HIE (No. 9)

CHANGE

The power of people is the power of change. Circumstances never stay the same. People never stay the same. Culture never stays the same.

Judaism did not fall from heaven. It was not invented by a divine spokesman. It was created by the Jewish people. It was molded by Jewish experience. It was flavored by Jewish sadness and by Jewish joy.

Holidays are responses to human events. Ceremonies are celebrations of human development. Music and literature are the expressions of human needs.

Life is an evolution, a continuous flow of transformations. And so is culture. When circumstances change, people change. When people change, their laws and customs change.

A healthy people welcomes change. It understands its history. It knows its own power. It leads the past into the future.

SONG: B'AYLE HAYADIEYIM (No. 22)

REASON

Human intelligence is the key to human survival. Jewish intelligence is the key to Jewish survival.

Blind faith is often so dramatic and so noisy that it diverts our attention from the quiet power of practical day-to-day decisions. Most people live by common sense. They test the truth of advice by its consequences. The ordinary people who learn to grow food, to build houses, to make friends, to fight disaster may easily be forgotten. But their undramatic efforts have more to do with human survival than priestly proclamations.

Jewish survival has a similar origin. We are so obsessed with the literature of prophets and rabbis that we ignore the unrecorded heroes of Jewish life, the people who day by day solved their problems and improved their world by adapting old advice to new situations. Peasants and merchants, workers and bankers, doctors and engineers—all of these are heroes of the unacknowledged tradition of Jewish reason.

When, two hundred years ago, the Enlightenment officially came to Jewish life, it was not entirely new. Science is only the refinement of the practical common sense of centuries of survivors.

SONG: MEE HAHAM (No. 65)

DIGNITY

A secular humanistic Jew affirms the power of people. He affirms the power of common sense and human reason. But above all, he strives for human dignity.

Pious people see themselves as weak and dependent. They see the world as a mystery too deep to fathom. They abhor change and search for everlasting guarantees. Divine power and divine guidance give them a sense of safety. For them, obedience is a small price to pay for eternal security.

People of dignity believe that they have the right to be strong and independent. They see the world as an orderly place to investigate. They welcome necessary change and are good-humored enough to know that nothing is permanent. Human power and human guidance give them some sense of safety. But they are willing—even desire—to live with risk. They avoid childlike obedience. They cultivate respectful equality.

Human dignity is Jewish dignity. Jewish dignity is our dignity.

SONG: AYFO OREE (No. 14)

MEMORIAL

Our past is a guide to our future. It is no sacred temple requiring reverence. It is no sacred book with immutable decrees. It is no sacred song with only one melody. It is a treasury of memories from which we can draw. It is a storehouse of wisdom from which we can borrow. It is a drama of endless creativity which we can imitate.

We are always the bridge between the past and the future. We are always the continuity between the old and the new. We do not betray the past by rejecting our roots. We do not betray the future by ignoring our needs. We pay tribute to both. We use the past to dream of our future.

SONG: Y'HEE SHALOM (No. 98)

6
ZIONISM

SONG: V'SHOOV ITKHEM (No. 95)

ZIONISM

Zionism is an important Jewish word. It is a word of hope, a sound of loyalty, an affirmation of Jewish dignity. It embraces a long history. It includes a twofold love—the love of a land and the love of a people.

Zionism flows from the nature of Jewish identity. If we Jews are an ancient nation, if we are a dispersed people, if we are the creators of an ethnic culture, then we must with integrity affirm this truth. We must resist the illusions that distort our reality. The Jewish people is neither a religious denomination nor a theological fraternity. It is a historic family, with all the roots and belonging that families provide.

In modern times, Zionism is the dramatic effort to recover our ethnic heritage and to give it a place to be real.

SONG: HATIKVA (No. 40)

PEOPLE

We Jews are a people. A people is both a nation and more than a nation.

A nation starts with families, clans, and tribes. It begins with dependence, loyalty, and commitment. It is molded by danger and opportunity. It grows up on its own land.

A people is a nation that moves beyond the boundaries of its own land. It enjoys the hospitality of many other countries. It seeks the citizenship of many other states. It pursues the welfare of many other nations.

As a people, we Jews may live in faraway places. We may pledge our allegiance to faraway rulers. But we never lose our sense of connection with other Jews. We never lose our attachment to the home of our ancestors.

SONG: BEHAREEM (No. 23)

CULTURE

A living people is a creative people. It is always responding in new ways to new circumstances. It invents holidays for celebration, songs for solidarity, lifestyles for survival, and the arts for beauty.

A living people is defined by its own creative work. It is distinguished by its own culture. A unique style shapes all behavior and gives it consistency. No kind of human effort is excluded. Working, laughing, and playing are as much a part of culture as praying. The music of love is as important as the songs of religious devotion. The secular side of life gives us more freedom to be creative.

Judaism is more than a religion. It is the living culture of a living people. Zionism is the expression of this reality in modern times.

SONG: ADAMA (No. 1)

HEBREW

To be human is to speak. Language makes us unique and gives birth to human community. Speech enables us to touch others without really touching. It gives us the power to share our thoughts and feelings, to transmit our memories. Without speech, each generation would have to invent its own culture.

Language is the cutting edge of culture. It is the most vivid and most elaborate creation of any people. If a nation has a unique style, its way of describing the world defines it. Every language compels us to see life through its own words.

Hebrew is the unique expression of the Jewish people. It is the mother of our childhood, the speech of our ancestors. Our history shines through its stories and sagas, poems and laws. Its strong sounds and powerful rhythms are the teaching instrument of our kings and priests, scholars and leaders. Even when we can no longer speak it, we sing its songs.

SONG: HAKH PATEESH (No. 34)

LAND

The Jewish people was born in a special land. Its personality was molded in a special setting. Its childhood memories include the blue of the Mediterranean Sea, the hills of Jerusalem, the olive trees of Galilee, the sands of the Negev. These remembrances are woven into our roots.

Even when we Jews became a world people, we did not forget the land of Israel. We did not forget Jerusalem. Our longing was more than a hankering for the past. It grew out of our need for dignity, our need to be a free people in a free land. In a setting of hostility and humiliation, we dreamed of being in charge of our own destiny.

The Zionism of Theodore Herzl and David Ben Gurion, the vision of Haim Weizmann and Golda Meir, was more than a return to roots. It was more than securing safety for refugees from hatred. It was a revolution in the Jewish spirit.

We would no longer consent to be the passive victims of fate. We would seize our own desiny in our own hands, defend our freedom, revive our culture, and restore our dignity.

SONG: MISSAVEEV (No. 68)

CENTER

Zion is one of the hills of Jerusalem. Jerusalem is one of the cities of Israel. And Israel is one of the countries in which Jews live.

But Israel is more than one of many. It is the historic homeland of the Jewish people, the very center of Jewish identity. As a world people, as an international nation, we Jews live comfortably as the citizens of many states. We participate in many cultures. Yet our extended Jewish family transcends national boundaries. It gives each of us a second culture and a second home.

If all Jews lived in Israel, we would lose our worldly character. But if Israel ceased to exist, we would be denied the heart of our culture.

We are bound together by mutual need. Israel needs the Jewish dispersion. We need the homeland of our identity.

SONG: AYFO OREE (No. 14)

MEMORIAL

Jewish memories are very deep. They go back through four thousand years of family history and melt into dim antiquity. They include traditions of heroism, mutual help, and generous love.

Our first attachment is not to land, but to people. A free land is only a setting for a free people. Rescuing a land is only part of rescuing a people.

When we remember our past, we do not dwell on holy cities and sacred hills. We do not linger on aged ruins and old possessions. We remember the living culture of living people. We pay tribute to the loving gifts of loving family.

Zionism begins with people. So do healthy memories.

SONG: SHEEM'OO (No. 83)

PART III
JEWISH
HOLIDAYS

Jewish holidays are the major vehicles of Jewish identity in the Diaspora—Jews feel most inclined to do something Jewish when holiday time comes around. Rosh Hashana, Hanukka, and Pesakh have become the major celebrations of Judaism in North America.

For traditionalists most Jewish holidays are divine inventions, creations of God at Mt. Sinai. For humanists Jewish holidays are human creations, developed over many centuries of popular experiments.

In the traditional perspective the theistic elements are intrinsic to the holidays and cannot be separated from their celebration without destroying the festivals themselves. In the humanistic perspective, theology was imposed on the holidays by clerical establishments. Humanistic Jews are just as comfortable, if not relieved, in a secular setting as in a religious one.

Jewish festivals emerged for three reasons: They were presumed to be unlucky days for work and activity; they dramatized the connection between nature and the lifestyles of farmers and shepherds; and they commemorated important historical events. Sometimes all three reasons merged to spawn a new holiday.

Ultimately, all holidays except the Shabbat found their niche in the lunar calendar. They were attached to new moons and full moons and were compelled to begin in the evening at moonrise.

Since Jewish holidays are popular inventions, there is nothing sacred about their remaining the way they are. If earlier generations were entitled to experiment, so are we.

HOLIDAYS

There are five kinds of holidays in the Hebrew calendar. The first kind is the ten-day New Year festival at the beginning of the year. Introduced by

Rosh Hashana and completed by Yom Kippur, these are humanistic days for self-reflection and personal change.

The second kind is the three great seasonal festivals—Sukkot for the autumn, Hanukka for the winter, and Pesakh for the spring. Each of these lasts either seven or eight days, perfect times for extended festivity. Two of them have historical connections also—Hanukka with the victory of the Maccabees and Pesakh with the exodus of the Jews from Egypt.

The third kind of Jewish holiday is the three ancient one-day holidays that precede and follow Pesakh. Tu Bi-Shevat has been rescued from oblivion and turned into a celebration of Israel's redemption by the Zionist pioneers. Purim now provides an opportunity to honor not only Mordecai and Esther (if indeed they were real), but also all the heroes of Jewish history. Shavuot has become the perfect time to celebrate graduations from community schools of Jewish studies since it arrives so conveniently at the end of the school year.

The fourth kind of holiday is the two contemporary one-day commemorations after Pesakh. They dramatize the two most important Jewish events in the twentieth century—one tragic and one joyous. Yom Hashoa remembers the Holocaust and Israel Independence Day points to the triumph of Zionism.

The fifth is the Shabbat, which has no place in the Hebrew lunar calendar. It is derived from an ancient agricultural calendar in which the number seven plays a decisive role. The Shabbat is one of the few remains of this once powerful time divider. Unlike the other holidays, which come only once a year, the Shabbat shows up at least 52 times in one year. Because of its frequency it provides an ideal weekly time for the community to celebrate the significance of Jewish identity.

CELEBRATION

The holiday programs follow the sequence of festivals in the Hebrew calendar. Each of them can be used in the community house or family home. Suggested songs follow each prose reflection.

The Zionism program can be used for Israel Day (Tu Bi-Sh'vat) and Israel Independence Day, and the special theme programs under either *Humanism* or *Judaism* can be utilized for the Shabbat.

1
ROSH HASHANA

SONG: SHALOM L'YISRAEL (No. 82)

AUTUMN

The summer ends. Autumn arrives. We feel the passage of time. Nature changes, and so do we. The fall season fills us with the anticipation of new adventures. The tempo of study and work increases. The pace of seeing and doing quickens. As nature cools, our activity warms. There is so much to do. We are bewildered by the options.

Change makes us aware of what is permanent in our life. Seasons come and go. Parents nurture us and die. Groups capture our loyalty and then lose their luster. Friends love us and depart. Landmarks rise and then decay. One reality persists amid all this drama: the power of our individual person outlasts each fleeting event and connects the chapters of our history. Attachments change, but our uniqueness survives.

SONG: NAE HAOR (No. 70)

INDIVIDUALITY

We sometimes underestimate our power. We see ourselves as part of something bigger than ourselves and imagine that we are too small to be real. We experience ourselves as dependent on special people and special places and fear that we will die if we are separated from them. Families and teams terrify us with the threat of rejection. They seem to possess our reality in their desire. If we do not resign ourselves to their power, we will cease to exist.

To be an individual is to know that each of us is a unique being distinct and separate from all others. We need other people. We are dependent. But we are not dependent on any one person nor do we need any single group. Individuality is the continuous road that enables us to move from group to group, from person to person. It is the strong chain of integrity which links all of our experiences and which allows us to taste the difference and remain the same. If many causes claim our loyalty, they may not claim it absolutely. If many people demand our commitment, they may not demand it without reservation. We are the possession of no single allegiance.

SONG: HANAAVA (No. 36)

COMPETENCE

Affluence and prosperity can be dangerous friends. They give us possessions to own. They fill our world with objects to care for. At first, we acquire things because they are useful, because they serve our survival and happiness. Later on, they become more seductive. They take on an additional allure. They promise us not only security, but identity. Our property ceases to be what we use. It becomes what we are. Our acquisitions become attached limbs that reach out for recognition and power. We develop a new self-image that envelops all that we own. We turn into heavy monsters that move gracelessly through life. Burdened by appendages we fear to lose, our identity becomes an external weight easily cut off, easily taken. Thieves of fortune can swiftly steal what we think we are.

To be an individual is to find identity in what we can do and not in what we come to own. Skills are weightless and effortlessly moved. They give grace to life. To read, to write, to paint, to sing, to build, to heal—these are the phrases of true personality. There is no mysterious inner self that gives us strength. There is no visible outer self that makes us independent. Individuality thrives on competence. It flourishes where people prefer doing to owning, training to seizing. If we are competent, we do not need to fear the loss of property. We do not need to fear the thief of fortune. We carry our identity in the security of our skills. Wherever we go, they follow.

SONG: Y'VARAYKH ADAM (No. 102)

COURAGE

Being afraid is so normal that we sometimes cultivate it as a virtue. To admit fear is often charming, since it establishes a special bond with all those who are equally afraid. As we grow older our enemies become fiercer. The stronger they are, the more justified we are in fearing them.

Resignation needs ruthless foes and insurmountable odds. If unacceptable relations are changeable, if unsatisfactory places are alterable, then fear can find few excuses. So we need to make destiny as terrifying as possible. We need to make society as cruel as imaginable. Cynicism is a convenient friend of fear. It makes it more respectable by turning it into reasonable caution.

Courage is the special passion that turns an entity into a person. To be an individual is to resist resignation. It is to defy the cheap excuses of contrived fear. If we are brave, we do not force our enemies to become more than they are. We do not add stature to public opinion we detest. We do not magnify authorities we do not respect: we look for their weaknesses as well as their power. Conformity may sometimes be unavoidable, but it should not receive our cooperation when it behaves badly. Individuality needs the willingness to make necessary changes even when others oppose our will. Cowards survive, but they are indistinguishable from the masses they surrender to. Bravery is the power to discipline our fear so that we are able to resist what is resistible, to defy what deserves defiance.

SONG: MEE HAHAM (No. 65)

RESPONSIBILITY

We often create the authorities we deserve. If we make decisions on our own, we will have to be responsible for what we do. If others make decisions for us, they will be responsible for what we do. Since responsibility is a heavy burden that we like to avoid, we hide from our own behavior. We turn our decisions over to others. And then we complain because they oppress us. Complaining is so much easier than the risk of failure. If we are good at resentment, then we never have to grow up. Like children we can rely on those who are willing to be adults. Like children we can resist our dependence. We defy our superiors just enough to be annoying, but never enough to be free. Resentful dependence is very secure. It requires only one decision, the decision to obey.

To be an individual is to be an adult.

Adulthood is more than physical. It is more than a chronological test. Many young people are more adult than their parents. Many old people are less adult than their peers. If we are adults, we prefer responsibility to resentful dependence. We may listen, but never parrot. We may defy, but never tease. We may decide, but never for the last time. If we are adults, we prefer the wisdom of authorities to their commands. We do not steal their insight and then give them our blame. We borrow from their example to train our shaky will. We will not be their servants. We will be our own masters. The complaining child must become the grateful adult.

SONG: BAMAKOM (No. 19)

FRIENDSHIP

Living alone is not the path to uniqueness.

Aloneness often leads to loneliness and to the deadening of our responses to people and to the world. Privacy is not the key to self-awareness. We are social beings, and we need the recognition of others. What is most vital within us only displays itself after the stimulus of other people. Friends, and even strangers, arouse our interest in life and make us aware of passions our private reflection never disclosed. Introspection reveals but a small part of our possibility because the catalyst of the human encounter is absent. When we are alone, away from the caresses and assaults of other human beings, we lose our sense of boundary. We begin to merge with what is around us. There is no point to being a person if there is no one to stand against.

To be an individual is to encounter others. Friendship is better than hostility. But hostility is better than indifference. Wanting to be alone may be appropriate to belief. It is rarely suitable to the excitement of personality. A private setting is not a human setting. It has very little to do with the evolution of our needs. Running away to nature may make us mystical. It will never make us individual. Self-awareness is learning the full range of our responses to others. We are most interesting to ourselves when we pursue others and they pursue us. Without two, one is less than one.

SONG: AYFO OREE (No. 14)

FIRST SHOFAR

Rosh Hashana is the day of aspiration. It is so easy for us to be deceived. It is so easy for us to imagine that we are what we are not. We become the victims of our own propaganda. Since others assault us with their accusations, we need to defend ourselves and to find our own excuses. If our excuses work, if indeed they are acceptable to others, we proceed no farther. Success is its own justification. Why should we disbelieve if we have been able to persuade others to believe? Why should we be testing if no one is asking us to test?

We must resist the easy assent of friends and strangers. They may think less of our excuses than we imagine. They may choose to ignore what they cannot change. Since we give them our approval, they courteously give us theirs.

We need to be less comfortable with ourselves than we are. We need to be open to the possibility that we are more needy than we think we are. We need to revive old dreams that challenge us with their visions and shake our complacency. We need to confront the strength of our own individuality and test its skills. We need to fill our lives with the anticipation of noble goals and strive to reach them. We need creative discontent.

CONGREGATION

With all our will we shall affirm our strength.
With all our hearts we shall pursue our dreams.

SUMMONS

May the ram's horn of old, which assembled ancient Israel for the task of new adventure, express our desire.

T'KEEA T'ROOA SH'VAREEM

SONG: TEEK'OO BASHOFAR (No. 87)

SECOND SHOFAR

Rosh Hashana is the day of earnest resolution. Wishing will not make us stronger. Hoping will not improve the quality of our individual power. The nature of our personality rests on the foundation of our skills. Without integrity, we cannot change. Without competence, we cannot safely move. Without decisiveness, we are condemned to blind obedience. Without friendship, we suffer the boredom of being less than human. Our individuality is a matter of degree. The more we cultivate the skills of independence, the greater will be the power of our person.

We cannot simply resolve to be an individual. We must first strive to acquire the skills from which personal uniqueness arises. If we lack integrity, we begin to practice it. If we lack courage, we start to discipline our fear. If we lack competence, we choose specific tasks to perform. If we lack decisiveness, we avoid dictatorial friends. If we are tired of privacy, we seek out human connection. The goal is clear. The way is hard. But the reward justifies the effort. A secure individual identity is no mean achievement.

CONGREGATION

With all our reason we shall train ourselves for freedom.
With all our strength we shall pursue the skill of competence.

SUMMONS

May the ram's horn of old, which proclaimed the defiance of Israel on the field of war, declare our resolution.

T'KEEA T'ROOA SH'VAREEM T'KEEA

SONG: TEER'OO BASHOFAR (No. 88)

MEMORIAL

The past is the teacher of the future. The men and women of earlier years are role models for those who follow. The results of what they chose to do are the recorded evidence of human history. When we consider the nature of the successful individual, we are not forced to use idle speculation. The testimony of the past stands up to instruct us.

History is a moral textbook. Integrity speaks through Einstein. Competence follows Maimonides. Decisiveness flows from Herzl. Courage is the reflection of Anne Frank. Friendship is the power of Martin Buber. Since the past is our teacher, we honor it.

SONG: TS'REEKHEEM (No. 91)

2
ROSH HASHANA YOUTH SERVICE

SONG: SHALOM L'YISRAEL (No. 82)

COMMUNITY

Today is Rosh Hashana.

Rosh Hashana is the first holiday of the Jewish year. Rosh Hashana is the Hebrew name of the Jewish New Year.

A Jewish holiday always reminds us that we are Jews, that we are members of the Jewish family, that we are part of the Jewish people.

The Jewish people is an old family. It began over four thousand years ago. It has a rich culture. It has famous heroes. It lives in many countries.

The Jewish people is our family. Jewish roots are our roots. Jewish culture is our culture. Jewish heroes are our heros. And Jewish men and women, boys and girls, wherever they may live, are our brothers and sisters.

As the Hebrew Bible says:

HINNAY MATOV OOMANAEEM SHEVET AHEEM GAM YAHAD.

It is good for brothers and sisters to live together in unity.

SONG: HINNAY MA TOV (No. 47)

NEW YEAR

Rosh Hashana comes with the fall.

Autumn is a good time to start the new year. Summer vacation is over. Everything is beginning again—parents go back to work, students return to school, new plans are being made, new projects are being designed.

Autumn lies between the comforts of summer and the hardship of winter. It is a time for us to think about the future and to gather our strength to face the problems that will come. The leaves of the autumn trees are a reminder to us that life is change. We must be wise enough to understand the change and strong enough to cope with it.

Our hope for the future does not lie in the kindness of nature. Summer does not last forever. Winter always follows. Our hope is within us and in our power to change.

Apples and honey are the traditional food of Rosh Hashana. They are symbols of hope. Their sweetness reminds us of our desires for the future.

SONG: TAPOOHEEM OOD'VASH (No. 85)

EVALUATION

When the New Year comes, we think about ourselves. We think about what we want out of life, our goals and ambitions. We think about all that we do well, all the skills we have to be successful. We think about all that we do badly, all the mistakes we have made that lead to failure and frustration.

There are so many things we need to do to make ourselves better and stronger people. But we cannot know what to do before we know what we need to change.

Our family is a very important part of our life. Mother, father, grandmother and grandfather, brother and sister give us the love and care we need to survive. Without their help, we would never grow up.

Our friends are an important part of our life. They share our pleasure and pain. They share our secrets. We can turn to them when our family cannot help.

Our teachers are an important part of our life. They train us for the future and give us skills we will need to fulfill our ambitions. Without education, we will never become what we want to become.

Getting along with family, friends, and teachers is necessary for our happiness. A wise person understands this truth.

SONG: Y'VARAYKH ADAM (No. 102)

STRENGTH

We need to be strong. We need to be strong enough to change our mind, strong enough to change our behavior, strong enough to give up bad habits we are used to.

Kindness to others does not come naturally. It requires self-control. Telling the truth is not easy. It means disciplining our fear. Sharing what we have needs more than a resolution. It means taming our jealousy.

We have to work very hard to encourage our good feelings and to control our bad feelings. Our power to be loving to family, friends, and teachers, our power to be successful in our studies, our power to be happy, takes more than wishing. It means giving up what is comfortable and walking new paths which are risky.

Our strength to do what we need to do does not lie in some mysterious place. It is not something we receive from others. It lives within us. It is the power of our will and determination. Either we discipline ourselves or nobody will.

Saying *yes* to our own strength is the first step in becoming strong.

SONG: AYFO OREE (No. 14)

RESOLUTION

Now is the time to plan our future for the coming year—to plan not only what we will study but also how we will behave.

We need to change our actions. We need to make fewer demands on our parents. We need to be more helpful to our brothers and sisters. We need to share more openly with our friends. We need to organize our time better for teaching and study.

False resolutions require no effort. They use only the mouth and the tongue. They substitute words for actions.

Good resolutions are hard work. They use our hands and our feet. They force us to change. They make us take risks. They make us uncomfortable.

Let us make good resolutions. Let us start with the words, but let us finish with action.

Let us say together:

We need to change our actions.

We need to depend more on ourselves.

We need to make fewer demands on our parents.

We need to be more helpful to our brothers and sisters.

We need to listen more carefully to our teachers.

We need to share more openly with our friends.

SONG: TS'REEKHEEM (No. 91)

SHOFAR

We need to change *now*. We need to be on the alert for action.

There is an old Jewish sound of warning, an old Jewish sound that calls us to action.

It is the sound of the *shofar*, the call of the ram's horn. The ram's horn was the first musical instrument of our Hebrew ancestors. It was the natural sound maker for nomads and shepherds.

The *shofar* did many things. It warned the people of danger. It called them to battle against attacking enemies. It summoned men and women to public meetings. It announced the election of new rulers.

In later years, it became the special instrument of the New Year, the special sound of Rosh Hashana. It warns us of the danger of doing nothing. It calls us to battle our excuses and alibis. It summons us to work together to make a better world. It announces that the time for change is *now*.

There are three *shofar* sounds. Each one is a warning.

Let us listen carefully.

T'KEEA T'ROOA SH'VAREEM T'KEEA

SONG: TS'REEKHEEM (No. 91)

3
YOM KIPPUR

SONG: SHALOM L'YISRAEL (No. 82)

JEWISHNESS

The day of atonement is a time when we feel at one with all our vital connections. We feel at one with the living world of nature, now displaying its glory in the beauty of autumn. We feel at one with ourselves as we seek integrity of mind and body, purpose and action. We feel at one with our family and friends, without whom our struggle would have little meaning. We feel at one with all creatures who bear our human form. Their needs and desires are also our very own. Above all, we feel at one with a living people whose unique style gives us a special identity. We are Jews. We share that destiny with each other and with millions beyond.

We do not really choose to be Jewish. We discover that we are. For some of us Jewishness is a minor enterprise, subordinate to what we deem more important concerns. For many of us Jewish identity is a major commitment, absorbing important energy and time.

The style of a healthy religion allows for many degrees of commitment and for many expressions of identity. If we all dance to the same Jewish tune, we will bore ourselves with uniformity. Some Jews see the Jewish future by looking at the Jewish past. They view identity through the eyes of the authoritarian state and believe that loyalty is obedience to the old way. But others view the Jewish future as a richness of options. We take what we receive and we mold it to our needs.

SONG: HANAAVA (No. 36)

SURVIVAL

The Jewish people did not begin with believers. It did not begin with a group of people who banded together to propagate a set of ideas. It began with families, clans, and tribes who came together to enjoy the unity of strength and to defend themselves against external enemies. Our people began as a nation, bound one to the other by blood ties and by mutual nurturing. Within this nation there were many points of view on all issues. Some liked many gods. Others preferred one. Some praised polygamy. Others chose monogamy. Some rallied for government by warriors. Others chose the government of priests. But all were Jews.

We Jews are a national family. Our tribal federation has gone through many changes. We have learned the skills of many new professions. We have absorbed the ideas of many new thinkers. But we have not lost the sense of our family origins. Family ties are a stronger glue than mere philosophy. Our bond, each with the other, remains what it was three thousand years ago. The family connection is irresistible. It is the power of survival and continuity, roots and the ease of birth identity. No set of ideas can substitute for that attachment. We are too big and too old for that silly test. We are a historic extended family. The music of our past expresses the power of that bond.

SONG: KOL NIDRAY (No. 55)

TRANSCENDENCE

Religion begins with transcendence. Transcendence is what we feel when we are part of something greater than ourselves. Transcendence is a natural experience, unrelated to gods and angels. It begins in infancy with the reverence we have for the power of parents. It grows in adolescence with our need to prove our worth to the community we depend on. It flourishes in adulthood with the approval we receive for useful work and useful children. Transcendence begins with our personal family and moves on to embrace the wider community that gives us identity.

The first and authentic religious experience is the experience of community. When we celebrate our membership in the Jewish people, when we dramatize our connection to the Jewish past and to the Jewish future, we transcend our own death and sense our part in an immortal enterprise. Without community there is no religion. Privacy may be appropriate to philosophy, but it is subversive of religion. Judaism did not begin with a sense of heavenly mysteries. It began with the transcendent experience of the Jewish people dancing out its will to live.

SONG: SHEEM'OO (No. 83)

WORLD PEOPLE

We began as a territorial nation. The land of Israel and the people of Israel were joined together in a bond of marriage that history arranges for every people. When our ancestors left this land and dispersed over the face of the earth, they felt the pain of separation. They also knew the terror of being aliens in someone else's land. Living in strange places made them feel like eternal strangers. The guilt of departure and the agony of rejection made them nostalgic for what they had left. They praised Zion and dreamed of it, although they did not return there. Even when they became a people of the world, they saw themselves as the people of one land.

Modern times will not let us hide from our new reality. The land of Israel is again a Jewish state, open to all who wish to return. Some do. Many do not. The dream has been put to the test of our own behavior. The dispersion is much bigger than the children of the homeland. Jerusalem is the center of a world people which encompasses the globe. We are the citizens of many states. We are the speakers of many languages. We are the lovers of many great cities. Our self-image is too big to be confined to one small territory. Our loyalties are too broad to be restricted by national boundaries. We are an international family.

SONG: Y'ROOSHALIEYIM SHEL ZAHAV (No. 101)

FUTURE

Ancestors are powerful beings. Even after their death they linger in memory to guide our lives according to their desire. Religion has made them very important. Since a living community exists not only in space but also in time, the past dominates the present. The will of our early fathers becomes more important than our will. The judgments of our distant parents become more significant than our own decisions. We revere the past and imagine that those who lived before were wiser and more noble than we are. We see our predecessors through a romantic vision. We believe that all they said was profound, even when it does not seem to be. Because part of us still remains the child, we are afraid of them and do not wish to displease them.

When we remember ancestors we must also think of our posterity. A living people not only stretches back to the past, it also reaches forward to the future.

Distant children are as important as distant parents. What will happen to our people is as important as what did happen. Just as our ancestors were the children of their past, so are we the ancestors of our future. Just as our forbears invented holidays and created ceremonies to serve their posterity, so do we alter the instruction of earlier years to serve our children. The story of Jewish survival is far more than the reverence of tradition. It is also the creative gifts of sensitive children who know they will some day be ancestors.

SONG: BAMAKOM (No. 19)

LIBERATION

Walls are comforting symbols. They speak to us of security and protection. They suggest the privacy of our homes. They keep out intruders. But walls are disturbing too. They close us in as well as keep others out. They imprison as well as protect. They hide the light, even when they seek to shield us from the darkness.

For many people the wall of tradition and the wall of segregation are the pillars of community survival. Even when these walls are breached by social change they believe in their strength and integrity. Even when the forces of history have torn them down, they still see them. They deny that they are face to face with a new and strange world. Although the walls have fallen, they still call for repairs.

We Jews once had strong walls which we bore with us wherever we went. Most of them were of our own creation. Some of them were built by our enemies. For many of our people, the walls were bastions of defense and safety. For others, they were tight and narrow prisons that offered the tyranny of custom as the price of security. Today the walls have fallen. They no longer exist except in the minds of those who refuse to admit their disappearance. They will not be rebuilt. The people who want them do not really want to forgo the freedom of not having them. Our choice is clear. We can either wax nostalgic about the walls and pretend that one day we will rebuild them, or we can train ourselves to enjoy a freedom we have never experienced before. Reason tells us that the second way is the way of integrity. We have no guidelines from the past for this new liberty. We will have to create our own.

SONG: AYFO OREE (No. 14)

FIRST RESOLUTION

Yom Kippur is a day of truth. We remember our past and do not hide from its reality. We peer into our future and do not fill its spaces with the fantasies of our desire. We want to be strong enough to live with the truth. We want to be bold enough to speak it even though others do not wish to hear it. Time will not allow us to return to the past, except in our dreams. It permits us only to step into the future. But each step is filled with the uncertainty of what has not already happened. It would be so much easier to walk backwards into what we already know!

We resolve this day to choose courage. We will not surrender to the fear of the unknown. We will not repair walls that have already fallen. We will not turn the sages of our past into infallible guides. We will not run away from wisdom even though it comes from strange lands and strange people. Our bravery is our dignity. It feeds our strength. If old laws no longer work, we will create new ones. If old ceremonies no longer fit, we will revise them. If old postures keep us from moving gracefully, we will find a new way to walk. A free world makes tradition only one of many options. There is more to life than imitation. Our ancestors created. So can we.

CONGREGATION

With all our will we choose the openness of courage.
With all our strength we choose the dignity of freedom.

SONG: B'KHOL ADAM (No. 24)

SECOND RESOLUTION

Yom Kippur is a day of hope. We remember that the survival of our people depended on no one skill and on no single strategy. We acknowledge that the will to live found new paths in the moment when it was necessary to see them. What is now old was once new, an unfamiliar action. What is now sacred was once profane, a bold insight that the fearful rejected. The danger is that we may imagine that what we did before we cannot do again. We exalt the past and demean our present. We ignore the trial and error of old decisions and view our own frustration as failure. We see ourselves as different and believe that we are dying.

We resolve this day to choose hope. We will not betray the future of our people by endorsing despair. We will not transform our past into such a fantasy of success that our future can become nothing more than failure. We will not turn problems into mysteries so that we can never learn how to solve them. Our optimism is our survival. It nurtures our will to live. If experience leads to new ideas, we will accommodate them. If science leads to new environments, we will test them. If opportunity creates a new dispersion, we will serve it. We are more adaptable than we imagine. There is no need for us to be surprised at Jewish survival. Our ingenuity speaks for itself.

CONGREGATION

With all our might we enforce the power of hope.
With all our will we affirm the pursuit of life.

SONG: B'KHOL ADAM (No. 24)

MEMORIAL

Yom Kippur is a day of memory. We offer our tribute to all who valued their Jewish identity and helped it endure. We salute the heroes of our past who did not hesitate to do something new in order to save something old. The assaults of our enemies have been so relentless that we are obsessed with losses and fail to see our gains. We notice the pain of our martyrs and ignore the pleasure of our survivors.

Jewish history is more than a tale of woe. It is a dramatic parade of splendid events and bold heroes. It is the saga of a small nation transformed into a world people. Triumph, as well as humiliation, belong to our memories.

We resolve this day to see the joy of the Jewish experience. We will not hover over our martyrs alone and ignore the countless millions who were happily Jewish. We will not remember the terrible lands from which we were expelled and forget the comfortable places that offered us hospitality. We will not accuse the outsiders who were our bitter enemies and discard the strangers who became our loyal friends. Our history deserves more than wailing. It has also earned laughter and cheers. We give honor not only to those who taught us how to cry, but also to those who were both Jewish and joyous. If we carried burdens, we also danced.

SONG: TS'REEKHEEM (No. 91)

4
YOM KIPPUR MEMORIAL

SONG: SHALOM LARAHOK (No. 81)

MEMORIES

We live with our memories. We cannot escape them. They have made their comfortable home within our brain and leave reluctantly. Good memories are easy to recall. Our conscious mind invites them to seize our attention and to comfort us with pleasant nostalgia. Bad memories are more difficult to find. They are banished to the underworld of our mind. They emerge without permission to make us relive old pain and old agony.

We are condemned to remember. It is the very nature of the human condition. Because we remember, we have culture. Because we remember, we have tradition. Because we remember, we are able to learn from our past. Even if we wanted to stop remembering, we could not stop. Even if we desired to forget our past, it would insist on intruding. We cannot be the creatures of our evolutionary past who lived from moment to moment without the assault of conscious memory. Our past stays with us vividly. We must learn how to live with it.

SONG: KAMIEYEEM (No. 51)

ACTION

Remembering is a skill. It can be done well. It can be done badly. Some of us always remember what we do not need to recall. Hosts of trivia dance in our mind and turn the past into a chaos of unimportant events. Others always recall what is sad and morbid. Memory becomes a road to despair and self-pity. Still others force their vision of the past through the tunnel of fantasy. History becomes a form of useless fiction. The power of memory is diverted to harmful ends.

When we remember well, we are not passive. We do not consent to be the quiet observer of a script we have not chosen. Time is too valuable to turn memory into nothing more than idle reverie. Our needs are too urgent to allow unedited stories to fill our hours with tales of symbolic horror. To remember well is to choose. To use memory constructively is to select. We do not want to deny what is in the album of our mind. But we do not have to dwell on every painful photograph or linger on every childhood scene we ought to outgrow. We can turn the page and find the picture that moves us to constructive action. We do not use the past to avoid our present. We use the past to shape our future. We remember in order to survive.

CONGREGATION

Who are the wise? People who understand themselves.
Who are the strong? People who rule themselves.
Who are the beautiful? People who are wise and strong.

SONG: MEE HAHAM (No. 65)

ROOTS

Our memories give us part of our identity. If we were unable to relate our present to our past, the moments of our life would be separate beads with no string to connect them. If we were unable to attach what we do now to what we did before, we would have no sense of being more than an instant experience. Our personalities derive their reality not only from space, but also from time. Our lives are events that flow one into the other, each happening bearing the mark of those that came before. Memory gives us our internal biography, allowing us to view each encounter with the world from the vantage point of history.

Our remembrance of the past also widens our identity and enables us to find our roots in the lives of other people. We are part of a long chain of human life that spans millennia. The memories of those distant years are locked up in our genes. They are also revealed in the tales of our ancestors and in the wisdom which we received from our parents and our teachers. Because we remember we lived before we were born, because our children can remember, we shall still live after we die. In one sense we are temporary and ephemeral, quickly arriving and abruptly departing. In another sense, we find ourselves part of the endless flow of the human stream.

SONG: SAHAKEE (No. 78)

EXAMPLE

We do not really learn from spoken rules. Words can inspire us, but they cannot transform our lives. We learn from people, from the living example of living teachers. Loving heroes enter our lives and guide us by what they do, not by what they say. They embody the ideal and make it real enough for us to understand. A cold ruler is marvelously transformed into a warm person. A noble concept takes on flesh and breathes its spirit on our senses. Sometimes the style is gentle, a graceful exposition of truth through behavior. Sometimes it is bold, assaulting our eyes with the strength of moral conviction. We first learn through imitation. The ideal follows the teacher.

Memory keeps alive the example of great men and women who taught us through action. It also preserves the behavior of more modest guides who entered our lives as parents and friends. They embodied ideals they would have found it difficult to articulate. The past is a school of morals, a drama of right and wrong. Some of the actors were villains, giving form to evil and vividly revealing what not to do. Other performers were heroes who made their lives their lesson. We too shall be part of the future's past. Each of us is a moral actor, teaching by what he does. Our actions will move others long after our words are forgotten.

SONG: MAASEEM TOVEEM (No. 61)

PROGRESS

Life is struggle. It is the solving of problems. It is the mastering of skills. Our brains are so complex that, unlike lower forms of life, we do not have a single response to a single stimulus. An infinite number of options greets us with each new intrusion of reality. Exploring and testing begin as childish games. They stay with us to become the special strength of maturity. We try— and blunder. We try—and succeed. Error and accuracy are the polar ends of our learning experience.

Pursuing knowledge makes us awkward. We fall and stumble so often along wisdom's way that we are embarrassed by our graceless action. We sometimes wish that we enjoyed the programmed ease of birds and cats. But we possess a freedom that they will never know. We can change what no longer works. We can alter what no longer pleases. We can transmit to future generations the fruits of our awkward struggle.

Memory is the storehouse of practical wisdom. The defeats of the past need not be preserved if we are willing to listen to its victories. The blunders of the past need not be repeated if we are willing to imitate its successes. Progress is the freedom to avoid doing what the past has already done. We stand on the building blocks of memory to reach higher and higher. The tower of human knowledge rises to heaven and allows us to visit the secrets of human existence that tradition forbade us to explore. Sometimes when we look up to confront the vast open spaces we have not yet attained, we despair. We forget how high we have already climbed.

SONG: LAM'TSAPPEEM (No. 56)

RESPECT

Religion begins with memory. It begins with ancestors. In a primitive world where change is slow and where the future is no more than an imitation of the past, our roots give us a sense of enduring community. We invoke the presence of those who died and make them live so that their strength can help us defeat the enemies of nature. The world of spirits and gods arises out of this lasting affection and desperate need. Since our ancestors offer their assistance, they exact their price. They want us to do what they did. They want us to make them live through imitation. Piety is the willingness to accede to this request.

A healthy religion forbids piety and substitutes respect. Since our forebears are only memories—not living beings, as many imagine—they cannot harm us with their anger. They cannot destroy us by withdrawing their affection. They become opportunities for our own pleasure and inspiration. We find in them our roots. We see in them models of noble action. We learn from them the tradition of practical wisdom. But we do not have to view them uncritically. They did not always do right. They did not always know the truth. Like us they were human. Like us they were the victims of their own circumstance. They were the prisoners of their own limitations. We will not give them the gift of blind obedience. We extend to them the more reasonable tribute of loving respect.

SONG: AYFO OREE (No. 14)

FIRST MEMORIAL

The Jewish family found its security within the larger family of the Jewish people. We enjoy the broader fellowship that clans and tribes and nations bring. The safety of numbers and the intimacy of a unique culture blend to make Jewish identity a comfortable style. Our genealogy passes back through forty centuries. We have tasted the freedom of nomadic tribes. We have experienced the power of a territorial nation. We have endured the fate of a dispersed and alien people. We have enjoyed the life of an international family, thriving on the challenge of new lands and new ideas. Our memories are rich and varied. They are not confined to Hebrew. They often speak to us in Yiddish and Ladino. They are not restricted to sunny Mediterranean scenes. They prefer busy cities and academic centers. Our experience is as universal as a parochial people can allow.

We offer our special honor to all the heroes of our Jewish past who gave vitality to our ethnic tale. Some of them achieved personal fame, remembered in legend and adoring biography. Others gave equal gifts but were forgotten by the injustice of fate. Tradition tends to honor prophets, priests, and warriors and to ignore the heroes of trade and scientific learning. But our survival needed the secular as well as the pious. The skills of daily life are more important than mystic turns. We pay them all our tribute. We will not betray their useful gifts.

SONG: Y'ROOSHALIEYIM SHEL ZAHAV (No. 101)

SECOND MEMORIAL

Our Jewish roots make us feel the power of our human roots. Our struggle for survival is a human struggle. Our search for happiness is a human search. Under the surface of national difference and ethnic flair lies the substance of universal human needs. We are bound together with all the people of the world through the very sameness of our desires. Chauvinists may prefer to stress the absolute uniqueness of their family style, but history embarrasses them by always finding twins. The tale of the human struggle is lending and borrowing. The useful discovery of one culture crosses the barrier of local pride and assumes its place under a new name. Skills and ideas move freely around the world because they serve human needs that know no boundary. Our human family is real even when we do not notice it.

We extend our respectful tribute to the heroes of all lands and all cultures. We will not allow the prejudices of war to assign whole nations to good and evil. Cyrus was as Persian as Haman. Plato was as Greek as Antiochus. Goethe was as German as Hitler. The models of nobility shine from many parts of the human sky. From the perspective of past evolution and future science the human fate is indivisible. The human past is our past. Human memory is our memory. Human hope is our hope.

SONG: ANEE MAAMEEN (No. 10)

THIRD MEMORIAL

The darkness of night will soon reach out to embrace us, but we are not afraid of it. There will be the brightness of moon and stars. There will be the flickering flames of man-made fires.

But the glories of our human connection will outshine them all. The energy of family and friends will warm us and keep us safe. The power of old loyalty and tested faith will give us strength and help us confront the darkness with courage. We are the children of love. We are the heirs of generous hope. Parents and peers are joined to us through mutual dependence. We need each other even when we do not wish to admit the need. We lean on each other, even when we deny the leaning.

We offer our loving tribute to all the people who gave us the gift of life. Some of them have died but stay with us in vivid memory. Some of them live on to repeat their gifts in every action. Each of us finds an intimate community of past and present, of memory and new experience that is the context of our survival. There are times when we are bored by its sameness. There are moments when we feel oppressed by its closeness. There are seasons when we resent our dependence. But we know that we cannot live on loneliness and thrive on scattered encounters with careless people. We honor the secure love of family and friends. We honor the powerful memories of those who gave their love when we needed it.

SILENT MEMORIAL

The memory of those I loved in life and still love in death blesses my thoughts and actions. The special grace of their years reaches out to touch my heart and give me hope.

CLOSING WORDS

The memory of those we loved in life and still love in death blesses our thoughts and actions. The special grace of their years reaches out to touch our hearts and give us hope.

SONG: TS'REEKHEEM (No. 91)

5
YOM KIPPUR YOUTH SERVICE

SONG: SHALOM L'YISRAEL (No. 82)

COMMUNITY

Today is Yom Kippur.

Yom Kippur is the closing holiday of the Jewish New Year celebration. The New Year festival lasts for ten days. It is called the High Holidays. It begins with Rosh Hashana. It ends with Yom Kippur.

Yom Kippur is the Hebrew way of saying "Day of Reconciliation." It is the time when we repair family relationships and friendships which may have been broken. It is the time when we bring together our hopes and our actions. It is the season when we return to the pursuit of our ideals, to what is most important in our lives.

The New Year festival gives us the opportunity to look back on the past and to plan for the future. It gives us the chance to think about our lives, to think about our behavior, to think about the people we need and love.

Yom Kippur is a special time for us and for all Jews.

SONG: HINNAY MA TOV (No. 47)

NEW YEAR

Yom Kippur comes at a good time.

The normal schedule of our life is starting up again. Work replaces play. Study makes leisure less available. New information has to be learned. New responsibilities have to be assumed.

There are many new demands we have to meet. There are many new problems we have to solve.

We need the strength to deal with the faster tempo of our lives. We need the insight to tell the difference between what we really want and what we think we want. We need the power to handle more than one problem at a time.

Yom Kippur is a time to gather our strength. It is a time to deepen our understanding. It is the season to discover the power we never knew we had.

SONG: AHAVA OOVEENA (No. 3)

EVALUATION

The ten days of the New Year festival give us the chance to change our life. Between Rosh Hashana and Yom Kippur, we have the opportunity to make important decisions. We therefore need to be serious about who we are and what we do.

We need to be serious about what comes first. It is very easy to run away from our most demanding goals and to waste our time with insignificant matters. It is very normal to avoid what frightens us and to pretend that we are not afraid.

Our family is very important to our survival. We cannot afford to abuse them. Our schooling is very important to our future success. We cannot afford to fail. Our health is very important to our safety and dignity. We cannot neglect good food and good rest. Fun and play are special. But family, education, and health are more important. Understanding this truth is part of growing up.

SONG: Y'VARAYKH ADAM (No. 102)

CHALLENGE

Self-control is necessary for the good life.

We cannot control our feelings. If we feel angry, if we feel jealous, if we feel mean, we cannot change the way we feel. Emotions are just there. And we have to be able to accept them.

But we can control our behavior. We do not have to express our anger. We do not have to express our jealousy. We do not have to express our meanness.

Some feelings, like love and caring, have good consequences, so we give them our energy. Some feelings, like hate and envy, have bad consequences, so we hold them back.

Self-control gives us a sense of being in charge of our life. Our feelings do not rule us; we rule our feelings.

Self-control gives us self-respect. If we can admire our behavior, we can admire ourselves.

The theme song of Yom Kippur is a song of self-control and self-respect. The words and the music have both sadness and hope. Even though the history of our people has often filled us with the sadness of suffering, we must resist the sadness and live with hope.

SONG: KOL NIDRAY (No. 55)

STRENGTH

We are responsible for all our actions.

Weak people always blame others for what they do wrong. They always find excuses. They always invent alibis. Weak people cannot take the risk of making a decision. They need to be right—always.

Strong people never blame others for what they do wrong. They do not look for excuses. They do not invent alibis. Strong people are willing to take the risk of making a decision. They do not need to be right—always. The sign of strength is the willingness to say "I am responsible." The act of courage is the willingness to take the blame as well as the credit.

When we have strength of character, we have dignity. Dignity begins with an inner determination and flows outward to our deeds.

SONG: AYFO OREE (No. 14)

RESOLUTION

Now is the time to do what we need to do.

Now is the time to think about our lives, to think about our behavior, to think about the people we admire and love.

Now is the time to gather our strength, to deepen our understanding, to discover our power.

Now is the time to choose first things first, to place our family, our education, and our health above mere fun and play.

Now is the time to become the masters of our lives and to rule our feelings.

Now is the time to discover our excuses and to take responsibility for all that we do.

Let us say together:

We will be honest about our behavior.

We will protect our family.

We will make learning important.

We will guard our health.

We will control our feelings.

We will take responsibility for all that we do.

SONG: TS'REEKHEEM (No. 91)

SHOFAR

We need to change *now*. We need to be on the alert for action.

There is an old Jewish sound of warning, an old Jewish sound that calls us to action. It is the sound of the *shofar,* the call of the ram's horn. The ram's horn was the first musical instrument of our Hebrew ancestors. It was the natural sound maker for nomads and shepherds.

The *shofar* did many things. It warned the people of danger. It called them to battle against attacking enemies. It summoned men and women to public meetings. It announced the election of new rulers.

In later years, it became the special instrument of the New Year, the special sound of Rosh Hashana and Yom Kippur. It warns us of the danger of doing nothing. It calls us to battle our excuses and alibis. It summons us to work together to make a better world. It announces that the time for change is *now*.

There are three *shofar* sounds. Each one is a warning.

Let us listen carefully.

T'KEEA T'ROOA SH'VAREEM T'KEEA

SONG: TS'REEKHEEM (No. 91)

6
SUKKOT

SONG: ADAMA (No. 1)

AUTUMN

We welcome the autumn season. No time of year equals its beauty. No other season touches the splendor of its glory. In a color symphony of brown and gold and red, nature plays its visual magic and fills our eyes with delightful wonder. The season is ironic. As the living things of summer approach their death, they defy their end and retire from the world more beautiful than their youth allowed. Fall resists a dignified decay; it prefers a radiant finale.

SONG: ZEMER LAKH (No. 104)

CHANGE

Autumn is more than the end of summer. It is part of an eternal circle of change which has neither start nor finish. Fall merges with winter; and winter ultimately yields to spring. If, in the drama of nature, death follows life, the eternal play of the seasons insists on resurrection. Out of the cold silence of winter the noisy warmth of spring emerges to announce its vital triumph. The splendid decay of autumn has both past and future, nostalgia and hope. It ushers out the old life in order to make way for the new. Like the Sukkot of Israel, it gathers in the harvest while it dreams of rain.

SONG: B'ROOKHEEM HAHIEYEEM (No. 25)

CREATIVITY

Nature has two faces. Like an indulgent mother it may smile protectively while caressing us with warmth and light. Or like some cruel tyrant, it may laugh at our suffering, devouring our life in devilish upheavals and tempests. Human survival is no product of a benign world. It is the perpetual struggle of humanity with a universe that is often less than friendly. If autumn, as the season of harvest, suggests the scenic beauty of the rural countryside it also announces the triumph of human ingenuity over the rocks and swamps and the unkempt wildness of empty fields. Farming is no passive art in which pastoral angels effortlessly pluck the fruits of life. History has made it a hard and taxing profession, by which human intelligence turns disaster into hope. Without the creative planning of human decision there would be no harvest. As the frail Sukka booth defies the winds of autumn and stands firm, so do creative farmers resist nature's hostility and by their wits survive.

SONG: SEESOO VSEEM'HOO (No. 79)

LIFE

The spirit of Sukkot goes beyond the harvest. Wherever man has tamed the primitive landscape of nature's face and turned it to the useful business of human pleasure, this holiday finds a congenial home. Wherever the creative talent of human thought has rescued the natural elements from moral indifference and put them to work to make men less afraid, this festival can be comfortably celebrated. The technical marvel of the modern city is no emotional stranger to the harvest season. It shares with the ancient farmer a persistent wish. In the golden barley fields of biblical Israel, as well as in the concrete vertical thrust of the new Manhattan, the human determination to live finds its expression.

SONG: SEESOO VSEEM'HOO (No. 79)

LOVE

Thanksgiving and gratitude are natural to this season. No person alone can subdue nature to human needs. Without the bonds of human love and cooperation, intelligence is useless. Our need for other people, our leaning on the efforts of other men and women, makes the claim of total self-sufficiency a pretense. Where people will not work together, there are no harvests. Where the ordered ties of human society are absent, there are no cities. Mutual dependence demands mutual gratitude. If we know that we need each other, thankful feelings arise from our awareness.

SONG: AL KOL AYLE (No. 6)

MEMORIAL

Autumn leaves are more useful than they seem. Although in final glory they fall to the ground in a wistful descent of death, the fertile earth pays them tribute. She embraces their forms and turns their hidden energies into the evolution of new life. In the drama of human love, a similar pattern prevails. The thoughts and ideals of those we admire survive death. They fall on the fertile earth of our minds and hearts and renew our lives through inspiration.

SONG: Y'HEE SHALOM (No. 98)

PROCESSION

Our ancestors matched the splendor of the harvest with the magnificence of their celebration. They seized the luscious fruits of their labor and paraded them in song-filled processions. Branches of the stately date palm and the fragrant citrons of perfumed orchards filled their hands. They did not hide the joy of their success behind solemn prayers but danced out the pleasure of their victory for life.

SONG: HOSHANA (No. 48)

7 SUKKOT YOUTH SERVICE

SONG: HINNAY MA TOV (No. 47)

S'TAV

Autumn is here. The days and nights are colder. The leaves are turning brown and gold and red. The sun spends less time with us and darkness arrives earlier than before.

Autumn is here. Everything is changing. Nothing lasts forever. What is born must also die. What is new must also grow old. Nature never stays the same. All the world is moving.

Autumn is here. Everything is beginning. School starts again. Work is renewed. Activity increases. While the life of nature ebbs, human energy grows stronger.

S'tav is the Hebrew word for "autumn."

SONG: SEESOO VSEEM'HOO (No. 79)

KATSEER

Autumn is harvest time. The seeds of spring have turned into the food of winter. The work of summer has brought forth the bread of life. We live with nature. It gives us grain and fruit. It yields up fish and fowl. It sends us survival.

But nature needs more than nature. Farming is far more than finding food. It takes human ingenuity to turn the earth into a field of corn. It requires human caring to change the sapling into the successful tree. The harvest does not happen all by itself. Nature and people work together. We need each other.

Katseer is the Hebrew word for "harvest."

SONG: ARTSA ALEENOO (No. 12)

SUKKA

Autumn is harvest time in Israel. The fruit on the trees is ready for picking. The grain in the field is ready for cutting. The land is filled with joy. The winter will be secure.

In olden times, Jewish farmers stayed all day in the fields at harvest time. They were very busy and had no time to return home. In the heat of the day, they stopped work for a while and rested in special huts nearby. The huts were frail structures, decorated with the special fruits of the harvest and open to the sky. Our ancestors sang songs, they danced, they ate their midday meal and returned to work.

Sukka is the Hebrew word for "hut."

SONG: HAVA NAGEELA (No. 42)

SUKKOT

Autumn is a special time for celebration. Like all the seasons of the year, it brings its own unique joy. Holidays are times of celebration. They make us aware of what is important in our lives. They make us notice the beauty of things and places and people.

As far back as we can remember, the Jewish people have always enjoyed a fall festival. They have taken the time to honor the autumn, to pay tribute to the harvest, to sing and to dance. There was so much to do, one day was never enough. Eight days were better. The autumn holiday needed eight days.

Sukkot is the Hebrew name for the fall festival.

SONG: ZOOM GALEE (No. 106)

LOOLAV

Holidays need parades. Parades need special things for people to hold and wave.

Sukkot needs a parade—not an ordinary one with flags and floats but a special one with harvest grain and harvest fruit.

In the land of Israel, the date palm grows tall and straight. At harvest time its dates are sweet and nourishing, its branches are long and graceful.

The palm branch is a beautiful Sukkot banner. For many years, Jews have marched with it to celebrate the harvest and to honor the autumn season. They decorate it with the leaves of myrtle and willow. They wave it to the sound of flutes and drums. They march with it in long processions.

Loolav is the Hebrew word for "palm branch."

SONG: HOSHANA (No. 48)

ETROG

The *loolav* did not stand alone. Tradition found it a partner, not long and thin and green but short, round, and yellow.

There is a special fruit that grows in the land of Israel. It grows nowhere else. It looks like a wrinkled lemon, but it does not taste like a lemon. Nor does it smell like a lemon. It has a special taste all its own. It has a special fragrance that is unique. People like to smell it because it smells like perfume.

This special fruit is the partner of the *loolav*. They always go together. They remind us of life: Some people are tall. Some of us are short. But all of us are important.

Etrog is the Hebrew name for this fragrant fruit.

SONG: HOSHANA (No. 48)

SIMHA

When holidays come we think of all the good things in life. We think of the beauties of nature, the love of family, the importance of friendship, the power of roots.

The good things in life bring us happiness. They give meaning to our existence. They offer us strength and hope.

Sukkot is a time of happiness. It is a time of joy. Just as in ages past our ancestors marched and sang and danced, so do we. We stamp our feet. We clap our hands. We proclaim our joy.

Simha is the Hebrew word for "joy."

SONG: SEESOO VSEEM'HOO (No. 79)

8
HANUKKA

SONG: SHALOM L'YISRAEL (No. 82)

WINTER

Winter is cold and dark. The pleasure of light and warmth is scarce. The sun is stingy, refusing us what we need. We feel less secure than we do in summertime. We feel more dependent on the goodwill of nature. Fantasies of warmer places fill our minds and divert us from the struggle to survive. Our evolutionary roots are in the tropics and winter makes us aware of how fragile we really are.

But challenge is the stimulus of progress. Had we lingered in our African Garden of Eden, had we chosen to stay in our tropical paradise, we would have become less than we are. Civilization was born out of our struggle with hardship and deprivation. We are at our best when we are neither content nor comfortable. The threat of pain and suffering makes us more creative and adds adrenalin to our ingenuity. In the season when everything dies, we become more aware of our will to live.

SONG: HANOOKKA (No. 37)

LIGHT

The energy of light is the source of life. It comes in such profusion during the summer that we take it for granted. Only in the winter, when it threatens to disappear, do we acknowledge its vital power and give it the tribute of our concern. A dark world is a dead world. Our ancestors affirmed this truth when they named the winter holiday the Feast of Lights. They kindled oil flames to encourage the sun to imitate their action. Human desire would force the flames to return the gift of life. As the winter days grew longer, it seemed to our forefathers that they had succeeded. In their eyes, the earthly flame had persuaded the heavenly fire to renew its strength.

We no longer fear the death of the sun, nor do we imagine that the stars heed the bidding of our magic. We know that the circling of the earth around the sun dictates the seasons and that the dearth of winter will be followed by the plenty of spring and summer. Our confidence in our own power has increased and has enabled us to manufacture our own light when we need it. The energy of light floats everywhere. With the vision of human reason, we can find it in the darkness and make it shine.

SONG: ASHRAY HAGAFROOR (No. 13)

COMMUNITY

We are not suited for the cold. We have no furry external mantle to keep us warm. We lack the arctic ease of the polar bear. Our limbs shiver and our teeth chatter in the face of icy blasts. Our clothing hides our humiliation and lets us pretend that we are hardier than our naked body would suggest. Indeed, the image of hell is not only the final fire but also the killing ice that numbs all consciousness and freezes the passions. Our feeling for life needs the heat of vitality.

When we are warmed by the sun, we become less needy of others. Protected by the kindness of nature, we are less dependent on the kindness of humanity. But the cold rescues us from our arrogance. We huddle together with those we love to share our precious heat and to warm each other with the presence of life. In the winter, families and friends become more important. They represent our vital link to survival. They reflect our need to be more than individuals. If nature chooses to be cruel, we shall offer each other the help that nature denies.

SONG: HINNAY MA TOV (No. 47)

COURAGE

Courage is the willingness to live with risk. People who choose security as their chief objective cannot be brave. They prefer places neither too hot nor too cold. They prefer work neither too hard nor too easy. They choose feelings neither too strong nor too weak. Moderation is safety, a comfortable fence to exclude all danger and to shut out all adventure.

Our human ancestors who risked the cold of winter to find new homes and to explore new places rejected this fence. They chose unknown worlds and the peril of death as the price of their search. Unlike their evolutionary cousins, they could not fall asleep to survive. Their will and their wits were their only guarantees of life.

Our human world has always been divided between those who prefer safety above all and those who are willing to risk survival for what they deem higher causes. The lovers of security can only admire bravery from the distance. They complain about evil conditions but never resist them. They denounce evil rulers behind their backs but never to their faces. They revere old heroes but never join new ones. When the Greek tyrant came to Israel, they mumbled their discontent and then offered obedience. The Maccabee rebels fought two enemies: they battled the armies of Antiochus; they also defied the fearful smugness of their Jewish brothers, who were prepared to join the struggle *after* victory was assured. Praising courage is very different from trying it.

SONG: MEE Y'MALLEL (No. 67)

NAYROT

The winter holiday is older than our Jewish memories. It has roots in dim antiquity, in the ancient fear of a dying sun and a dark, dead world. *Nayrot,* the Feast of Lights, was an important part of the popular religion and joined autumn Sukkot and spring Pesakh in a trio of tributes to the seasons. Like wedding celebrations before the age of the relentless urban time clock, they lasted for a week and a day, public celebrations of the collective will to live.

In the human scene, history supplements nature. Great national events heighten the drama of survival. *Nayrot* took on the second name of *Hanukka.* The new name was the gift of the Maccabees, who sought to preserve the memory of their victory by attaching it to an old celebration. Having defeated the Greek king, having resisted his attempt to turn the Jews into Greeks, they chose to rededicate the great Temple of Jerusalem to Jewish use on the first day of the winter holiday. How appropriate to light the seven lights of the Temple Menorah on the very day that the Jewish nation gave honor to light. How timely to celebrate the bravery of resistance in the very season that gave birth to human courage. *Hanukka* means dedication, a reminder of ideals more important than mere survival.

SONG: MACCABEES OF OLD (No. 62)

MENORAH

The Temple Menorah had seven candles, a reminder of the sun, moon, and five planetary stars that the ancients believed controlled the destiny of the human race. Unlike the Menorah of the Nayrot festival, the flames of Hanukka, it was hidden in the Temple building, accessible only to priestly eyes and priestly care. No ordinary Jew could enter the sacred home of divinity and gaze on its light. It was a mystery to be glorified by rumor, not an event to be understood by experience.

The Hanukka Menorah was less pretentious. It was the creation of every Jewish home, of every Jewish family. Its proportions were domestic, small and cozy. Its materials were ordinary, clay and fire. Its light was public, available to human eyes in a thousand and one open windows. Unlike the Temple lamp, whose flames were lit at one time, the Hanukka Menorah had its fires kindled in sequence, one more each day. The holiday lights were the expression of hope. They expanded their power and their strength with time. No secret event in a forbidding temple, they announced the vision of better things to come. Each Menorah did not stand alone. It merged with all the others to proclaim to all who would see the power of hope that community brings.

SONG: Y'MAY HANOOKKA (No. 99)

MEMORIAL

Our past is filled with people who never surrendered their courage to fear, who never yielded their hope to apathy. They were ancestors who valued dignity more than life. They were citizens of other lands who ventured forth to explore new places and to test new ideas. They were grandparents and parents who refused the safety of pious obedience to create freer alternatives. They were Jewish idealists who denounced the resignation of waiting to return to the home of the Maccabees to rebuild it.

The Maccabees did not invent Hanukka, but they gave special meaning to its celebration. Hope is an action more than a belief. It is the willingness to try even when trying seems dangerous. It is the boldness to resist even when the resistance seems hopeless. The splendor of the Maccabees was not their routine military action. It was their spontaneous bravery that inspired the masses to attempt a rebellion that the cautious denounced. We remember the Maccabees with great affection. Five brothers led their people to victory against the predictions of the wise. They proved that reason is harmful when it is only an excuse for cowardice. Like the Maccabees, reason needs courage to keep it honest.

SONG: SHEEM'OO (No. 83)

CANDLELIGHTING

Our present is filled with the hope of courage. We are no different from our ancestors. We are human in our desires and fears. Like all people, we crave safety and we are comfortable with routine. Like all people, we need dignity and we yearn for excitement. Like many of our ancestors, we can choose resignation and invent noble reasons for doing what is not noble. But like others of our past, we can swallow our fear and go forth to change what needs to be changed. The power to change defines our self-esteem.

The eight lights of our Hanukka Menorah do not speak to us only of the courage of the past. After all, we cannot use the credentials of old heroes. We cannot survive for long on the glory of others. We need to affirm our own strength. We need to prod our own bravery. The Hanukka lights remind us of the risks we must take, of the changes we must effect. We must not use the winter season to reinforce our despair and to justify our apathy. We must try all the harder to overcome the cold of the outside with the heat of our inner passions, to overwhelm the darkness of the world with the light of our long-run vision. We kindle these flames to express this determination.

SONGS: BAROOKH HAOR (No. 20)

MACCABEES OF OLD (No. 62)

9
HANUKKA YOUTH SERVICE

SONG: SHALOM L'YISRAEL (No. 82)

HOREF

Winter is coming, a new season. The cold gets colder. The rain turns to snow. The wind blows. And the darkness grows longer.

In the winter, we need to be strong. Since nature is cold, we need to make our own fire. Since nature is dark, we need to make our own light.

Horef is a Hebrew word. It means "winter."

Hanukka is the winter holiday, the holiday of *Horef.*

SONG: HANOOKKA (No. 37)

NAYROT

The darkness of winter is all around. The sun shines less and less. The blackness of night stretches farther and farther.

Many years ago, in the land of Israel, when winter came, our forefathers did not fear the dark. They took oil and wicks and made lamps. And they lit the lamps to brighten the darkness.

They lit the lamps for eight days. And they made a holiday out of this celebration, repeating the ceremony of the lights every year.

Nayrot is a Hebrew word. It means "light."

Hanukka is the feast of lights, the holiday of *Nayrot*.

SONG: AYFO OREE (No. 14)

ADAM

Even though the winter is hard, we are not afraid of it. If we are cold, we are smart enough to make our own fire. If we cannot see because of the dark, we are clever enough to make our own light.

We are people. We do not have to wait for nature to help us. We are smart enough to help ourselves. We have brains to think with. We have tongues to speak with. We have hands to work with. And we also have each other, doing together what we cannot do alone.

Adam is a Hebrew word. It means "people."

Hanukka is the festival of people, the holiday of *Adam*.

SONG: HANOOKA (No. 37)

YISRAEL

Many centuries ago, all the Jewish people lived in their own land, the land of Israel. The land was very beautiful, with mountains and valleys and the shores of the sea. There was also a big city called Jerusalem. And in the city, a big temple. And in the temple, a big Menorah.

One day, a strange people came. They were called the Greeks. They had a big and strong army. They defeated the Jews and conquered the land. They closed the temple. They put out the lights of the Menorah. They forced many Jews to become Greeks. But the people of Israel refused to die. They wanted to live.

Yisrael is a Hebrew word. It means "Israel."

Hanukka is the holiday of the Jews, the feast of *Yisrael*.

SONG: AM YISRAEL HIE (No. 9)

MACCABEE

In the small town of Modin, in the land of Israel, lived an old man with five sons. These young men were called the Maccabee brothers. They were brave and strong, and they wanted to drive the Greeks from the land of the Jews. Judah Maccabee, the second son, was the bravest and strongest of the five boys. He encouraged many Jews to fight the Greeks and formed an army of resistance.

The Greeks outnumbered the Jews ten to one. But the Jews were fighting for their freedom and their land. With Judah Maccabee as their leader, the Jews faced the Greeks bravely and drove them from the land.

SONG: MEE Y'MALLEL (No. 67)

HANUKKA

When the land of Israel was free again, Judah Maccabee came with his army to the great city of Jerusalem. He walked up to the great temple. He opened the gate of the courtyard. He saw the dirt and disorder and commanded that the place be made clean and beautiful again.

The time was winter, the season of the great festival of lights. On the first day of this holiday, Judah Maccabee entered the temple and relit the lights of the great Menorah which the Greeks had put out. The people cheered. And Judah Maccabee changed the name of the holiday from *Nayrot* to *Hanukka*.

Hanukka is a Hebrew word. It means "the dedication of the Temple," the dedication of the Temple to the freedom of the Jewish people.

SONG: MACCABEES OF OLD (No. 62)

S'VEEVON

Hanukka is a happy holiday. We light the lights. We come to Temple. We play games.

The special toy of Hanukka is the draydel. It is a top with four sides. On each side is written a Hebrew letter. The four letters—*noon, gimmel, hay, shin*—are the first letters of the four words in the Hebrew sentence *"NAYS GADOL HAYA SHAM,"* which in English means "A great victory happened there." The victory is the victory of the Maccabees over the Greeks in the land of Israel.

S'-vee-von is a Hebrew word. It means "top" or *draydel.*

SONG: I HAVE A LITTLE DRAYDEL (No. 49)

L'VEEVA

Hanukka is a delicious holiday. We not only light the lights. We not only come to Temple. We not only play games. We also eat delicious food.

The special food of Hanukka is a potato pancake. Fried crisp and brown, it gives a special taste to our holiday. In the winter, when meat was expensive and green vegetables were not available, the humble potato became a food that could be enjoyed by rich and poor. The potato and the winter festival go together. The potato and Hanukka go together.

L'vee-va is a Hebrew word. It means *latke* or "pancake."

Hanukka is the holiday of *L'veeva,* the feast of the latke.

SONG: Y'MAY HANOOKKA (No. 99)

MENORAH

There are two candlesticks in Jewish history. The first had seven lights, one for each day of the week. It was very big and stood in the great Temple of Jerusalem. It was the light of this candlestick that the Greeks put out. This was the candlestick Judah Maccabee recaptured and rekindled. Today, this lamp is one of the signs of the Jewish people.

The second lamp had eight lights, one for each of the eight days of the winter festival. It was small and stood in every Jewish home in the land of Israel. This was the candlestick that proclaimed the victory of light over darkness. This was the candlestick that announced the victory of Judah Maccabee over the enemies of Israel.

Menorah is a Hebrew word. It means "lamp" or "candlestick."

Hanukka is the holiday of *Menorah,* the festival of the lamp with eight lights.

SONG: BAROOKH HAOR (No. 20)

CANDLELIGHTING

FIRST CANDLE (HOREF)
This first light is the light of *horef,*
the winter season that tests our will to live.

SECOND CANDLE (NAYROT)
This second light is the light of *nayrot,*
the power we have to create our own fire in the face of darkness.

THIRD CANDLE (ADAM)
This third light is the light of *adam,*
our need for other people in our struggle for life and freedom.

FOURTH CANDLE (YISRAEL)
This fourth light is the light of *Yisrael,*
our loyalty to the Jewish people and to our Jewish roots.

FIFTH CANDLE (MACCABEE)
This fifth light is the light of *Maccabee,*
the courage of Judah Maccabee and his brave army in their fight for Jewish independence.

SIXTH CANDLE (S'VEEVON)
This sixth light is the light of *s'veevon,*
the *draydel* which proclaims the victory of the Maccabees and of the Jewish people.

SEVENTH CANDLE (L'VEEVA)
This seventh light is the light of *l'veeva,*
the food of joy and celebration and family togetherness in this season of the year.

EIGHTH CANDLE (HANUKKA)
This eighth light is the light of *Hanukka,*
the dedication of the Jewish people to the ideals of freedom and national survival.

SONGS: MACCABEES OF OLD (No. 62)

10
HANUKKA HOME CELEBRATION

FREEDOM

Many years ago the Jews in the land of Israel were not free. They were not free to rule themselves or to live in the way their hearts and minds desired.

A foreign king made their lives miserable. He sent many soldiers to make the Jews do what he wanted them to do. He took away their Temple and gave it to their enemies. The Jews rebelled. They rose up against the king. Under their brave leader, Judah Maccabee, they defeated their enemies and won their freedom.

The Jews decided to celebrate their victory. They set aside eight days for a special festival. The temple was made ready for the celebration. The lights of the Temple Menorah were kindled and gave forth a bright light.

Judah Maccabee dedicated the Temple to the service of the people. He called this special festival Hanukka. *Hanukka* is a Hebrew word which means "dedication." Judah Maccabee asked the Jews to celebrate this holiday every year at the same time. He wanted them to remember this victory.

The Jews of this story were our ancestors. Our ancestors suffered the cruelty of a foreign king. Our ancestors fought for their freedom. Our ancestors restored the Temple in Jerusalem. Our ancestors heard the words of Judah Maccabee when he asked them to remember their victory. Our ancestors saw the lights of the Temple Menorah rekindled.

Let us, therefore, remember what our ancestors did. Let us kindle the lights of our Menorah in the memory of their courage.

CANDLELIGHTING

BA-ROOKH HA-OR BA-O-LAM
BA-ROOKH HA-OR BA-A-DAM
BA-ROOKH HA-OR BA-HA-A-NUK-KA

Radiant is the light of the world.
Radiant is the light of humanity.
Radiant is the light of Hanukka.

SONG: MACCABEES OF OLD (No. 62)

11
ISRAEL DAY YOUTH SERVICE

SONG: SHALOM L'YISRAEL (No. 82)

TU BI SH'VAT

Tonight is Tu Bi Sh'vat, the fifteenth day of the Hebrew month of Shevat. Tonight is a special holiday, a time when we honor the place from which we came, the land of our ancestors, the home of our people.

We call Tu Bi Sh'vat Israel Day. Israel is the oldest name of the Jewish people. It is also the name of our birthplace, of the country where we began.

Many years ago, all the Jewish people lived in the land of Israel. All the Jewish people spoke Hebrew. All the Jewish people were close together. But enemies came and drove our ancestors out of the land. For two thousand years, we traveled over the face of the entire earth, settling in many lands, becoming the citizens of many countries. Yet the memory of our homeland remained fresh in the minds and hearts of our people. They dreamed of returning someday. They hoped to see again the place of David and Solomon, Hillel and Akita.

And, in this century, their dream came true. The state of Israel was born again.

Erets Yisrael is a Hebrew phrase. It means the "land of Israel." Tu Bi Sh'vat is the holiday of *Erets Yisrael*.

SONG: ARTSA ALEENOO (No. 12)

AM YISRAEL

Without the people of Israel, the land of Israel would have no meaning. Without the love and devotion of a living nation, the piece of earth that we call *erets yisrael* would be nothing more than earth.

The Jewish people found this land, farmed this land, built on this land, struggled to defend this land. Every hill and valley, every desert and green place, speaks to us of Jewish history, tells the tale of the Jewish will to live. The memories of our people cannot be separated from the memories of this place. Wherever Jews may live, the land is part of them. Whoever lives on the land is part of the Jewish people.

Am Yisrael is a Hebrew phrase. It means "the people of Israel."

Tu Bi Sh'vat is the feast of *Am Yisrael.*

SONG: AM YISRAEL HIE (No. 9)

Y'ROOSHALIEYIM

Three thousand years ago, David, the king of Israel, chose a special city to be his capital. He built his palace there, and his son, Solomon, built his temple there.

The name of this city is Jerusalem. It is also called the city of peace, the city of Jewish unity. Many quarreling Hebrew tribes came together to make one nation. Many fighting clans joined together to make one people. Jerusalem is the sign of that unity. It belonged to no clan and to no tribe. It belonged to all the Jewish people.

Y'rooshalieyim is a Hebrew word. It means "Jerusalem."

Tu Bi Sh'vat is the celebration of *Y'rooshalieyim.*

SONG: Y'ROOSHALIEYIM SHEL ZAHAV (No. 101)

HATIKVA

For two thousand years, the Jewish people lived outside the land of Israel. They wandered eastward to Persia and China. They moved westward to Europe and America.

But wherever they went, they never forgot the place where their journey began. They never stopped hoping that they would be able to return some day. Whenever their enemies were cruel to them, they turned their thoughts to the future and dreamed of freedom and independence in the land of their fathers. Whenever their friends were kind to them, they valued the kindness and imagined how marvelous it would be to return the favor as the host, not as the guest.

For many of our ancestors, hoping was waiting for destiny to bring them back. For others, hoping was action, action to create a new state of Israel. Those who waited accomplished nothing. Those who acted rebuilt our state.

Hatikva is a Hebrew word. It means "hope."

Tu Bi Sh'vat is the holiday of *Hatikva*.

SONG: HATIKVA (No. 40)

HALOOTS

The enemies of the Jewish people conquered the land of Israel and made it a wasteland. For twenty centuries Greeks, Romans, Arabs, and Turks took their turns in ruling our national birthplace. They left it worse than they found it.

When, eighty years ago, our people were able to return, they did not find the land they had abandoned. They encountered a ruin. Desert and swamps covered the places of former cities and farms. Sand and salt replaced rich earth and watered plains.

The Jews who returned discovered that coming back was not enough. They had to rebuild and restore. They had to work and to pioneer. Those who were weak did not stay. Those who were strong changed the face of the land. They drew farms out of the swamps, cities out of the sand.

Haloots is a Hebrew word. It means "pioneer."

Tu Bi Sh'vat is the feast of *haloots*.

SONG: ZOOM GALEE (No. 106)

AYTS

In olden times, Israel was filled with trees. Cedar and cypress, eucalyptus and oak covered the hillsides and gave the land a blanket of beauty.

But the foreign rulers of Israel did not care about beauty, nor did they respect the gifts of nature. In their wastefulness, they cut down the trees and destroyed quickly what took centuries to grow. The beautiful land became the ugly land. Flood washed away the soil. Flowers no longer bloomed.

For the Jewish pioneers who returned to their land, planting trees was very important. Trees meant new soil. Trees meant water. Trees meant survival. To plant a tree was to express the hope that the dead land could be brought to life again, that the lost beauty could be restored.

In the state of Israel, Tu Bi Sh'vat is the special day when new trees are planted. By planting trees, the people of Israel express their love of their land, their struggle for survival, their love of beauty.

Ayts is a Hebrew word. It means "trees."

Tu Bi Sh'vat is the celebration of *ayts*.

SONG: ANEE NOTAYA (No. 11)

DEGEL

Every nation has a flag. The Jewish people has a flag. It is the flag of the state of Israel.

Our national banner has two colors, blue and white. Blue is the color of the Mediterranean Sea that washes the western shore of our homeland. White is the color of the snow on the top of the northern mountains.

Our national banner has a blue star. It is called the Star of David. David was the second king of Israel. He made his nation strong, free, and independent. When we look at the star, we remember how important strength, freedom, and independence are to the Jewish people.

Israel Day Youth Service

Like the American flag and the world flag, the Jewish flag is *our* flag. It is a sign of our attachment to the land of Israel and to the people of Israel.

Degel is a Hebrew word. It means "flag."

Tu Bi Sh'vat is the holiday of *degel*.

SONG: OOSH'AVTEM MIEYIM (No. 74)

MENORAH

Every nation has an emblem. The Jewish people has an emblem. It is the emblem of the state of Israel.

Our national emblem is a candlestick with seven lights. It is just like the candlestick that stood in the great Temple of Jerusalem and gave light to the interior of the shrine. Its seven lights represent the seven days of the week. It reminds us of the passage of time and of our continuing love of the land of Israel.

The seven lights speak to us of our past, present, and future. We do not have the power to change our past, but we do have the power to mold our future. That sense of strength is the source of our joy and happiness.

Menorah is a Hebrew word. It means "candlestick."

Tu Bi Sh'vat is the feast of the *Menorah*.

SONG: HAVA NAGEELA (No. 42)

12
PURIM

SONG: SHOSHANNAT YAAKOV (No. 84)

HOPE

Life needs hope. Without the prospect of better things daily routine would be too dismal to bear. The anticipation of pleasure and the expectation of beauty bring luster to present dullness, while the vision of progress gives our feelings an upward momentum. In the gray cold of winter's landscape, we find not only the memory of January's fury, but also the promise of April's spring. Purim is the bearer of good news. It declares the imminent end of nature's death and bids us prepare ourselves to greet the earth reborn.

SONG: B'AYLE HAYADIEYIM (No. 22)

POSITIVENESS

The cruelty of winter finds its human counterpart in the love of death. For the passionate bigot, death holds a strange fascination. Killing the enemy becomes the goal of life. Exterminating evil becomes his obsession. Hating villains seems preferable to loving people.

Too often we fanatically feel what we are against, but never discover what we are for. The tragedy of the legendary Haman lies in his wasted talent, in his directing his energies to negative ends. In his will to destroy others he destroyed himself, for hatred breeds only more hatred, and the lust for death, once unleashed, devours its own author.

SONG: ZEMER LAKH (No. 104)

COURAGE

The anticipation of spring is a realistic hope; it thrives on the performance of the past. The succession of seasons, in their regularity, suggests the secure potential of other things. In almost every age of vicious tyranny great men and women have arisen to defy the present evil and to demand the dignity of life. Like the persistent possibility of vital energy that lies beneath the white cover of winter, the boldness of bravery hidden by the security of peace reveals itself in the hour of crisis.

Mordecai is the expression of his power. Too proud to endure oppression and too selfless to flee for his safety alone, the need of the moment made him the hero. In another season and in another land he would have remained the plain peasant. But before the rage of the tyrant he awakened to his talents and found his just fame.

SONG: OOTSOO AYTSA (No. 75)

REBIRTH

As we imagine the glory of the earth revived, nature reveals herself the eternal woman. The earth is our immortal mother who, after the barrenness of winter, conceives and gives birth to the beauties of spring. The fertility of the land is no fantasy; it is manifest in the lush promise of Purim time. Mother Nature has conceived her child of hope and awaits its momentary deliverance. Like the earth goddess of ancient myth who rescues life from the death of winter, Esther of Persia is the queen of life. Without her power and compassion, death is triumphant and destruction victorious. Without her devotion and courage, the fields lie barren and despair stalks the land. Through her the wailing of the Jews is turned into laughter, while the hour of massacre is transformed into a festival of exultant joy.

SONG: OOTSOO AYTSA (No. 75)

SPRING

Purim rehearses the vital cycle of the eternal seasons. Haman is wintry death, who seeks to maintain the power of his cold reign through the fury of human hatred. Mordecai is the king of life, who strives to bring courage to the hearts of the oppressed. Esther is the mother of spring, whose every act is hope and whose every deed is redeemed by the success of love. As for the Jews of our story, they are, like all people, rescued from passive despair by the bravery of action.

SONG: HAG POOREEM (No. 33)

MEMORIAL

The joy of Purim is the pleasure of hope. As the end of the winter is also the beginning of spring, so is the March wind the prelude to April's rain. When Haman dies, Mordecai rules, and Esther becomes the queen of queens.

SONG: ZAYKHER (No. 103)

MEGILLAH

The problem with so much religion is that it is far too solemn. Piety shuns laughter and turns stuffiness into a virtue. How delightful, then, is the spirit of Purim. The festival despises the pompous in heart and shows no mercy to those who wear the mask of propriety. If spring is coming, sad faces must be outlawed and gaiety must be the law of the land. The Book of Esther can be no pious tome that we must listen to with straitlaced severity. As an ode to the season, it deserves our laughter. The villains of the story may appear too villainous and the heroes too heroic—all the better! For what we really want to do is to hiss cruel Haman loudly and to cheer good Mordecai and brave Esther with lusty hearts.

SONG: HAG POOREEM (No. 33)

MEGILLAH READING

SONG: HAG POOREEM (No. 33)

13
PURIM YOUTH SERVICE

SONG: HAYVAYNOO SHALOM ALAYKHEM (No. 44)

GIBBOR

We are human beings. We have our human strength. We have our human power. We have our human wisdom. Sometimes, when we are afraid, we do not see what we are and what we have. We do not see our strengths and power. We do not value our wisdom.

Many people, many Jews, think of themselves as weak and helpless. They run away from problems and refuse to face their enemies. But others stand their ground and challenge their foes. They value their courage.

Brave people become leaders. They become human examples to follow. They become heroes.

Gibbor is a Hebrew word. It means "hero."

Purim is the holiday of *gibbor*, the festival to honor heroes.

SONG: OOTSOO AYTSA (No. 75)

ESTHER

Jewish history has many heroes. They are both men and women. They are both old and young. They are both ancient and modern.

Esther was a Jewish hero. She was a brave women who saved her people from death and destruction. When she discovered that wicked Haman was plotting to kill all the Jews, she refused to run away and cry. With the help of her good cousin Mordecai, she persuaded her husband, King Ahashverosh, to protect the Jews and to send Haman away.

Esther never thought of herself as a hero. But she used her courage and common sense and discovered that she was stronger than she ever dreamed she could be.

Esther is a Hebrew word. It comes from the name of an ancient goddess of life.

Purim is the festival of *Esther,* the season of life.

SONG: A WICKED, WICKED MAN (No. 97)

MEGILLAH

The story of Esther and Mordecai is a book in the Bible. Some say that the story is true. Others say that the tale is a legend. But it makes no difference. Esther and Mordecai stand for all the heroes of Jewish history. They are symbols of strength, power, courage, and loyalty.

The Book of Esther was written many centuries ago. When it was first copied, it was copied on a scroll. The scroll was decorated with beautiful Hebrew letters and many pictures of events in the story.

Every Purim, the holiday of Esther, the scroll of Esther is taken out from its special box and is read to the people. In this way we are reminded of what it means to be here.

Megillah is a Hebrew word. It means "scroll."

Purim is the time of the *megillah,* the season of the scroll.

SONG: SHOSHANNAT YAAKOV (No. 84)

RAASHAN

Our world features both good and evil. People who defend the good become heroes. People who pursue evil become villains. Being human, all heroes are never completely good. Being human, all villains are never completely bad.

Haman was a wicked man. He tried to hurt people who had done him no harm. But he was also good to his wife and children and was loyal to his friends. When we denounce Haman, we are not denouncing all of Haman. We are simple expressing our fear of evil, our fear of the power of hatred.

When the story of Esther is read, we remember Haman's hatred for the Jews. When Haman's name is read, we make a noise, a noise against evil, a noise against hatred.

Raashan is a Hebrew word. It means "noisemaker."

Purim is the holiday of the *raashan*, the festival of the noisemaker.

SONG: HAG POOREEM (No. 33)

TSEDEK

Heroes have been part of the Jewish people from the very beginning. Moses, David, Deborah, Isaiah, Ezra, Hillel—these and many more helped their nation in times of trouble.

Heroes are still with us. In this century, Theodore Herzl, Haim Weizmann, Albert Einstein, Golda Meir, Jonas Salk—and many like them—offered their strength and their wisdom to the Jewish people and to the world.

All of them firmly believed that justice was possible, that human effort could make things better.

Tsedek is a Hebrew word. It means "justice."

Purim is a celebration of *tsedek*, a feast of justice.

SONG: AM YISRAEL HIE (No. 9)

MASAYKHA

Celebrations need the power of strong feelings. Not just serious ones, but happy ones too. Laughter and fun are important experiences. They express our commitment to life.

Purim time is a time of hope, hope for life. Spring is coming. The earth will be reborn. The trees will bring forth their leaves. The flowers will bloom. The snows will melt away. And nature will warm us with sunlight and beauty.

Purim time is a time for singing, a time for dancing, a time for playing games. The heroes of our past become masks and costumes. We change our faces and, for a day in this season of hope, we become whoever we dare to be.

Masaykha is a Hebrew word. It means "mask."

Purim is the time of *masaykha,* the season of masked celebration.

SONG: HAVA NAGEELA (No. 42)

PURIM

Hero-day is Purim. Fun-day is Purim. Waiting-for-spring day is Purim.

We need Purim. We need to remember our heroes. We need to laugh, to sing, and to dance. We need to look forward to something good and exciting.

Legend tells us that when Haman plotted to kill the Jews, he cast lots to determine the day of the massacre. But his plans were foiled, and the day of destruction turned into a day of celebration. Despair turned into joy.

Purim is a Hebrew word. It means "dice."

Purim is the holiday of games, the festival of joy.

SONG: HAG POOREEM (No. 33)

14
PESAKH

SONG: HINNAY MA TOV (No. 47)

SPRING

In the coming of spring, the year has proved faithful to its eternal cycle. Although winter seemed coldly persistent, it finally surrendered to the warm promise of new life. Although the harshness of wind and snow seemed stronger than death, it inevitably yielded to the soft rains of budding vitality. A passion for green has seized our world and dismissed the ugly regime of uniform gray. If the earth rejoices in the freshness of new strength, can we resist her song? Must we not feel her gladness and dance to the music of her happy fulfillment?

SONG: DODEE LEE (No. 27)

EXODUS

Tonight is a night of memories. Many years ago our fathers were slaves in the land of Egypt. In bitterness and in hardship they struggled to please their masters and win the precious opportunity of mere survival. Many died from the heat of work; others perished from the cold of despair. Through the agonies of oppression they searched their hearts for the one thing that would make life bearable. They searched for hope and found it. They dreamed of freedom and believed that one day it would be theirs.

Tonight is a night of hope. Ancient legend has it that, in a moment of surprise, a prophet called Elijah will return to earth and make all people free. In his time he protected the weak and the poor and fearlessly challenged wicked authority. In all ages his name was a word of comfort and pleasant expectations. Passover invokes his presence and, with it, the vision he brings.

SONG: AYLEEYAHOO HANAVEE (No. 16)

FREEDOM

They say that birds are free. In their flight to the skies they express an easy liberty. With a brush of the wings they can flee the terrors of the grounded life and escape to the safety of airy fantasy. Fickle in their contact with the earth, they taste the pleasure of speedy departure. Yet their freedom is only appearance, for they are prisoners of their instincts. To act without consciously choosing to act, to do without knowing the alternatives of doing, is to deny the substance of liberty. Human beings can be free because they know the anguish of decision. And they can only remain free when they are willing to endure this anguish.

Voluntary slaves are those who cannot bear the challenge of alternatives. How pleasant it is to exchange the discomfort of decision for the security of obedience. The delightful irresponsibility of childhood is sometimes too attractive to abandon. Fathers often seem indispensable, if only to tell us what to do. Genuine liberty is a constant threat to our human frailty. To choose without the sanction of higher authority is its special passion; to risk decision without the guarantee that others will take the blame is its special courage. Passover is the season of our freedom, the thrilling independence of human decision.

SONG: ADEER HOO (No. 2)

RESPONSIBILITY

The fear of freedom is a human fear. Our fathers languished in the torture of Egyptian suffering. They stood afraid before the destructive might of king and taskmaster. But they feared their liberty even more. Escaped from the brutality of bondage, they marched into the open wilderness and came face to face with the frightful reality of their freedom. Summoned to be masters of their own destiny, they pleaded to return to slavery.

Like our fathers of old, responsibility for the consequences of an action is often too much for many of us to bear. We need Pharaoh as much as Pharaoh needs us. If power without an accounting for power is the dream of every child, it is also the dream of numberless "children" who look like adults. When we wish to be secure, we cannot be free. When we wish to be free, we cannot dispense with the risk of decision. Safety and freedom are the opposite poles of human desire. Their reconciliation is the noble task of sensitive men.

SONG: ADEER HOO (No. 2)

COURAGE

Free people are people who know the risks of living and are not afraid of them. There is danger in every breath and they accept it. To act only when there is a guarantee of happiness is never to act at all. Only death provides complete security.

Moses plunged our fathers into the desert in search of a new home and a new destiny. He was a bold man who faced the uncertainties of life with the firm confidence that he could meet the unexpected and win it over to his side. While he knew that every deed requires thoughtful preparation and that every decision demands a survey of the consequences we can see, their essential riskiness is inevitable. Without the bravery of daring, there is no freedom; without the courage to plunge into the uncertain there is no progress.

SONG: DIEYAYNOO (No. 26)

MEMORIAL

As an individual, separate and distinct, each of us is temporary, an ephemeral chapter in the saga of the universe. Death is all too personal and particular. Yet as a fragment in the never-ending process of life, each of us is immortal, a participant in the persistent thrust of vital energy. The leaves of last year's summer have died and have vanished into the arms of mother earth. But, in a special sense, each lives on in the renewal of every spring. Every person dies, but humanity survives. Every living thing perishes, but life is indestructible.

SONG: ZAYKHER (No. 103)

HAGGADA

Spring is the season of freedom. The powers of life, long imprisoned by the tyranny of winter, escape and run wild with the pleasures of liberty. The free man finds spring congenial to his spirit. The vital explosions of human history have vanquished the winters of slavery and covered the human landscape with the happy colors of courage and creativity. The deeds of brave men and women reflect this excitement.

SONG: HAD GADYA (No. 31)

CLOSING WORDS

May we be strong enough to be brave.
May we be brave enough to be free.

15 REMEMBRANCE DAY

SONG: HINNAY MA TOV (No. 47)

HOLOCAUST

Tonight is a night of memorial.

We remember six million innocent victims who were brutally murdered by a heartless enemy. We remember six million men and women who died because they were Jewish. The assault was unprovoked. The fury was without reason. The crime was immeasurable.

It is too late for justice. If there was a divine providence, it failed to rescue the condemned. If there was human help, it never reached them.

The past is regrettably unchangeable. We cannot bring the victims back to life. We can only remember and never forget.

SONG: L'MAAN TSEEYON LO EHESHE (No. 58)

SURVIVAL

The Jewish people lives.

For two thousand years, our enemies have conspired to destroy us. For two thousand years, our foes have planned our destruction. The Greeks sought to turn us into Greeks; the Romans burned Jerusalem; the Crusaders gave us massacres; the Spaniards tied us to the stake.

The Jewish people lives.

Adolf Hitler made the twentieth century unique. Never had evil been so pure. Never had wickedness been so bold. Never have so many Jews died for so little reason. A mad union of hate and technology gave us gas chambers and genocide.

And yet—the Jewish people lives.

SONG: AM YISRAEL HIE (No. 9)

LOVE

The Jewish people lives.

If our story were only the story of hate, persecution, and massacre, we would not be here to tell the story. If our saga were drenched only in blood, the Fates would long since have dispensed with us.

But we have many skills for survival. Even through the horror of horrors, we never lost our will to live and our will to love.

Love is a Jewish theme. Our enemies surrounded us with hate, but we found loving family and friends to give us support. Our persecutors sang songs of destruction, but our teachers and leaders wrote poems of peace.

We remember not only the hate of hateful people, but also the love of loving men and women.

SONG: TUM BALALAIKA (No. 92)

DIGNITY

The Jewish people lives.

Many of our martyrs went to their death passively, bewildered by torture, unable to believe in the plans of their enemies, overwhelmed by starvation and cruelty.

But many of our people offered defiance even when resistance seemed more than futile. They knew that they were going to die. Yet they were determined not to perish like slaves but to depart with dignity.

Dignity is easy when prosperity and freedom provide the setting. But it is hard when success is no longer there. In the face of triumphant injustice, self-esteem seems a thin reward.

Yet resistance is part of the Jewish story. Warsaw, Vilna, and Bialystok are witnesses to that truth. We did not consent to our own humiliation. Death might steal our lives, but not our determination.

SONG: ZOG NIT KAYNMOL (No. 105)

SOLIDARITY

The Jewish people lives.

We are the children of a great nation. We are the heirs of a warm and loving culture.

Not long ago we had a European homeland. It teemed with vital people. It was filled with bustling cities. Its music was powerful. Its language was unique.

We were no strangers to this place. We were no aliens to this land. Neither Germans nor Slavs were there before us. Its rivers and mountains were part of our lore. Centuries of ancestors were buried in its fields.

The holocaust of people was also a holocaust of culture. A nation and its identity were sent to execution.

This culture and this identity are our roots. We dare not forget.

SONG: OIFN PRIPETSHOK (No. 73)

DEFIANCE

The Jewish people lives.

We were not only victims—the genocide of Auschwitz, Buchenwald, and Treblinka are only part of the story.

We were also fighters in battle. With no army, no weapons of power, and no freedom we fought a war. We offered national resistance.

Our defiance took many forms. Some simply refused to die. Others joined the ghetto uprisings. Still others became partisan soldiers.

Even in the darkest hour, we dreamed dreams of a better world and sang songs of defiance.

SONG: MISSAVEEV (No. 68)

HOPE

The Jewish people lives.

We live because we are stubborn—because we will not surrender to humiliation, because we will not give our enemies the satisfaction of vanishing from the face of the earth.

We live because we remember—because we recall the adversaries who came up against us in every century and did not prevail—because we will not betray the cry of our martyrs.

We live because we defy the Fates—because we will not endorse the blind cruelty of blind destiny—because we will not allow the death of our slaughtered to be entirely without meaning.

Above all, we live because we hope—because we reject the pessimism of the bitter—because we refuse to imitate the cynicism of our persecutors—because, despite all, we still believe in the possibility of a decent world.

We hope and strive to realize our hope.

SONG: AYIT (No. 15)

MEMORIAL

We remember. We remember the six million of our people who died in the whirlwind of Hitler's fury. We remember the many millions of many other peoples and other nations who were the victims of fascist terror. We remember the fighters for freedom, from many lands and from many places, who rose up to free the world of the Nazi plague and who were killed in battle.

We also remember our loved ones who died in peace but who are linked in solidarity with our martyrs as children of one people.

CANDLELIGHTING (in honor of the six million martyrs)

SONG: ANEE MAAMEEN (No. 10)

16
SHAVUOT

SONG: KALLANEEYOT (No. 50)

COMMUNITY

Community is a feeling of identity, a sense of sharing with others what is one's very own. The possession may be a family, a home, a friend, a place of work. It may embrace a common love or a common hate. A fiery cause that needs the fuel of many hearts may forge an alliance of feeling and deed; or the glamour of a new idea may unite the minds of men and women in an intense devotion. Even a shared grief may draw hearts closer together in their quest for the sympathy of understanding.

But the surest bond is the invisible hold of the past. A common history strikes the roots of memory with clannish pride and envelops us in the thick vine of tradition. We are the heirs of past events that mold our fears and hopes; we are the children of ancient suffering and joy that leave their trauma in our sense of life. The inertia of old excitement pushes the stream of culture ever onward and opens new channels of meaning for the venerable thoughts of great men and women. We are joined together in a mighty fellowship with our past. The legacy of our ancestors is our own legacy too.

SONG: AM YISRAEL HIE (No. 9)

WISDOM

Israel is a people of darkness and light. The annals of our history are black with defeat and destruction while the horror of martyrdom hovers over our years. Terror shrieks in our corridor of passing time and allows little intrusion of human compassion. If our suffering has become the classic test of social cruelty, our humiliation also knows no equal. The chill of death has been colder in the place of our destiny. Yet all is not darkness. There is the light of creative achievement. Even without military might and political power, we make our presence felt. Instead of weapons we manufactured words and ideas. Instead of victories and conquests we produced artful discussions and books of law. The courage of our people was sustained by visions in poetry.

SONG: EMET L'YISRAEL (No. 29)

DIVERSITY

The literature of a people reflects no single opinion or thought. Nations are not persons with minds of their own. They are only ethnic collections of diverse individuals. Some citizens believe one thing; others are convinced of its contradiction. Yet each is an intimate of the culture. Civilization thrives on the give and take of controversy; uniformity petrifies progress. Jewish culture is not a consistent harmonious whole. It is a collection of many moods and thoughts. The bitter fights of three thousand years created its history. Judaism is not the product of some ancient commitment. It embraces all that we Jews have managed to agree on—and disagree on.

SONG: LAM'TSAPPEEM (No. 56)

PROGRESS

Too often Jewishness seems to be an ancient thing. World culture has chosen the Bible for special honor and makes it seem the most important Jewish achievement. We are flattered by the choice and are reluctant to challenge it. Yet Judaism is far more than the Bible. While Moses and David, Micah and Isaiah, spoke their way to immortality, they did not exhaust the Jewish possibility. People of later ages took advantage of new ideas and were inspired to write new books equally profound. Hillel and Akita, Spinoza and Bergson are all heroes of Jewish creativity. Jewish wisdom is as old as Moses and as new as Einstein.

SONG: SAHAKEE (No. 78)

USEFULNESS

The quality of things is often found in their familiarity. We like the places that are filled with happy memories. We like the words that centuries have hallowed by repetition. It is so comfortable to be surrounded by approved sounds and sights! It is so warmly secure to utter the same words our ancestors found delightful! The pleasure of tradition is the ease with which it merges us with our past and rescues us from the pain of personal decision.

But no heritage can defy the critique of each age. It must face the continuous test of human usefulness. Nostalgia can be both friend and foe. When it uses the gag of conformity to stifle conscience, it is the enemy of integrity. True wisdom is not afraid of reason's probe and human need; it welcomes the challenge of every mind and seeks to confirm its right to live. Tired teachings plead the virtue of old age and old affections and resist the test of utility. They summon the virtues of ancient love in order to justify present survival. But tradition does not exist to make us the prisoners of our past; it endures to enrich our future with the reality of proven values.

SONG: AYFO OREE (No. 14)

MEMORIAL

Poets and sages wandered through the centuries of our history and wove the strands of our heritage with the flair of their talents. In the special joy of Shavuot we remember their gifts and reach out with gratitude to use their creation. To be Jewish is to bask in the sun of their fame. To be human is to sense the urgency of their words. People of the past who plant the seeds of wisdom in the minds of others bequeath to the present the harvest of a better world. Others have sowed and we have reaped; we shall sow and others will reap.

SONG: SHEEM'OO (No. 83)

CLOSING WORDS

Let peace embrace those who are far and those who are near.
Let peace embrace all the world.

SONG: SHALOM LARAHOK (No. 81)

17
SHAVUOT YOUTH SERVICE

SONG: SHALOM L'YISRAEL (No. 82)

SHAVUOT

Spring is here. Summer is about to begin. The school year is ending. Vacation time is near.

Shavuot is here. Shavout is an old spring holiday. In the days when all of our ancestors lived in the land of Israel, the holiday marked the completion of the spring harvest. What began with Passover found its finish in Shavuot.

In olden times, our fathers and mothers took garlands of flowers, put them around their heads and danced in the fields. Even today the farmers of Israel celebrate the end of the spring harvest at Shavuot time.

The harvest lasts for fifty days—seven weeks and one day.

Shavuot is a Hebrew word which means "weeks."

The holiday of Shavuot is the Feast of Weeks.

SONG: DODEE LEE (No. 27)

YAHADUT

When most of our ancestors moved away from their farms and left the land of Israel, the holiday of Shavuot took on a new meaning.

The rabbis declared that the writing of the Torah began on Shavuot. The Torah was the first Hebrew book that was ever written. A new harvest of good books was added to the harvest of wheat and barley.

Jewish books, like Jewish farming, are part of Jewish culture. A culture includes all the things a living people tries to do in order to stay alive, in order to be happy. Jewish culture includes all the things the Jewish people tries to do in order to stay alive, in order to be happy.

The name for Jewish culture is Judaism.

Yahadut is a Hebrew word which means "Judaism."

Shavuot is the holiday of *Yahadut,* the feast of Judaism.

SONG: AM YISRAEL HIE (No. 9)

YISRAEL

Judaism is the culture of a living people. Every people has a homeland. We Jews have a homeland. Israel is the name of our homeland. It is the place where our people was born, the fatherland of our dreams, the motherland of our hopes. It was there that we first spoke our language, sang our songs, danced our dances. It was there that we first farmed our land, wrote our books, defended our homes.

A strong culture has strong memories. Judaism is a strong culture. Judaism has strong memories. Even though we Jews now live all over the world, we cannot forget Israel, we cannot forget our homeland.

Yisrael is the Hebrew word for "Israel."

Shavuot is the festival of *Yisrael,* the holiday of Israel.

SONG: HATIKVA (No. 40)

IVREET

Almost every culture has its own language, its own way of speaking. Judaism has its own language. It has its own way of speaking.

The first Jewish language was Hebrew. At one time all Jews spoke Hebrew. They taught their children in Hebrew. They did their business in Hebrew. They told their jokes in Hebrew. Even today, many Jews still speak Hebrew as their everyday language. In the land of Israel, Hebrew is still the language of the Jewish people.

When we speak in Hebrew, we feel Jewish. When we sing in Hebrew, we feel Jewish.

Ivreet is the Hebrew word which means the "Hebrew language."

Shavuot is the feast of *Ivreet*, the celebration of the Hebrew language.

SONG: Y'ROOSHALIEYIM SHEL ZAHAV (No. 101)

SIFROOT

Jewish writers have been writing for three thousand years. They have written prayers and poems, stories and sayings, legends and facts. Most of what they have written has been forgotten, lost in the dim memories of bygone days.

But some of what they have written was so good that our ancestors saved it. The books of the Bible, the books of the Talmud, the poems of Halevi, Bialik and Tchernikhovsky, the stories of Peretz, Sholem Aleichem, and Agnon—are still with us.

All famous Jewish writers did not answer the questions of life in the same way. They often disagreed. Some were humanistic Jews. Others were not. Our literature has many different opinions.

A culture needs many points of view to be a rich culture. Judaism is a rich culture. The Jewish people has a rich literature.

Sifroot is the Hebrew word for "literature."

Shavuot is the festival of *sifroot,* the holiday of Jewish literature.

SONG: KEE NAYR MITSVA (No. 53)

MOOSEEKA, RIKOOD

Reading, writing, and speaking are important for a strong culture, but they are not enough. A strong people has strong feelings. It needs to sing and dance to give space to its feelings.

Jews always loved to sing songs. Whenever they were happy, they wanted to sing happy songs. Whenever they were sad, they wanted to sing sad songs.

Jews always loved to dance dances. Whenever they were free, they danced for their freedom. Whenever they were slaves, they danced against their bondage.

Jewish music has many moods. So does Jewish dance. Our history has included so many places and so many happenings that no human feeling has escaped its moment. Since we are Jews, we enjoy singing Jewish songs. We enjoy dancing Jewish dances.

Mooseeka is the Hebrew word for "music."

Rikood is the Hebrew word for "dance."

Shavuot is the celebration of *mooseeka* and *rikood,* the time to honor Jewish music and dance.

SONG: HAVA NAGEELA (No. 42)

MAZON

A culture begins with people. A people begins with family. A family begins with children. Children need food, clothing, and shelter.

In olden days, when life was hard, most parents spent most of their time growing food, making clothes, building houses. They spent most of their time trying to stay alive.

Today, in a land of plenty, we sometimes forget the human struggle. We take our food for granted. We take our clothing for granted. We take our home for granted. We do not remember how important they are.

As Jews, we eat special foods at special times. The matsa of Passover, the hamentasch of Purim, the potato latke of Hanukka, the cheese blintz of Shavuot are more than decorations. They are reminders of our history, of our struggle for life.

Mazon is the Hebrew word for "food."

Shavuot is the feast of *mazon*.

SONG: ZOOM GALEE (No. 106)

MISHPAHA

Most of the Jewish things we do are done with our families.

Holidays need families. Mitsvas need families. Confirmations need families. It is hard to celebrate them alone. It is hard to celebrate them with strangers.

What we do with our family is an important part of our culture. Our style has its roots in the way we respect our parents, deal with our brothers and sisters, love our children, talk to our husband or wife.

Every small family can be part of a larger family. Each of us is part of the Jewish family. Each of us has a home wherever Jews live. Even though most of them live far away, they are still our brothers and sisters.

Mishpaha is the Hebrew word for "family."

Shavuot is the season of *mishpaha,* the feast of the family.

SONG: HINNAY MA TOV (No. 47)

TARBOOT

A culture cannot survive all by itself. It is caring people that make it live. It is loyal children who make it survive.

If we value Judaism, we use it. If we like Judaism, we study it. If we think it important, we will also add to it.

There are so many books to read. There are so many songs to sing. There are so many dances to dance. There are so many holidays to celebrate. There are so many foods to eat. There is so much love to give—to our family and to others.

At the end of the school year, we remember all that we have studied and learned. We are also aware of how much more there is to study, of how much more there is to learn.

Understanding Judaism is a life-long project. Knowing our culture is a never-ending responsibility.

Tarboot is the Hebrew word for "culture."

Shavuot is the festival of *Tarboot,* the holiday of Jewish culture, the feast of Judaism.

SONG: HATIKVA (No. 40)

18
SHABBAT HOME SERVICE

FAMILY DAY

The Shabbat is a family day. It is the time when we honor all the families to which we belong.

Parents and grandparents are our family. The Jewish people is our family. The human race is our family. We remember them all on this Shabbat eve.

The lights of the Shabbat are the lights of family love.

CANDLELIGHTING

BA-ROOKH HA-OR BA-O-LAM
BA-ROOKH HA-OR BAA-A-DAM
BA-ROOKH HA-OR BA-SHAB-BAT

Radiant is the light of the world.
Radiant is the light of family and love.
Radiant is the light of the Shabbat.

(Candles are kindled)

CUP OF WINE

The Shabbat is a day of peace. It is a time when we remember all the feelings and actions that bring people together in love and in hope.

It is a time when we affirm our power to be generous, caring, and loyal.

This cup of wine is a sign of this power and of the happiness it brings.

(Wine is drunk)

SONG: HINNAY MA TOV (No. 47)

PART IV
HUMANIST HOLIDAYS

Humanist holidays supplement our Jewish holidays. They are reminders that we are not only Jews but also humanists and members of the human race. They dramatize our connection with humanists all over the world and with people of all cultures.

Since humanism is a comparatively new philosophy, and since, for most of its short history, most humanists have been unorganized, there are no venerable old holidays that have won wide acceptance. Right now, humanists have to invent their own.

In the Birmingham Temple we have adapted five secularized holidays to humanistic use. Instead of starting from scratch and inventing festivals that have no place in public recognition, we chose holidays that have lost their traditional religious significance, whether Christian or pagan, but which still have a strong hold on public awareness and public observance.

New Year's Day is a universal holiday for all cultures. The Roman calendar has become the world calendar and a symbol of human unity. The beginning of the year is a time for celebration for all the peoples of the world.

People Day (May 1) is another name for May Day. As a pagan and socialist holiday, it has certainly mobilized millions of people to participate in its celebration. Now secularized, it dramatizes the human struggle for equality and justice as well as the power of people to make positive changes. Just as World Day once marked the beginning of the winter season in northern climates, so did People Day announce the advent of summer.

Humanism Day falls on the summer solstice (June 21), a day honored in northern European custom. It has been designated by the International Humanist and Ethical Union, the world organization of humanists, as the annual celebration of humanism. The symbol of light is significant.

World Day (November 1) is built around the persistence of Halloween celebrations. Since it comes so close to the birthday of the United Nations it seems an ideal occasion to celebrate the unity of the human race. United Nations flags and pledges of world citizenship are very appropriate additions. Even a special ritual for children has emerged. They go "begging" with UNICEF boxes.

Thanksgiving is an American holiday with obvious theistic overtones, although most Americans celebrate this special day in a secular fashion with family gatherings. But gratitude is a significant humanist virtue also—not the thank-yous that are directed heavenward to unresponsive deities, but the thank-yous that we need to offer to all the people of significance in our lives. We depend on the loyalty and generosity of others, just as they depend on our gifts of support.

Other humanist holidays have been created and are being tested all over the world. Only time will tell which ones will capture the imagination of the humanist public.

1
NEW YEAR'S DAY SERVICE

SONG: SHALOM L'YISRAEL (No. 82)

PEACE

Peace on earth. Goodwill to all men and women.

These are not uniquely Christian words, nor uniquely Muslim words, nor uniquely Buddhist words. They are universal ideals shared by people of all cultures and affirmed by the teachers of every moral nation. They are humanistic words. Their value derives from no religious myth and is independent of any parochial dogma. They are Jewish words, expressing the hopes and ideals of countless prophets and sages, who preferred world tranquility to national glory.

SONG: NAASE SHALOM (No. 69)

NEW YEAR'S DAY

New Year's Day was the creation of the Romans. It was the opening festival of the Roman year, the symbol of the turning of the seasons. The fall harvest was done. The spring planting was yet to begin. January lay between the achievement of the past and the anticipation of the future. It was a season of satisfaction and a time of hope.

New Year's Day is no longer Roman. It has become universal. Not only have the Christians made the sun year of Julius Caesar their way of counting time, but also every civilized nation in every distant place has done the very same. The Roman year is the world year. From Tokyo to Buenos Aires, from Helsinki to Singapore, it reigns supreme.

SONG: AHEE ADAM (No. 4)

LIGHT

The Romans began their new year with the winter. For them, the beginning of winter was the renewal of hope. In the autumn, they despaired. Every day the light of the sun was weaker than the day before. Every day the world grew darker and colder. They imagined that the sun was dying and that its life-giving rays would vanish from the heavens. Without light there would be no life and death would rule the earth.

January changed the mood of despair into the celebration of life. The darkness halted. The daylight was reborn. Pessimism was dismissed. Optimism seized command. It was a time of joy and celebration.

Every year, in this season, we also suffer the absence of light and heat. But we also sense their renewal: although the earth about us is dark and cold, we shine with the glow of our own hope. Our optimism is not naïve. It reflects the subtle return of the earth's own power.

SONG: ASHRAY HAGAFROOR (No. 13)

UNIVERSALISM

The world new year is a time of courage. In our fear of assimilation to other cultures, we are sometimes hesitant to take the steps which goodwill requires. We imagine that if we share any celebration which the Gentile finds meaningful we will become less Jewish, less loyal to our ancestors, less affirmative of our own traditions.

The fear is groundless. Our humanist holidays do not replace our Jewish holidays. They supplement them. They remind us that we are not only Jews but also human beings, sharing with all other men and women common desires and common needs.

We Jews celebrate two new years. We celebrate the New Year's Day of the Hebrew calendar which unites us with the life of the people of Israel and which binds us together with Jews of all lands. We also celebrate the New Year's Day of the world calendar which unites us with the life of the peoples of all nations and which binds us together with the citizens of all lands.

New Year's Day Service   293

SONG: HINNAY MA TOV (No. 47)

LOVE

Our ancestors, like the forefathers of every people, divided humanity into insiders and outsiders. To the insider they extended kindness, tenderness, and tolerance. To the outsider they offered anger, fear, and distrust. As long as the weapons of war were primitive, this mutual rejection was bearable. But in an age of sophisticated arms it is fatal to all people.

Unless the barriers between insider and outsider fall resoundingly, unless our common humanity becomes more important than our cultural difference, there will be no world to divide.

We have a choice. We can choose to live in the past, to be obsessed with the memories of old hate and old crimes. Or we can choose to live in the future, to commit ourselves to the possibility of new love and new respect. The past cannot become the future, but the outsider can be invited inside.

SONG: V'AHAVTA (No. 93)

WORLD CITIZENSHIP

The world new year is a time of humility. Nations sometimes live with false pride. They imagine that they are self-sufficient and that everything worthwhile, everything good and beautiful was invented by them, without the assistance of other peoples. We Jews often forget our cultural debt to the Egyptians, Greeks, and Romans. Western nations forget their debt to the Jews and to Oriental lands. Each ethnic group, in its own arrogance, turns what is universal into a parochial achievement and pretends to give what has really been achieved. In this striving for special recognition, goodwill is destroyed. Brotherhood cannot exist where nations foolishly argue about who invented brotherhood.

Each of us is a citizen of the world. Each of us is the heir of all peoples and all nations. We have given to each other. We have borrowed from each other. We have brought our creations to other lands, and other lands have been equally generous. If we are wise, we are sensitive to our inheritance. We refuse false patriotism. We humbly choose to be universal.

SONG: AYFO OREE (No. 14)

MEMORIAL

The world new year is a time of hope. Just as the power of the sun's light is renewed at the beginning of every winter, so is the power of life renewed with each human generation. For most of nature, the revival of life is repetitious. But for us, it is unique. Every new year is different from the one that preceded. Every succeeding generation is distinct from the one that came before. In the world of human culture, each of us lives on the work of the past. We have inherited the ideas and inventions of our ancestors. We shall bequeath our own useful work to the future. This year is the cultural child of last year. It is also the cultural parent of the year to come. We acknowledge our debt to the past. We affirm our obligation to the future.

SONG: SHEEM'OO (No. 83)

2
PEOPLE DAY

SONG: HAYVAYNOO SHALOM ALAYKHEM (No. 44)

PEOPLE DAY

May Day is People Day.

People Day is a holiday, a humanist holiday and a humanistic Jewish holiday.

May Day is an old celebration. It has deep roots. It comes from cold countries. In cold places, there are really only two seasons. There is the winter season of snow and ice. There is the warm season of sun and growing things. November Day ushers in the winter. May Day announces the summer.

May Day has a long history. In Rome, they made it a festival of love. In England, they sang and danced around the Maypole. In Israel, they held archery contests and called the holiday Lag Ba-Omer. In Germany, the workers transformed it and made it a celebration of the working class.

No matter what the label, no matter what the ceremony, May Day always was a day of hope. It made the people feel good about themselves and about their future. Like the coming of summer, it filled them with a new sense of life and strength. It still does.

SONG: SAHAKEE (No. 78)

HUMAN NEEDS

People Day is about people. It is about men and women, boys and girls.

In many places and during many centuries, people were ignored. What they needed and what they wanted were less important than what the gods needed and the gods wanted. Filled with fear and terror, the people offered gifts of clothing, gold, and silver to the spirits they imagined ruled the world they lived in. Meekness and humility accompanied their sacrifices. They were afraid that human pleasure and human dignity would arouse the envy of the gods.

But people should not be afraid to pursue their own pleasure and to achieve their own dignity. Our needs are the most important needs we have. Our pleasure is the most important pleasure we can imagine. Our dignity gives meaning to life. When people think little of themselves, they feel guilty about their needs and desires. But when people esteem themselves, they value what they need and want. We have a right to happiness. We have a right to dignity.

SONG: EREV SHEL SHOSHANNEEM (No. 30)

HUMAN DREAMS

People Day is about human dreams. It is about what people are and what people can become.

Many people live from day to day. They think neither of the past nor the future. They make no plans for better times to come. They are content with what they receive from destiny. Although they may have dreamed good dreams when they were young, they gave up dreaming long ago to protect themselves against the hurt of disappointment, to shield themselves against the pain of frustration. For them, the fear of failure outweighs the pleasure of life.

But hope is part of human dignity. To endure the winter with no dream of the summer is to surrender to fate. It is to accept without protest what destiny delivers. We may not be able to change what happens, yet we do not have to consent to it. Our imagination is our resistance. Our determination to make the world a better place to live in is our defiance. Without the power of our dreams, the present has no meaning.

We can be better than we are. The world can be better than it is.

SONG: MAHAR (No. 63)

HUMAN POWER

People Day is about human power. It is about our power to change what needs to be changed.

In the wintertime, we become very much aware of our limitations. The cold freezes our courage and makes us huddle in the dark. Obsessed with thoughts of warmth and survival, we have little energy left over for other needs and other wants. And for many people, even the summer is like the winter. They cannot open up. They cannot grow. They cannot take risks. They firmly believe in human weakness. They firmly believe that they only have enough strength to survive.

But human power is as real as the reborn earth. There are many things we cannot do. Yet there are so many things we can do. There are so many things to change. We have the power to learn. We have the power to love. We have the power to work with others. Our confidence is a reflection of our self-image. If we insist that we are weak, then we shall be weak. If we insist that we are strong, then we shall be strong.

We can do more than we think we can, especially if we let ourselves believe it.

SONG: LAM'TSAPPEEM (No. 56)

HUMAN SUCCESS

People Day is about human success. It remembers what we do well.

It is so easy and so fashionable to condemn the human race. There is so much cruelty and deceit. There is so much hate and selfishness. War is still popular. Holocausts are still possible. Even the educated still do wicked things. Indeed, the visions of many prophets remain unfulfilled.

Yet human failure is only part of the story. Death has not been conquered, but we are living longer than ever before. Ignorance has not been defeated, but we have more knowledge than ever before. Fighting has not been stopped, but we are talking about peace more than ever before. In our determination to see our failures, we often do not notice our successes.

Perhaps we prefer to lose. Perhaps we are afraid to win. Perhaps despair places fewer demands on our talents.

The truth is that if we have much to regret we have also much to be proud of.

SONG: SAHAKEE (No. 78)

HEROES

People Day is about the people who believed in people. It is about the heroes who never lost their faith in humanity.

Throughout human history there have been many voices of despair. There have been many teachers who denounced the human race, many philosophers who saw us as terrible sinners. They told us not to trust ourselves, not to have faith in our own judgment, not to rely upon our own power. If we were to be saved from our own incompetence, we would not be responsible for that happy ending.

But many men and women refused despair. They defended human desire. They applauded human power. They enjoyed human success. They encouraged human dreams. Sometimes they did their work quietly, acting out their faith in personal behavior. Sometimes they proclaimed their thoughts publicly, defying public opinion, and giving hope to those who would listen.

Sometimes they did both. Einstein did, Sanger did, and so did many others.

SONG: AYFO OREE (No. 14)

MEMORIAL

People Day is about real people, the people we know and once knew.

Our families and our friends are so close to us that we often take for granted what they do. What is familiar has a tendency to appear ordinary. We lose our perspective. We imagine that what is far away is superior to what is close at hand.

We need to see the special in the familiar. There are parents who give us love. There are children who give us hope. There are friends who give us courage. In their own unique way—without the privilege of spoken philosophy—they make us feel worthwhile.

In this hour, on this special day, we offer them our tribute and our recognition.

SONG: SHEEM'OO (No. 83)

3
HUMANISM DAY

SONG: SHALOM LARAHOK (No. 81)

SUMMER

Winter is darkness, the darkness of the night. But summer is light, the light of the sun. When the end of June comes, darkness surrenders to light and withdraws to its small corner of time. The sun, the star of life, takes over and fills the world with the warmth and brilliance of its healing rays.

The blackness of winter tames our spirits and makes us fearful. But the sunshine of summer brightens our days and revives the energy of our hope. In the comfort of this season we are more aware of our power. We feel stronger, more confident, more vital, more optimistic. We greet the future with a joyous anticipation.

SONG: BASHANA HABAA (No. 21)

ENLIGHTENMENT

History is like the seasons. Sometimes forces of darkness overwhelm humanity and fill the world with the winter of ignorance and superstition. Sometimes the power of light shines down on the human scene and illumines the earth with the summer of knowledge and wisdom.

Summer is the season of light and enlightenment. The rays of the sun give us vision in the same way that the inspiration of reason helps us to see reality. Lovers of darkness cultivate mystery and fantasy. Lovers of light prefer openness and clarity.

Three hundred years ago a new age of light emerged for humanity. The defenders of reason and science entered into battle with the powers of darkness. They revealed the vast heavens of stars and galaxies. They exposed the richness of planetary life. They uncovered the secrets of the human body. They explored the past of a universe much older than they had ever imagined. What was once mystery now became knowledge. What was once obscure now became clear. What was once frightening now became comprehensible. The Age of the Enlightenment had dawned.

SONG: SAHAKEE (No. 78)

REASON

Blind faith is darkness. It believes because it is traditional to believe. It believes because it needs to believe. It believes because it chooses to believe. No evidence is required. No facts need intrude their support. Both absurdity and common sense take equal place before this tribunal of commitment. Too much light would dispel the mystery and expose the arbitrary foundation of such trusting belief. Where we cannot see and do not want to see, faith thrives.

Good-humored reason is light. It even believes what it is not traditional to believe. It even believes what it does not need to believe. It even believes when it does not choose to believe. The harsh landscape of reality is its guide. Both pleasant and unpleasant facts, both kind and unkind events demand recognition and insist that truth be not self-serving. The world we have may not be the world we want. But we cannot change it for the better if we cannot see it. Our reason is our strength. It enables us to stand face to face with reality. Living in the light often takes more courage than living in the darkness.

SONG: NAE HAOR (No. 70)

NATURE

The sun shines in the world of nature and makes it visible. But some people do not like what they see. There are so many things about the natural world that bother them. They see death and fear it. They see change and despise it. They see moral disorder and find it unacceptable. They dream of another world quite different—a world where there is no change—a world where the good are always rewarded and the wicked are always punished. They look forward to leaving the realm of the sun and to entering the more awesome realm of gods and deathless souls.

But children of the light prefer nature. They revel in change, enjoying the adventure of movement and growth. They defy death, filling their lives with pleasure and achievement. They confront moral disorder, striving to bring justice to those who deserve it. Nature is the disaster of earthquakes and plagues. It is also the ecstasy of sunrises and sunsets, of flowers and friendships. Good things may not last forever. But their value does not lie in eternity. It emerges from the intrinsic beauty of their own existence.

SONG: LAM'TSAPPEEM (No. 56)

HUMANITY

Many people hate what people are. They always think about the darker side of human nature. They always concentrate on whatever is mean and despicable in human behavior. After all, there is so much human cowardice and human cruelty. There is so much lying and cheating. There is so much betrayal and humiliation. If one insists, one can always portray humanity as the the devil incarnate. And for many centuries, most of the world did.

But many people love humanity. They do not love it in a sugary utopian way that dismisses human faults as trivial and our darker side as really light. They love it in a realistic way that goes beyond the negative to the shining, positive potential of every man and woman. After all, there is so much human talent and human ingenuity. There is so much loyalty and devotion. There is so much strength and endurance. If one insists, one can always celebrate the human power to nurture, to love, to strive for beauty and dignity. For the sons and daughters of the enlightenment this is the celebration the world needs.

SONG: OUT OF THE NIGHT (No. 76)

FREEDOM

It is not easy to be free. To be free means more than the power to do what you want to do. It means the determination to take control of your own life. It means the willingness to be responsible for the consequences of your own actions. It means the sensitive awareness that other people want their autonomy too.

For many people freedom is frightening. They do not want to control their own lives. They do not want to be responsible for their deeds. They do not want to set limitations on their own desires. They prefer to remain children. And they crave parents and governments that will rescue them from freedom.

But the lovers of light want their freedom. They understand the risks and perils that liberty brings. They understand the burdens of self-control that the free person must always bear. The security and safety of paternalistic societies hold no attraction for them. To live without dignity is to live in a prison of self-denial. To live without personal independence is to forgo integrity. Freedom is the passion that reason needs in its battle against the darkness.

SONG: HATOV O HARA (No. 41)

HUMANISM

The season of light is the season of humanism. This day of light is Humanism Day.

Humanism is the child of the light, the son and daughter of the enlightenment. When we embrace the life of reason, we embrace humanism. When we strive to fulfill the human potential, we strive to fulfill the promise of humanism. When we celebrate the dignity of freedom, we celebrate the vision of humanism.

The light of the sun is not under our control. But the light of human wisdom is. And so is the light of human self-esteem. May we keep it burning when the day is strong. May we keep it burning even in times of darkness.

As we light this light of humanism, may we renew our commitment to all that it represents.

KINDLING OF THE FLAME

SONG: AYRO OREE (No. 14)

4
WORLD DAY SERVICE

SONG: HINNAY MA TOV (No. 47)

WORLD DAY

We are human. We are part of the human race, part of the whole world.

This evening is World Day. It is a special time of the year. Winter is coming. Darkness grows. Cold gets colder.

At the end of October, at the beginning of November, we think about the winter. We think about nature, the fallen leaves, the strong winds. The fires that warm us will no longer come from the burning sun and the heat of summer. They will no longer come from the world of nature. They will arise from within us. They will be kindled by our own power. Even when the winter is cold and dark, human love will keep us safe. Human love will keep us warm.

SONG: V'AHAVTA (No. 93)

WORLD CITIZENSHIP

We are more than Jews. We are more than Americans. We are also citizens of the world. Every people is our people. Every nation is our nation. Every land is our land. The earth is our mother. And we are her children.

On World Day we dream a dream. We announce a vision. Someday soon the world will be one country. The people of the world will be one nation. Boundaries will vanish. Barriers will come down.

The dream is important. Because if we believe in it hard enough, we will make it come true.

SONG: AHEE ADAM (No. 4)

UNITED NATIONS

At the end of October we celebrate a birthday, not the birthday of a person, but the birthday of a dream.

Almost forty years ago, after a terrible war, the nations of the world came together. They had a vision. They held on to a dream. They wanted peace.

The United Nations is their creation. It is the congress of all the people of all the world. It is an opening to peace. It is the beginning of world citizenship. It is a sign of better things to come.

The United Nations is more than it was. It is less than it ought to be. But it keeps the dream alive.

We belong to the United Nations, not only as Americans but also as world citizens. We will not be impatient with it. We will not lose hope. We will work to make it better.

SONG: LO YISSA GOY (No. 60)

UNITY

We are Jews. We are Americans. But, above all, we are human beings.

Sometimes we forget this truth. Sometimes we only think about our own family. Sometimes we only think about our own friends. We look at other people and see them as strangers. The color of their skin is often different. The language they speak is not our own. We turn them into enemies before we give them a chance to become our friends.

But World Day makes us see the truth. Underneath the different color, underneath the different speech, underneath the different costume, every person is a human being. Every person needs the dignity we need. Every person wants the happiness we want. Every person feels what we feel.

SONG: SAHAKEE (No. 78)

WORLD FLAG

The Jewish flag is our flag. The American flag is our flag. The world flag is our flag.

The world flag is the flag of the United Nations. It is the symbol of no one country. It is the emblem of no one people. It belongs to everybody.

The world flag is blue and white. It is blue like the circle of air that shields our earth. It is white like the mountain snows that hold the water of life.

Although the world flag has only two colors, it represents a rainbow of people.

SONG: NAASE SHALOM (No. 69)

UNICEF

UNICEF is the name of a group that belongs to the United Nations.

UNICEF helps children all over the world. It gives them food and clothing, schools and medicine. It lets them know that they are part of the human family, that people in all nations want to help.

UNICEF is an orange box. If it has our cooperation, it collects money to buy what these children need. It gives us a chance to do good. It makes us feel useful.

UNICEF is Halloween, a time to help, in honor of World Day.

SONG: EEM AYN (No. 28)

ADAM

Adam is a Hebrew word that means "people."

Adam is the sound of World Day.

Adam is the people of the world, our human family.

This evening we pledge our loyalty to the people of the world, we pledge our allegiance to the human family.

Let us all rise and say together:

We are members of the human race. We are citizens of the world. The earth is our home. Every boy and girl, every man and woman is our brother and sister.

We pledge our allegiance to the flag of the world and to the dream of justice, beauty, and peace for which it stands.

We shall always be loyal to our human family.

SONG: WE SHALL BROTHERS BE (No. 96)

5
THANKSGIVING SERVICE

SONG: AYTS HIEYEEM (No. 17)

WINTER

Winter comes and brings with it the chill of dying nature. The power of the sun is weaker now and cannot melt the frost of midday. We look for warmth and cannot find it in nature's stingy gifts. Without the luxury of summer's heat, standing alone is a cold enterprise. We become aware of our need of others, of our desire for human warmth. If we are to survive the coming icy reign of winter's cruelty, we shall have to pool our fires.

Thanksgiving is a celebration of our shared dependence. Summer is deceptive and makes us feel comfortably self-sufficient, but the advent of winter returns us to reality and reminds us of our frailty. The struggle for survival rescues us from individual arrogance and restores our sense of social balance. Gratitude to those we depend on is no impulsive gift. It arises from necessity.

SONG: HINNAY MA TOV (No. 47)

HARVEST

The harvest is our friend. It gives us food even when nothing grows. Science is our ally. It transforms the elements of the earth and gives us heat even when nature freezes. Love is our protector. It encloses us with the strength of others and makes us strong even when our own power fails. Without the harvest, we would die. Without science, we would never reach out beyond survival to happiness. Without love, we would shrivel from loneliness.

The harvest is not an individual creation, nor are science or love. They are not possible as solo achievements of single men and women. They arise out of collective work. They live in community. Without cooperation, there would be no harvest. Without the free exchange of ideas, there would be no science. Without the experience of mutual dependence, there would be no love. Thanksgiving is an expression of our intimate tie to others. Grateful words do not rise to the heavens. They move horizontally, driven by the power of our need and affection.

SONG: HALBEESHEENEE (No. 35)

DIVERSITY

America is a land of immigrants. Our people have come from everywhere. We are no homogeneous race that enjoys ethnic solidarity. We are no smooth blend of ancient invasions that time has mixed. We are no ancient nation so old that we cannot even remember when we came to our sacred soil. Our language bears the name of some foreign shore. Our technology brings us swiftly to our ancestral home. We cannot enjoy the isolation of earlier nations.

The Pilgrims were the first of many immigrants. They did not arrive in some massive tribal invasion. They came in boatloads, in human dribbles. As English men and women, they shared the comforts of a common culture, which softened the hardships of a harsh environment. Their descendants were less fortunate. They invited strangers to do their work and to increase their wealth. The strangers were a formidable challenge. New cities and new work made it impossible to enclose them, to keep them separate. The task of integration was overwhelming. How does one unite such difference without the bonds of shared race and religion? The tension of that enterprise is still with us. It defines both our agony and our triumph.

SONG: LAM'TSAPPEEM (No. 56)

SOLIDARITY

America started with scarcity. The early pioneers struggled to survive. Thoughts of personal happiness and individual fulfillment were driven from their minds by necessity. Without labor and nurture, without cooperation and generosity, without loyalty and self-control, the community would have perished. America did not begin with rugged individualism. It was established on the foundation of group solidarity. The true religious experience of the Thanksgiving Puritan was no isolated mystery. It was the transcendent sense of belonging that needy and intense groups give to all their members.

Affluence gives us illusions. The security of material comfort weakens our loyalty to others and makes us imagine that we need no one else, that we are self-sufficient and independent. We fail to remember how fragile we are, how dependent on the work and knowledge of others. No one of us can master all of science. No single person can undertake to learn all the vital skills of our world of industry. The very energy we use so freely in our quest for freedom may be easily exhausted and return us to the life of scarcity. We are frail parts of a greater whole we can scarcely comprehend. If we remember this reality, we will not be seduced by selfishness. Our society lives because it breathes the air of giving and sharing.

SONG: WE SHALL BROTHERS BE (No. 96)

RELIGION

Patriotism and religion are not easy to distinguish. They arise from the same source, from the same human experience. Loyalty to community is the beginning of patriotism. It is also the beginning of religion. The reverence for dead heroes, the legends of epic beginnings, the tearful response to old symbols, fill both commitments. Unlike Israel, America is too young for the patriotic and the religious to merge completely. Every immigrant brings the memories of older nations and older loyalties. The Pilgrims and the Founding Fathers are not as old as Moses and David. But they give us national roots.

Our American religion is the celebration of our American experience. Thanksgiving is part of that celebration. It is more than the memory of Pilgrims on a Massachusetts shore. It is more than a reminder of our colonial beginnings. It is the dramatic symbol of the undramatic source of national power. The effort of being part of an enterprise greater than ourselves, the willingness to share our work with those who share our loyalty, the courtesy to caress each other with words of grateful affection—all these quiet deeds are the security which makes bold adventure and individual glory possible. Thanksgiving makes us turn from the glitter of national heroes to the substance of human community.

SONG: O BEAUTIFUL (No. 72)

IDENTITY

Each of us has many identities. We belong to many communities. We are Jews. We are Americans. We are also part of humanity, citizens of the world. Loyalty to a community is harmful to ourselves and to others when it is absolute and fanatic, when it excludes our other commitments. It is healthy when it is reasonable and good-humored, when it allows us to enjoy the richness of all our attachments. To be an American and only an American is too narrow a vision. In a world where no nation is independent and where no people is self-sufficient, chauvinism is more than super-loyalty. It is dumb arrogance.

The grandeur of America is its connection to all humanity. Too diverse to be confined to English memories, it embraces all the races of the world among its citizens. Too young to forget the origins of its people, it finds its homeland in many distant places. Too powerful to confine its creations to local places, it reaches out to many nations to give and take. Our American and our human loyalties complement each other and rescue us from the sin of parochial pride. All of us stand on the mountain of human culture, which is universal, and which no nation can claim as entirely its own. We are human, even before we are American, even before we are Jewish. Our thanksgiving to others must go beyond familiar boundaries.

SONG: AYFO OREE (No. 14)

MEMORIAL

Religion has always had a fondness for ancestors. It is that part of patriotism that turns to the past and reveres our roots. Too often this reverence easily becomes worship, changing the stories of our past into myths and the heroes of our past into gods. But when this tribute has self-control and keeps its respect within the bounds of reason and honest affection, it ceases to be pious and becomes grateful attachment. Communities exist in time, as well as in space. America is more than miles of land. It is also years of history. It is more than the needs of the living. It is also the enduring work of the dead.

Thanksgiving reaches out in three directions. It embraces the present of our living friends with gratitude. It touches the future of our dependents with hope. It honors the past of our ancestors, real and adopted, with the pleasure of belonging and the respect of strong commitment.

SONG: ZAYKHER (No. 103)

PART V
LIFE CYCLE

Every culture arranges dramatization of the personal life cycle. Judaism is no exception. After all, the major transitions in an individual's life are important not only to the individual but also to the community. When a child is born, when young men and women assume responsibility for their actions, when a couple marries with the prospect of offspring, when a person dies, the community will be affected either positively or negatively.

There are four traditional times of transition for which all cultures have provided some rite of passage or some ceremony: birth, growing up, marriage, and death.

BIRTH

Ritual circumcision remains the traditional Jewish way of marking the formal entrance of baby boys into the Jewish community. Nothing significant is provided for girls.

The *brit* (*bris*) presents several problems for humanistic Jews. First, it is built around a tension-filled surgery, with blood and screaming babies. Secondly, there seems to be no logical connection between trimming penises and welcoming children into a community. Thirdly, and most importantly, it is a male chauvinist ceremony which excludes girls by its very character.

The humanistic Jewish alternative is a welcoming ceremony at which children receive Hebrew names as a sign of their membership in the Jewish community.

GROWING UP (MITSVA)

The now familiar Bar Mitsva ceremony did not emerge in Jewish life until the middle of the fourteenth century in Germany. Originally and appropriately modest in scope, it allowed the thirteen-year-old to demonstrate his skills by reading a selection from the Torah and the prophets during the morning prayer service. In the afternoon of the same day he presented a *d'rasha*, a commentary on some Biblical or Talmudic passage. In more recent years the commentary has been replaced by an enormous party.

The Bar Mitsva, like the *brit*, presented many problems to Jewish humanists. It occurred at an age when young men were no longer entering adulthood; it sponsored a ritual that seemed to have no significant connection to growing up. It excluded girls from participation.

What has emerged as a humanistic response includes the following developments. Girls now have the opportunity to become a Bat Mitsva. The ceremony has been made more relevant by having the students choose Jewish heroes from Jewish history to serve as role models for their growing up. They prepare special research papers on their respective heroes and present them at their celebrations. An alternative Bar Mitsva/Bat Mitsva (Confirmation) ceremony at sixteen is offered to students. They can have both or either, although if only one is chosen the sixteen-year ceremony is obviously more important.

The Mitsva ceremony is an affirmation of the equality of boys and girls.

MARRIAGE

Traditional Judaism, like all traditional cultures, used marriage as the community's way to license reproduction. Men must get married, and women must be mothers.

The traditional ceremony included two parts: the betrothal, in which the bride becomes the possession of her husband; and the wedding, in which the bride and groom are blessed. Wine is used for both the betrothal and the wedding. A canopy surrounds them. One ring is used and presented by the groom to the bride during the betrothal, and glass is broken at the end of the ceremony to frighten away evil spirts. A betrothal document (Ketuba) is signed and presented to the bride.

Humanistic Jews have several problems with the traditional approach: marriage is confined to a reproductive purpose; the role of women is restricted; the concept of husbands owning wives is morally offensive; a betrothal document that reinforces this inequality is equally offensive; and, finally, intermarriage is forbidden.

The humanistic Jewish marriage ceremony is based on alternative values. Marriage is defined as a friendship of equality in which reproduction is an option. Two rings are used to reinforce this concept. The Ketuba is replaced by a simple document of confirmation signed by witnesses. Canopies, wine, and broken glass remain as nice traditional touches.

DEATH

Rabbinic Judaism approached death with a resolute faith in immortality and in the ultimate resurrection of the dead. The dead were quickly buried to keep their angry spirits from harming the living; cremation was forbidden to preserve the body for the resurrection; the Kaddish prayer was recited to win a reduction of punishment for the loved one in the afterlife; mourners humbled themselves with neglect and discomfort to dissuade the angel of death from returning.

Humanistic Jews start from the reality of death and the need to honor the needs of the living. Quick burial is necessary. Cremation is encouraged. The Kaddish prayer can be replaced by the humanistic *SHEEM'OO*, and the style and length of mourning is a personal choice.

A memorial service is necessary in order to allow family and friends to say their "farewells," to make final the reality of death. This service can be held in the community house, in the home, or in the funeral chapel.

OTHER CELEBRATIONS

Two other life-cycle celebrations are possible. The first is the *Educational Achievement* ceremony to honor members of the community who have completed a program of college or university study. If we can honor thirteen- and sixteen-year-olds at a time of life when they have accomplished very little, how much the more so if someone has acquired a B.A., M.A. or Ph.D.

The second is the *Confirmation* ceremony for adults. This ceremony is preceded by an intensive study of humanistic Judaism. When the orientation is completed the student is invited to confirm his membership in the community and in the larger fellowship of humanism and humanistic Judaism. Non-Jews who wish to join the Jewish people can use the *Confirmation* ceremony as the "Adoption" celebration.

1
BIRTH

ORDER OF CELEBRATION

1. WELCOME
2. CONFERRING OF A HEBREW NAME
3. CUP OF CELEBRATION
4. SONG

1. WELCOME

(Choose One)

LIFE

We affirm the power of life.
We affirm the power of life in every human being.
We affirm the power of life in every newborn child.

HOPE

We need hope.
We need the hope that comes from loving and nurturing.
We need the hope that comes from loving and nurturing a newborn child.

LOVE

We come together in love.
We come together in the love of family and friends.
We come together in the love that new life needs.

Birth

2. CONFERRING OF A HEBREW NAME

(Choose One)

ANTICIPATION

Life needs hope. It needs anticipation. It needs striving. It needs the future. So often our days are filled with the past, with regret for things not done, with the thought of events we cannot change. But when a new child is born, the direction of life turns forward. We become aware of our power to mold the shape of the world to come. We become aware of our power to create, to share, to teach, to train. A child is the gift of the future in the present. It is a potential waiting to be fulfilled. If we extend to him/her the gift of our love, s/he will share with us, in return, the gift of hope.

May your new son/daughter fill your life with new excitement and new anticipation. May s/he give you a new sense of positive power. May s/he bring forth from you all your capacity to love and to nurture. May the name s/he bears, _____, be a sign of the strength of your commitment to him/her and of his/her commitment to life.

AUTUMN

Autumn is a beautiful season. It suggests not only the fulfillment of summer but also the more distant promise of spring. The cycle of life is persistent. Even in the decay of autumn we are filled with the hope of new life to come.

Newborn children are expressions of this hope. They are affirmations of our confidence in the future. They are possibilities waiting to be fulfilled. If there is patience and tenderness, if there is gentle discipline and honest guidance, they will realize their potential and discover their strength. The radiance of life will shine through them and give them happiness and dignity.

May your new son/daughter always be an expression of your hope in the future. May s/he grow to maturity confident in his/her strength and strong in his/her purpose.

May the name s/he bears, _____, accompany him/her through a life of worthwhile achievement and happy anticipation.

BONDING

Newborn infants have a way of changing the lives of those who love them. They are so warm, soft, and cuddly that it is very hard to resist picking them up and holding them. They are so charmingly naïve, fresh, and curious that it is difficult not to be touched by their innocence. They are so helpless and in need of love that it is easy to reach out to help and to love.

Although they appear to be powerless, babies have a power all their own. They know how to hold their audience in thrall. They know how to reduce adults to cooing playmates. They know how to turn off all the terrible anger of our daily struggles and bring us so much joy with only the silliest of smiles.

_____, you have entered our lives like a breath of fresh love. Your adoring audience of parents and grandparents surround you with admiration ready to record your slightest achievement with oohs and aahs! In your small body you represent the future, a picture of hopes and dreams waiting to be fulfilled.

May the Hebrew name you bear, _____, be a sign of your membership in the Jewish people and of your connection with all your ancestors. You have brought us so much happiness. We hope that you will do the same for yourself.

CREATIVITY

Love is an expression of our strength. To nurture another human being with the gift of our time and our talents is to affirm our own power to create. True love is never self-sacrifice. It is the overflow of vitality which allows the force of life to pass from one to another.

To love a child is to love life. To nurture an infant is to express hope. Children do not steal our strength. They allow us to go beyond ourselves to discover the power of our own creative talents in their success. To be a father or a mother is more than a profession. It is more than a social calling. It is the fulfillment of one of our deepest needs—our need to touch the future and to make it live.

You have touched the future with your own creative power. You have brought a new child into the world. You are parents by choice and desire. May your newborn son/daughter bring you more life through his/her life. May s/he always enable you to reach out beyond yourselves to love and to nurture. May the name you have given him/her, _____, always be an affirmation of life.

FAMILY

Life offers the gift of many blessings. None is more precious than the love of family. In the strength and compassion of parents, in the loyalty of brothers and sisters, in the mutual devotion of husband and wife, we find the security of our love. Even the sweet affection of children brings its special charm and warms our attachment to life. The landscape of our days is peopled by the secure presence of open hearts that exact no price for the gift of themselves.

Your child is now an intimate part of your family circle. S/he needs your strength. S/he needs your compassion. S/he needs your nurturing love. In turn, s/he will give you the warmth of new life.

May the name s/he now bears, _____, be a reminder of his/her family connection. May it always be a sign of his/her firm attachment to life.

FULFILLMENT

New life is a vision of realities to come. Every living thing comes into the world with the promise of possibility, with the drive of potential. Every newborn child reaches out to the earth with its desire for fulfillment. There is a special beauty in infant children, not only the beauty of what they are but also the splendor of what they can be, of what they can become.

Your new son/daughter is now part of your fulfillment as you are part of his/hers. For s/he depends on you not only for the food, clothing, and material goods which you will give him/her, but especially for the love, the empathy, the laughter, and the moral strength which every child yearns to receive.

May the two of you be the agents of his/her fulfillment. May the name which you have chosen to give him/her, _____, accompany him/her through many years of joy, growth, and human success.

HOPE I

Children are the signs of the future. They are messengers of hope. When we think about the past, we are filled with regret for all that cannot be changed. But when we think about the future, we enjoy the anticipation of all that we will be able to do. Children remind us of our power to create, mold, teach, and change. They are tests of our love, imagination, and commitment. Immortality does not point to some distant supernatural world. It is part of the here and now. Our children will inherit more than our genes. They will inherit our vision of the good life. They will bear our gifts of kindness and strength and hand them down to those who will follow. Through them, we go beyond ourselves and touch the future.

Today we celebrate the birth of your new son/daughter. S/he is a unique human being. But s/he is also part of that chain of life which you reinforce through your love. May the name s/he bears, _____, accompany him/her through a long life of achievement and hope.

HOPE II

When a child is born, hope is born. A baby makes us look forward with anticipation and excitement. So often we become prisoners of the past, dwelling on events we cannot change, filled with regret. But newborn children make us love the future, with all its possibilities and with all its opportunities. They unleash the power of our love and creativity and let us discover how much we need to nurture. When we give life to others, we give life to ourselves. We become alive with hope.

Your new son/daughter is the living expression of the power of your own love and the vitality of your own hope for the future. May s/he give you dreams as s/he fulfills his/her own. May the name s/he bears, _____, always be a sign of the happy visions s/he inspires at this hour.

INDIVIDUALITY

Love is a creative act, especially the love of parents for children. When we love a child we want to help it grow, we want to make it strong. We want to love it enough so that it will love itself.

But parenting is not always easy. Children do not always to conform to our expectations. They have their own way of doing things, of being who they are. They often dance to their own music and not to the music we give them.

Creative discipline encourages them to become what they need to become. It also guides them with firmness and with gentleness so that they never betray their potential through fear or through impulse. Children are an affirmation of our power to create, of our faith in the future. They help us discover the profound joy of nurturing through love.

_____, you are a unique human being with unique needs and unique talents. May you always be aware of your needs. May you always use your talents to become a strong and achieving man/woman.

322   *Birth*

We welcome you into the Jewish people with the Hebrew name of _____.

JOY

Life is worth living because it presents the opportunity of joy and happiness. Many pleasures, both profound and simple, adorn our fleeting days, but none is more creatively exciting than the experience of parenthood. Newborn children are challenges to our patience, our understanding, our willingness to give; they are also an invitation to hope and fulfillment. In their helpless infancy, they cry out for love; and we need to love.

May your new son/daughter bless your home with his/her zest for life. May the name s/he bears, _____, serve as the sign of her/his continuing happiness.

LIFE

Life is the beauty of the world. In the vitality of our universe, we find the possibility of warmth and surprise—and, above all, the opportunity of love. In the needs and desires of newborn children, this vital force reaches out to touch the hearts of their parents with the pleasure of youthful promise. Infants are irresistible. In their helplessness, they invite our love and concern. In the hidden potential of their talents and drives, they shine with the possibility of happiness.

May your new son/daughter bring a special joy to your lives. May the name of s/he bears, _____, become for all who will know and love him/her a symbol of life fulfilled and happiness achieved.

LOVE

Love is not an abstraction. It is a passion of the heart, an expression of the body, deeply rooted in life and human existence. Our first experience of love starts when we are helpless infants, when we are completely dependent on the care and attention of our mother and father. They hold us and feed us and make sure that we are warm. They respond to our needs and do for us what we cannot do for ourselves. They make us feel safe and secure. Above all, they give us a sense of specialness and significance. Without their love, we would not come to love ourselves and to find our self-esteem. Nor would we ever learn to love others.

Your new son/daughter will learn love from you. S/he will learn to love herself/himself because you love her/him. S/he will learn to love others because you have shown him/her how it is possible to reach out to another human being and to embrace him/her with caring warmth. Right now you are teaching him/her the most important lesson of life, the lesson of love.

May this experience fill his/her life with deep satisfaction. May the name s/he bears, _____, unite him/her with all his/her family roots, the hopes of the past and the promise of his/her future. May the love s/he now receives be an intimation of the love s/he will in turn give to others as s/he assumes the responsibilities of his/her own life.

PARENTING

Love is ironic. It is never exhausted by use; it is stimulated by every new opportunity. Two people who love each other and who share in the creation and nurturing of a child find in this experience a special unity. Your child is the product of your love, and what s/he will become is the result of your consistency. Through your self-esteem, s/he will find his/her self-esteem. Through your compassion, s/he will find his/her compassion. Through your willingness to be free, s/he will desire to be free.

May your son/daughter, whom you have called _____, enrich and strengthen your love and may you ultimately give to him/her the respect that you feel for each other. May s/he take the gifts of your caring and make them a secure foundation for happiness and fulfillment.

PROMISE

In a season when darkness overwhelms the world, the light of new life is precious. A new child is a reminder to us that in the midst of winter the promise of spring is always there. The warmth of the child is the warmth of life; and the cry of the child is the cry of hope. In his/her infant helplessness, s/he yearns for love and finds in the arms of his/her parents the security of belonging. If life makes love possible, then love makes life meaningful.

May your newborn child find his/her fulfillment in the love s/he will receive and in the love s/he will give. May the name s/he bears, _____, accompany him/her through long life to the honor of good deeds and the pleasure of happiness.

SELF-ESTEEM

Love begins with family. Without the nurturing care of mother and father we would never survive and never know that we are worthwhile. Without the tender discipline of those who give us life, we would be too frightened to reach out beyond ourselves. In order to be strong enough to give love we must first know what it is to receive love. Newborn children are the continuity of love. They allow their parents to express their need to nurture. And they, in turn, take the love they are given and grow with it into self-esteem. Some day they too will reach out to others and help as they have been helped.

Your newborn son/daughter needs the love you give him/her. S/he will use it well. S/he will grow strong on it. S/he will come to trust the world. S/he will learn that s/he is supremely worthwhile. S/he will be able to love others.

May the name s/he bears, _____, be a sign of the bond between her/him and you and all her/his family. May it accompany him/her through many years of fulfilled dreams.

SPRING I

In this spring of the year, the earth is made young again and awakens to new life. The freshness and hope of this season expresses itself in the wonder of birth. Infant children embody the mood we feel. Their presence is the victory of life and love. Their cry, a challenge to the world they grow to know. The joy of parenthood is this continual exposure to spring—this persistent invitation to vitality, to fulfillment, to creative work. In a world with so many winters, children warm our hearts with the hope of their promise.

May your newborn son/daughter heighten the excitement of your life and intensify the power of your love. May the name, _____, which you have chosen to give him/her, represent, in the years to come, the strength of useful achievement and the courage of self-respect.

SPRING II

The season of spring is the mother of new life and new hope. As the world is reborn, as the earth is renewed, the fresh infancy of nature seizes our sight and makes us respond to its beauty. Spring is like the pleasant touch of parenthood. New children are born and reach out with all their innocence and charm to find the love of their mothers and fathers. They begin as helpless infants, but breathe the hope of growth and fulfillment. In their irresistible presence nature smiles and confesses that life is good.

Your new daughter/son is like the promise of spring. May the name s/he bears, _____, be a mark of her/his continuing vitality and an invitation to the warm summer of happiness s/he shall grow to find.

SPRING III

Spring is here. The season of rebirth makes its warm entrance. New life announces its arrival in the beauty of leaves and flowers. The exciting anticipation of summer fills the air.

Babies are born. Like the spring, they are the living expression of hope. They are the promise of better things to come. They are small realities suggesting big possibilities. But infants do not grow as easily as trees and flowers. They need loving parents. They need holding, touching, and tender caring. They need soft words of assurance. They need encouragement, kindness, and consistent discipline. Above all, they need guides and teachers, mothers and fathers whose behavior fits their words. Adults with integrity mold children of integrity.

May your newborn son/daughter receive all that s/he needs from you and from others who love him/her. May his/her name, _____, accompany him/her through a long life of self-esteem and creative happiness.

SPRING IV

Spring is special. In the spring we experience the rebirth of nature and the revival of the earth. In the spring we sense the power of new life and new hope. Like the spring, the birth of a child speaks to us of hope. The infant is the sign of our immortality, helping us to reach out beyond ourselves to the possibilities of the future. Every child is unique, entitled to the fullfillment of his/her unique potential. But s/he is also a line in the chain of life, receiving from the past his/her talents and needs and bequeathing to the future his/her skills and his/her strength. Each of us is more than an individual. We find our happiness and sense of worth in the love and warmth of family, in the acceptance of the communities we grow up to serve.

We celebrate today the birth of your new daughter/son in the spirit of spring. May s/he grow to womanhood/manhood, conscious of the power of love and aware of her/his own strength. May the name s/he bears, _____, accompany her/him through a long life of self-esteem and generous service to others.

SUMMER

Summer is a lovely season. It is a time when spring realizes its full glory and opens our eyes to the beauties of the world. Nothing is more beautiful than new life. In its freshness, it thrills us by its promise; in its modest splendor, it excites us by its opportunity. The infant child is an invitation to all the vitality within us—to our love, to our hope, to our creative work. By his/her presence, we are renewed and awakened to the happy challenge of parenthood.

May your newborn son/daughter heighten the joy of your living and intensify the power of your love. May the name _____, which you have given him/her, represent in the years to come the strength of useful achievement and the courage of self-respect.

TEACHING

We speak through our own behavior. Our lifestyle becomes a personal message. If we are generous, then our action teaches others how to be generous. If we are creative, then others can see how to be creative. If we are strong, then our strength becomes a vivid example to those around us. Good teachers teach by what they do, not by what they say. Good parents are good teachers. They mold the lives of their children by the beauty and integrity of their own actions.

May your new son/daughter learn from you what it means to be a loving and effective human being. Since you have the power to share yourselves with a newborn infant, you also have the power to give him/her the greatest and most intimate of all gifts—the gift of your loving behavior. May the name s/he bears, _____, become the sign of the gentle virtue you so clearly value. It is your ultimate message to your child.

UNIQUENESS

To love children is to love the future. Infants are only human possibilities: They need the imagination of parents to grow. They need the patient tenderness of understanding adults to become real and personal. To love a child is to love the creative. Every individual is unique. Although humanness is shared, it allows a wide range of difference. Infants need more than the wisdom of the past. They need people who see them as new and special. They need protectors who shelter them from the tyranny of old scripts and who teach them to write their own.

To love a child is to love more than to speak of love. Strength and generosity are more than words. They are deeds.

Your newborn child needs your love. S/he needs your optimism, your respect, and your reliability. S/he needs your enthusiasm, your warmth and your good humor. S/he deserves to be happy. You can train him/her to achieve that happiness. May the name you have given him/her, _____, always identify his/her uniqueness.

WINTER I

The assault of winter reminds us of how fragile life is. When the summer sun shines we imagine that it is easy to survive, but the darkness of winter makes us feel vulnerable and puts our independence into proper perspective.

We are dependent not only on the kindness of the weather but especially on the kindness and love of other people. We are born into a world of many opportunities for happiness and personal fulfillment. Growing up successfully is not easy. It needs the caring love of mothers and fathers. It needs the indulgent support of grandfathers and grandmothers. It needs the protective guidance of teachers and friends. It needs the encouragement to be brave.

When a child is born, a potential is born. A new flame is kindled to illumine the darkness. If parents give their love, if grandparents extend their support, if teachers and friends offer their guidance, the flame will grow brighter, the child will become strong and self-reliant, the possibility for happiness will turn into something real.

May your newborn son/daughter fulfill his/her potential. May the flame of his/her power shine strong and clear. May the name s/he bears, _____, become for him/her and all who love him/her an affirmation of life and hope.

WINTER II

In this season of darkness we dream of the light, not only the light of the sun which is renewed in every winter but also the radiance of new life which the sun makes possible. In the face of every infant child there is a beauty that rivals the grandeur of the stars. There is the beauty of innocence, of trust, and of joy. There is the loveliness of hope, of wonder, and of sudden discovery. Young children make our world brighter by their optimism and richer by the wealth of their unfulfilled talent. In their dreams lies the future of all people.

Your new child is a child of hope, filled with the promise of his/her own potential. May s/he never betray this promise. May s/he always see life through positive eyes. May the name you have given her/him, _____, connect her/him to the past of his/her roots and to a future of realized talents.

WINTER III

The winter is cold. But life is warm—warm as hope, warm as love. In a season of icy darkness, new life is the promise of better things. A newborn child speaks to us of the promise of a boundless world—the promise of joy and human fulfillment. A newborn child speaks to us of the opportunity of parenthood, the opportunity of loving and creating and giving.

May your son/daughter, to whom you have given the name _____, add to the richness of your own fulfillment. May you, through your own wisdom and care, lead him/her to discover the pleasure of living and the strength of happiness.

WINTER IV

Winter is a cold season. It chills our bones and makes us grateful for the warmth of human life. In the luxury of summer's heat, we do not notice our need for other people. But in the winter, the value of life and living things becomes more vivid.

When new life appears in the cold season, when a child is born, the fire of renewal warms our hearts and gives us hope. A child is a sign of the spring to come, a symbol of all the possibilities of human existence. Nature renews itself and gives us the opportunity to love, to nurture, to care. Even in the winter, infants grow and reach out to the world. In the secure setting of home and family, they discover their will to live and their power to become more than they are.

Your newborn child is both a present reality and a future dream. S/he needs your love, your tenderness, your discipline, your optimism to fulfill all the vital possibilities that are within him/her and to express all the need for joy and happiness that motivates his/her being. May the name s/he bears, _____, bring honor to those who bore those names before and give pleasure to those who see him/her grow from the winter of birth to the spring of youth and adulthood.

3. CUP OF CELEBRATION

(A cup of wine is filled and presented)

(Choose One)

LIFE

This cup of wine is the cup of life. It is the symbol of family life and the sign of continuity from generation to generation. _____ is more than an individual. S/he is part of the chain of the life which stretches from the past into the future.

Let us raise this cup to life. *L'-HIE-YEEM*.

LOVE

This cup of wine is the cup of love. It reminds us of our power to care and to nurture. _____ needs our love as we will ultimately need his/hers.

Let us raise this cup to love. *L'-A-HA-VA*.

HOPE

This cup of wine is the cup of hope. It speaks to us of joy and fulfillment. It touches our lips with the promise of good things to come. _____ is this day our hope for the future.

Let us raise this cup to hope. *L'-TIK-VA*.

> (The cup is passed around to all who are assembled. Each person pays tribute to the newborn child. At the end, a drop of wine is taken from the cup and placed on the lips of the child.)

4. SONG

(Choose One)

HINNAY MA TOV (No. 47)

SHEEM'OO (No. 83)

BASHANA HABAA (No. 21)

2
GROWING UP (MITSVA)

(Choose one of the five celebrations)

MITSVA I (ETHICS)

SONG: SHALOM L'YISRAEL (No. 82)

ADOLESCENCE

The cycle of life is like the cycle of the seasons. It never stops. It expresses itself in the story of every living thing. It repeats itself in the biography of every human being. Although we are wiser and more powerful than any other living being, we are, like all other creatures, obedient to an eternal rhythm. The winter of the womb is followed by the spring of youth. The summer of maturity yields to the autumn of decay. We cannot remain forever young. Whether we accept or resist reality, we must grow up.

SONG: B'AYLE HAYADIEYIM (No. 22)

GROWING UP

(Choose One)

To be thirteen is to stand between two worlds, the past of childhood and the promise of adolescence. The middle years of teenage are often very hard to cope with. They are a testing ground for adult life. If we are too dependent on others, we must learn to become more independent. If we think too little of our talents, we must train ourselves to respect them. If we are afraid of

Growing Up (Mitsva)

the future, we must grow accustomed to live with the surprise of challenge. Adolescence can be wasted in fear and laziness so that growing up is too painful to bear. Or it can be a time of happy excitement when new responsibility becomes a pleasure and new learning becomes our hope for success.

To be sixteen is to stand in the doorway of adulthood. It is to confront the meaning of what growing up is all about. It is to experience both the terror and the joy of being in charge of your own life. To be sixteen is to know that childish behavior no longer works and that new skills have to be learned. We need to be more honest, more decisive, more creative, more responsible, more loving and more open than we have ever been before. We need to affirm our own potential for happiness.

SONG: AL SH'LOSHA D'VAREEM I (No. 7)

HONESTY

Honesty begins with behavior. What we really think is reflected in what we do. Too often we imagine that we know what we want and believe. We check our conscious mind and encounter numberless ideas and convictions which claim to be the essence of our being. But they are obvious frauds. Our tongue speaks love, but our hands speak hate. Our mouth exudes serenity, but our eyes exude fear. Our lips utter friendship, but our whole body screams anger. We feel sincere and imagine that we are sincere. We feel honest and imagine that we are honest.

If we listen to our hearts alone, we shall never discover the truth. It is only when we coldly watch our own behavior that we confront reality. Our deepest convictions about ourselves and others can never really be hidden. They boldly proclaim themselves through our actions. While our mouths spin tales of fantasy, our bodies speak with honesty. When we plead that we cannot act on our own beliefs, we are self-deceived. We *always* act on what we believe. When we run away from what we say we love, then our love is an illusion. And when we embrace what we say we hate, then our hatred is unreal. We simply are what we do.

SONG: HAEMET YOTSAYT (No. 32)

SELF-RESPECT

Self-respect is never a gift. It is always an achievement. Neither the flattery of friends nor the reassurance of family will give us the feeling of self-worth.

Neither the counseling of therapists nor the comforts of religion will elevate our dignity. Self-esteem is the child of competence. It is the offspring of personal skill. People who believe that they have the power to help themselves and to help others will respect themselves.

People who like themselves believe that they have power. They believe that they have the power to determine the course of their own lives. They believe that they have the competence to be useful to others. They believe that they have the strength to make decisions even when the consequences of their decisions cannot easily be predicted. They even know that when they give to others they do not threaten their own welfare, for their own security lies in no possession. It resides in their own creative skill.

SONG: EEM AYN (No. 28)

COMMITMENT

Some of us hate to make decisions. Decisions are so risky. They may lead to failure. They may sponsor embarrassment. They may expose our fantasies. Decisions burden us with responsibility. They make us confront our freedom to choose. They make us shoulder the blame. They make us apologize for our mistakes.

Avoiding responsibility may be unattractive. But it seems so much safer than the risk of being wrong. It seems so much safer to find respectable ways to be irresponsible. Our genes, our social conditions, our helplessness are comfortable excuses. Gods, dictators, and bossy bosses are convenient blame takers, even though we choose to forget that we consent to our own obedience.

Our lifestyle is defined by the way we make decisions. Some of us prefer to be children, always pleading our innocence and dependency. Some of us prefer to be adults, taking responsibility for our actions and confronting other people with the dignity of our self-esteem.

SONG: HATOV O HARA (No. 41)

MATURITY

Many men and women are physical adults. But they remain spiritual children. They possess an insatiable need to please—a fearful desire to win the approval of others—a persistent wish to conform to the expectations of their peers and superiors. They are the prisoners of their childhood. Hostility and disapproval terrorize them. Public opinion fills them with dread. Self-respect eludes them. They become the perennial followers who never create, who never resist.

Maturity is the power to control fear. When our fears and anxieties overwhelm us, they paralyze our will. We cannot choose between alternatives. We cannot make decisions. As dependent children, we seek the protection of a strong leader who will assume the burden of our will, who will tell us what to do. Tyrants may indeed be bossy. They may be pushy and oppressive. But they love to take responsibility. Rational fear is the fear of losing control. Irrational fear is the fear of being in control.

SONG: LAM'TSAPPEEM (No. 56)

LOVE

Newborn infants come into the world in helpless dependency, with only the knowledge of how to receive. As they grow up, as they cease to be children in mind and heart, they sense a new power—not the power to demand love, but rather the power to express love.

To sense that we not only need to be helped but also need to help, to feel that we not only require the care of others but also are able to give care, is the beginning of inner security. We do not transcend our loneliness by only finding others to love us. We transcend our sense of separation by finding others to love. In the act of being useful, in the work of fulfilling the desires and needs of other human beings, we feel our creative power and discover our strength. True love is an ironic deed. It binds us closer to other people while it awakens within us the thrill of independence. The more we help, the stronger we feel; and the stronger we feel, the more secure we become.

Love is the developed art of expressing our human power through the act of giving to others. It overwhelms our fears and gives us hope through the promise of our strength.

SONG: SHEEM'OO (No. 83)

FRIENDSHIP

Family and friendship are like the air we breathe. We cannot really live without them. We are not designed for loneliness. We thrive on the opportunity of human response. We need to give our love. We need to receive the love of others.

Life is sustained by our will to live. It also finds its meaning in the affection of others. Parent and friend, husband and wife pay us the tribute of caring. Our pain is their pain. Our happiness is their happiness. Through their love, we come to love ourselves and to find our self-esteem.

SONG: HINNAY MA TOV (No. 47)

CREATIVITY

Life without imagination is dull. People without imagination are boring. Imitation and conformity are necessary for survival. But they need to be challenged if life is to go beyond survival, if life is to yield the excitement of happiness.

Successful people are creative people. They refuse to accept the world as fixed. They refuse to believe that life offers only one script for living. They see old things and imagine new ways of putting them together. They see new things and fancy old settings which they will transform. They gaze at one scene and envision a hundred ways to describe it. They experience one life and imagine a thousand ways to live it.

SONG: B'AYLE HAYADIEYIM (No. 22)

OPENNESS

Youth is not so much a condition of the body as it is a state of the mind. Many people are old at thirteen/sixteen, their curiosity chilled by fear. Others are young at eighty, their perceptions warmed by the courage to love surprise. Physical youth fades quickly, but the springtime of our mind lasts as long as we will it. To find in each new event a teacher and to see in each new day the excitement of hope is never to grow old. Wisdom is not the product of wintry age. It is the special gift of the eternally young.

SONG: AYFO OREE (No. 14)

MITSVA PRESENTATION

RESPONSE

(From a representative of the community)

CANDLELIGHTING

(Family and friends light the lights of the Menorah)

SONG: HAVA NAGEELA (No. 42)

MITSVA II (SELF-ESTEEM)

SONG: V'SHOOV ITKHEM (No. 95)

ADOLESCENCE

(Choose One)

Thirteen is an important age. It is a time of important change. We have to move from being a child to being a teenager. We have to rely less on our parents and more on ourselves. We have to deal with our new body and the fact that we are growing up. We have to live less in the present and to plan more for the future. We have to make decisions we never made before.

Sixteen is an important age. It is a time of important change. We have to move from being a child to becoming an adult. We have to learn how to become less dependent and more independent. We have to think about work and training for work. We have to prepare for taking care of ourselves. We have to make decisions we never made before.

SONG: AYFO OREE (No. 14)

CHANGE

Life is change. It never stands still. It does not like eternal shapes and forever forms. It does not enjoy peace and quiet. Birth, growth, decay, and death define its busy rhythms. As living beings, we are always on the move. We are always experiencing change. We are always becoming different.

336 *Growing Up (Mitsva)*

Healthy people do not resent change. They use it. If they are growing up, they do not resist their experience. They do not strive to remain children. They try to understand what is happening. They try to prepare for what will be. Since our childhood is so long, it is very tempting to remain the child. It is very appealing to continue to do what we do so well. Our willingness to grow up is often very weak. We have to work very hard to do what we need to do.

SONG: EEM AYN (No. 28)

DIGNITY

All of us look for security, but we pursue it in different ways. Some of us chase things. We imagine that if we own more and more objects, control more and more money, acquire more and more promises, we will be safer. We find our identity in our possessions. But our advantage turns out to be a problem. Our attachments can be stolen, either by people or by fate. And when they leave, they bear us no fundamental loyalty. They are as happy to be with others as to be with us. Because they are so fickle, they make us very vulnerable.

Others prefer to pursue self-esteem. To have self-respect is to find identity in what we can do and not in what we come to own. Skills are weightless and effortlessly moved. They give grace to life. To read, to write, to paint, to sing, to build, to heal—these are the phases of true personality. There is no mysterious inner self that gives us strength. There is no visible outer self that makes us independent. Self-respect thrives on competence. It flourishes where people prefer doing to owning, training to seizing. If we are competent, we do not need to fear the loss of property. We do not need to fear the thief of fortune. We carry our identity in the security of our skills. Wherever we go, they follow.

SONG: MEE HAHAM (No. 65)

AUTONOMY

We often create the authorities we deserve. If we make decisions on our own, we will have to be responsible for what we do. If others make decisions for us, they will be responsible for what we do. Since responsibility is a heavy burden that we like to avoid, we hide from our own behavior. We turn our own decisions over to others. And then we complain because they oppress us. Complaining is so much easier than the risk of failure. If we are good at resentment, then we never have to grow up.

Adulthood is more than physical. It is more than a chronological test. Many young people are more adult than their parents. Many old people are less adult than their children. If we are adults, we prefer responsibility to resentful dependence. We may listen, but never parrot. We may defy, but never tease. We may decide, but never for the last time. If we are adults, we prefer the wisdom of authorities to their commands. We do not steal their insight and then give them our blame. If we are to be our own masters, the complaining child must become the thoughtful adult.

SONG: OUT OF THE NIGHT (No. 76)

COMPETENCE

Wishing will not make us stronger. Hoping will not improve the quality of our individual power. Our personality rests on the foundation of our skills. Without integrity, we cannot change. Without competence, we cannot safely move. Without decisiveness, we are condemned to blind obedience. Without friendship, we suffer the boredom of being less than human.

We must always strive to acquire the skills we need. If we lack integrity, we begin to practice it. If we lack courage, we start to discipline our fear. If we lack competence, we choose specific tasks to perform. If we lack decisiveness, we avoid dictatorial friends. If we are tired of privacy, we seek our human connection. Strength is the gift of training.

SONG: MAASEEM TOVEEM (No. 61)

LOVE

When we are born, when we are very young, we need more love than we are able to give. As infants we are helpless and dependent, without even the power to move and to feed ourselves. As children we are frightened and awkward, aware of how much we do not know and how much we do not control. Without the loving help of mother and father, teachers and friends, we would never grow up. We would never discover our strength.

When we leave childhood, we begin to learn a new skill. We begin to understand the difference between being loved and loving. We come to know the distinction between care and caring. New power and new wisdom make us aware of our ability not only to receive but also to give. Just as many reached out to us, we can now reach out to others. Just as family and friends helped us, we can now help them. Just as generous people tended to our needs, we can now serve theirs. Growing up fills us with the joy of a new discovery. We are strong enough to love.

SONG: SHEEM'OO (No. 83)

COMMUNITY

The past lives in our present. Each of our genes is much older than we are. It has traveled through thousands of years, dozens of places, and countless biographies. It is a bossy thing, controlling our shape and behavior, while arrogantly doing the same for other members of our family. Parents look into the faces of their children and see themselves. Brothers and sisters watch each other and discover that they are more alike than they would prefer. Just as our bodies are communities of cooperating cells, so are we, as individuals, part of societies greater than ourselves. We are all bound together by mutual convenience and shared roots.

Families and friends are mirrors. They reflect our form and desire. Because they are human, because they share our evolutionary past, they can see what we see. They can feel what we feel. They need what we need. We are extensions of them. They are extensions of us. We are no less individual because we are tied to them with the bonds of biology. Our uniqueness is only possible when we are relating to others.

SONG: HINNAY MA TOV (No. 47)

ROOTS

When we grow up, we must not forget our roots. They give us stability and depth. They give us identity and a place to belong.

Our families are our roots. They gave us life. They shared our childhood. They guided our behavior. When we celebrate our own achievement, we also celebrate theirs.

The Jewish people is our roots. They presented us with our place in history. They endowed us with famous ancestors. They reinforced our will to live. When we honor our past, we also honor theirs.

Growing Up (Mitsva)

Humanity is our roots. They gave us needs and desires. They passed on to us the gifts of human invention. They provided us with brothers and sisters all over the world. When we pay tribute to our own future, we also pay tribute to theirs.

SONG: AYFO OREE (No. 14)

MITSVA PRESENTATION

RESPONSE

(From a representative of the community)

CANDLELIGHTING

(Family and friends light the lights of the Menorah)

SONG: HAVA NAGEELA (No. 42)

MITSVA III (LIFESTYLE)

SONG: HAYVAYNOO SHALOM ALAYKHEM (No. 44)

OPENNESS

Youth is not so much a condition of the body as a state of mind. Many people are old at thirteen/sixteen, their curiosity chilled by fear. Others are young at eighty, their perceptions warmed by the courage to love surprise. Physical youth fades quickly, but the springtime of our mind lasts as long as we will it. To find in each new event a teacher and to see in each new day the excitement of hope is to never grow old.

SONG: BASHANA HABAA (No. 21)

CREATIVITY

Life without imagination is dull. People without imagination are boring. Imitation and conformity are necessary for survival, but they need to be challenged if life is to go beyond survival, if life is to yield the excitement of happiness.

Successful people are creative people. They refuse to accept the world as fixed. They refuse to believe that life offers only one script for living. They see old things and imagine new ways of putting them together. They see new things and fancy old settings which they will transform. They gaze at one scene and envision a hundred ways to describe it. They experience one life and imagine a thousand ways to live it.

SONG: SAHAKEE (No. 78)

EDUCATION

Education is life. From the moment we are born, we begin to learn. And until the day we die, we continue to learn.

We are born incomplete. Our possibility is so much greater than our reality. Since neither instinct nor destiny are enough to guarantee our future, our brain and open mind respond to the world and help us go beyond our inheritance to understanding and wisdom. Something is always happening to us. And we change with every experience.

Long after our body ceases to grow, our mind continues to grow. Even when we become physical adults, the curious child never completely leaves us. Maturity is as elusive as perfection.

SONG: MEE HAHAM (No. 65)

PURPOSE

Life is purpose. Without goals and aspirations, we would cease to be vital. We would also cease to be human.

Purpose comes from our needs, our instinct for survival, our desires for pleasure and dignity. They give us the motivation and the passion to go beyond our present condition and to strive to become more than we are. They are the fire which fuels our ambition.

No life is long enough to satisfy all our desires. There is so much we want to be, so much we need to be, that our years are inadequate to accommodate all our dreams. No sooner do we complete one task than another awaits us. Sometimes we have to make painful choices, choosing one path over another, forgoing one dream to fulfill another vision and never knowing for sure that the decision we made was the right decision.

Growing Up (Mitsva) 341

If we are naïve, problems are burdens, curses of the present to be dismissed by the future. If we are wise, problems are opportunities, challenges to the future that give meaning to our present. We know that we do not solve problems in order to live. We live in order to solve problems. Foolish people may find the secret to mountain climbing in the love of mountain tops. But wise people are never naïve. They know that the value of the climbing is always in the climbing; and the value of the game is in the game.

SONG: LAM'TSAPPEEM (No. 56)

DISCIPLINE

Wishing is never enough. If we wait for success, it will most likely elude us. And if we rely on luck and destiny to get what we want, they will prove less dependable than their reputation suggests.

Dreams need work and self-control to become more than dreams. They need planning and the postponement of pleasure. Running away from frustration and the tedium of daily tasks is only a momentary satisfaction. The wisdom we want, the skills we need, demand training. Our potential is a weak muscle that needs constant exercise. Our intentions alone will never make it stronger. It requires an earnest discipline.

Talent is useful for the successes of life. But it is rarely sufficient. Too many talented people betray their promise by their laziness. Effort and the willingness to work make the difference. True education is not a gift. It is an achievement.

SONG: BAMAKOM (No. 19)

GROWTH

When we are children, we want so desperately to grow up. We see the power and privileges of adults and we want them for ourselves.

When we are adults, we are less naïve. We see the obligations more than the privileges, and we know that we have tasted only a small part of our power. In fact, we realize that we never really stop growing up.

Our power to learn and to change keeps us younger than our body suggests. Our self-awareness and our actions take longer than our limbs to reach maturity. Awkwardness is more than physical. It is also a mental condition, a roughness of the human spirit that comes from too little knowledge and too little experience. Grace is an inner strength and refinement which emerges from hard striving and long-run achievement. Every fulfilled dream makes it smoother and more satisfying.

Growing up does not end at thirteen—or sixteen—or twenty. It has barely begun.

SONG: EEM AYN (No. 28)

SELF-ESTEEM

Self-esteem is our dignity. It is our sense of personal independence. It is the awareness of our own responsibility for our own lives. It is the experience of turning the power of our possibility into reality.

There are times in our lives when we feel our self-esteem most strongly. When an important task is finished, when a course of study is completed, when a new skill is mastered, when the people we respect give us their respect for the things we do—then our perception of our own dignity becomes bolder and fills our lives with a deep satisfaction. It is good to know that we can do what we want to do and that others can see our competence.

If we pause for a moment to congratulate ourselves, the acknowledgement is appropriate. But we must not linger too long on our achievements. There are many more mountains to climb.

SONG: AYFO OREE (No. 14)

FAMILY

Family and friendship are like the air we breathe. We cannot really live without them. We are not suited for loneliness. We crave the warmth of human concern. We need to give our love and we need to receive the love of others. Family and friends pay us the tribute of caring. Our pain becomes their pain; our pleasure becomes their pleasure. Through their love, we come to love ourselves and find our self-respect.

There are many families to which we belong which deserve our love and devotion. There is the family of our mother and father, brothers and sisters, grandparents and cousins. Without them we would have no life. There is also the family of the Jewish people in which our ancestors grew up for over four thousand years with the help of many brave and wise teachers. Without them we would have no past. There is even the family of humanity into which every child is born which reaches out to cover all the world, and which makes each of us the brother and the sister of the other. Without them we would have no future.

SONG: Y'ROOSHALIEYIM SHEL ZAHAV (No. 101)

LOYALTY

Loyalty is life. We live through the loyalty of others, not only the devotion of living family and friends, but also the loyalty of the past to the future. Countless numbers of our ancestors worked, saved, and gave up their pleasure to provide for generations yet unborn. They pursued distant goals they knew they would never reach in order that their children and grandchildren could enjoy the fruit of their efforts. The mountain of human culture is built out of many layers of human achievement, each generation resting on the work of the one before.

We are here today because the people of the past did not forget us. Our ancestors have planted and we have reaped. Let us also live for more than the present. Let us also work for those who will follow.

SONG: NAASE SHALOM (No. 69)

MITSVA PRESENTATION

RESPONSE

(From a representative of the community)

CANDLELIGHTING

(Family and friends light the lights of the Menorah.)

SONG: HAVA NAGEELA (No. 42)

MITSVA IV (HUMANISM)

SONG: SHALOM L'YISRAEL (No. 82)

SEVEN PRINCIPLES

A religion is a philosophy of life. Our religion is our philosophy of life. It is the set of principles and beliefs by which we seek to guide our lives. It is that set of ideas and ideals which we seek to transmit to our children. It is that combination of hopes and aspirations which defines the future we try to achieve.

Our religion determines the way we see reality, both the reality outside and the reality within ourselves. What we truly believe about ourselves and others, what we truly feel about our power and the power of other people controls what we do. If we think of ourselves as nothing, then we shall be nothing. If we think of ourselves as strong, then we shall act with strength.

SONG: HINNAY MA TOV (No. 47)

HUMANISM

The world we live in is ageless. It has no beginning and no end. It has no author and no conclusion. It may explode and contract. It may expand and shrink. But it never dies. It is simply there—with its infinite variety and its never ending change.

People give meaning to the universe. If we call to the stars and say "Tell me the purpose of life," the stars are silent. If we caress the earth and ask "What shall I do?", the earth gives no reply. If we pursue the wind and plead "Let me know the path that I must follow," the wind has no answer. The universe with all its complexity is dumb. It can neither love nor hate. It can neither be born nor die.

People give meaning to the universe. The commands of the gods are only the echo of our own striving. Although we are part of the world, we are different from all other things. We can hear and speak. We can love and hate. We can choose and deny. Out of our needs arise desires. And out of desire arises our passion for life. We are not told to be happy. We simply want to be.

SONG: SAHAKEE (No. 78)

SELF-RESPECT

Self-respect is never a gift. It is always an achievement. Neither the flattery of friends nor the reassurance of family will give us the feeling of self-worth. Neither the counseling of therapists nor the comforts of religion will elevate our dignity. Self-esteem is the child of competence. It is the offspring of personal skill. People who believe that they are able to help themselves and to help others will respect themselves.

People who like themselves believe that they have power. They believe that they have the power to determine the course of their own lives. They believe that they have the competence to be useful to others. They believe that they have the strength to make decisions even when the consequences of their decisions cannot easily be predicted. They even know that when they give to others they do not threaten their own welfare. For their own security lies in no possession. It resides in their own creative skill.

SONG: LAM'TSAPPEEM (No. 56)

AUTONOMY

Many people choose to live without dignity. They choose to be like little children and to place the responsibility for their lives in the hands of outside powers. So if they are happy, it is not because of their decision. And if they suffer, it is not because of their desire. They are blameless and powerless before the might of the world.

People of dignity are men and women who see their freedom and value it. They perceive that the quality of their life is their decision and that no suffering justifies passive acceptance. Although they are limited by the human condition, although they are assaulted by every natural provocation, they refuse to surrender their self-esteem. For what else is human dignity than to acknowledge that we are masters of our fate and captains of our soul?

SONG: OUT OF THE NIGHT (No. 76)

SELF-RELIANCE

People who respect themselves respect their own power. They understand their potential and do not avoid fulfilling it. If they confess their weaknesses from time to time, they do so realistically and with no intention of escaping action.

If they feel despair in the hour of crisis, they admit their fear and seek to dispel it.

Many people make a religion out of pleading helplessness. They devise rituals of despair to dramatize their conviction that they can do nothing to change their condition. Apathy becomes their best friend and self-pity becomes their constant companion. Their morality is reduced to two commandments: do nothing, and feel sorry for yourself.

The reality of human power gives the lie to this religion. Ordinary people can do extraordinary things if they have the strength to see their strength. Ordinary people can fulfill extraordinary dreams if they have the will to use their will. Arrogance is less the enemy of humanity than cowardice.

SONG: AYFO OREE (No. 14)

REASON

The age of science is the age of uncertainty. No more eternal answers console the human heart. No more changeless doctrines pacify the human mind. Religious dogma has been replaced by the humility of testing. Mythical fantasy has yielded to the careful search for reality.

The age of science is the age of courage. Bravery is not possible when all is predictable. Only the danger of surprise gives people the dignity of true freedom. The heroes of modern times are no fanatic believers. They are the people of patience who are strong enough to live with uncertainty. They are the people of integrity who are honest enough to wait for reasonable answers. They are the men and women of good humor who can value what they cannot totally explain.

Love is no less lovely because we do not yet know the chemistry of feeling. Beauty is no less beautiful because we do not yet understand the physics of thought. Even the wonders of nature are no less wondrous because she has not yet revealed to us the secret of her evolution. If the experience of these mysteries inspires us, what more is required?

SONG: KAMIEYEEM (No. 51)

LOVE

Newborn infants come into the world in helpless dependency, with only the knowledge of how to receive. As they grow up, as they cease to be children, they sense a new power—not the power to demand love, but rather the power to express love.

To sense that we not only need to be helped but also need to help, to feel that we not only require the care of others but also are able to give care, is the beginning of inner security. We do not transcend our loneliness by only finding others to love us. We transcend our sense of separation by finding others to love. In the act of being useful, in the work of fulfilling the desires and needs of other human beings, we feel our creative power and discover our strength. True love is an ironic deed. It binds us closer to other people while it awakens within us the thrill of independence. The more we help, the stronger we feel; and the stronger we feel, the more secure we become.

Love is the developed art of expressing our human power through the act of giving to others. It overwhelms our fears and gives us hope through the promise of our strength.

SONG: SHEEM'OO (No. 83)

JUDAISM

Each of us is the total of his yesterdays. Layers of experience rise in solid succession to build the personal present out of past performance. We can never escape our memories nor elude the imprint of daily experience. The power of our nostalgia always shapes our desire and decision.

Jewishness is not a matter of religious belief. It is not a matter of ritual practice. Jewishness is the memory of our family past and the irresistible attraction of family roots. Einstein and David were both Jews. But they were bound together by neither shared values nor shared ideas. They were united through time by the force of family loyalty.

Since family tradition is part of our uniqueness it deserves our wise respect. If it plays the taskmaster and beats us with the whip of conformity, then we shall, with justice, resist its malice. But if it acts the teacher and guides us gently to wisdom, we shall embrace it with the tribute of our consent.

SONG: Y'ROOSHALIEYIM SHEL ZAHAV (No. 101)

ADOLESCENCE

The cycle of life is like the cycle of the seasons. It never stops. It repeats itself in the individual story of every plant, every flower, every bird, and every beast. Although we are wiser and more powerful than any other living beings, we are, like all other creatures, obedient to an eternal rhythm. The winter of the womb is followed by the spring of youth, and the summer of maturity yields to the autumn of decay. We cannot remain forever young. Whether we accept or resist reality, we must grow up.

SONG: B'AYLE HAYADIM (No. 22)

GROWING UP

(Choose One)

To be thirteen is to stand between two worlds, the past of childhood and the promise of adolescence. The middle years of teenage are often very hard to cope with. They are a testing ground for adult life. If we are too dependent on others we must learn to become more independent. If we think too little of our talents, we must train ourselves to respect them. If we are afraid of the future, we must grow accustomed to live with the surprise of challenge. Adolescence can be wasted in fear and in laziness so that growing up is too painful to bear. Or it can be a time of happy excitement when new responsibility becomes a pleasure and new learning becomes our hope for success.

To be sixteen is to stand in the doorway of adulthood. It is to confront the meaning of what growing up is all about. It is to experience both the terror and the joy of being in charge of your own life. To be sixteen is to know that childish behavior no longer works and that new skills have to be learned. We need to be more honest, more decisive, more creative, more responsible, more loving, and more open than we have ever been before. We need to affirm our own potential for happiness.

SONG: NAE HAOR (No. 70)

FAMILY

Family and friendship are like the air we breathe; we cannot really live without them. We are not suited for loneliness. We crave the warmth of human concern. We need to give our love. We need to receive the love of others. Family and friends pay us the tribute of caring. Our pain becomes their pain; our pleasure becomes their pleasure. Through their love we come to love ourselves and find our self-respect.

There are many families to which we belong which deserve our love and devotion. There is the family of our mother and father, brothers and sisters, grandparents and cousins. Without them we would have no life. There is also the family of the Jewish people in which our ancestors grew up for over four thousand years with the help of many brave and wise teachers. Without them, we would have no past. There is even the family of humanity into which every child is born, which reaches out to cover all the world, and which makes each of us the brother and the sister of the other. Without them, we would have no future.

SONG: HINNAY MA TOV (No. 47)

MITSVA PRESENTATION

RESPONSE

(From a representative of the community)

CANDLELIGHTING

(Family and friends light the lights of the Menorah)

SONG: HAVA NAGEELA (No. 42)

MITSVA V (WOMEN)

SONG: SHALOM L'YISRAEL (No. 82)

LIFE

We live and find it good to live. We feel the invitation of doing and rush to the surprise of new excitement. We sense the opportunity of our talents and hurry to taste their fulfillment. Interesting events seize our attention and make us want to understand them. Unselfish acts capture our heart and fill our being with boundless promise. If we let the light of our possibility shine through, it will give us hope.

SONG: B'ROOKHEEM HAHIEYEEM (No. 25)

HAPPINESS

The meaning of life is happiness. Yet happiness is not some faraway goal we strive to achieve, some future joy we suffer to reach. It is the awareness of what is valuable in the here and now. It is the special pleasure of helping others, the beauty of friendship, the thrill of running, the excitement of learning, the opportunity of challenge. Happiness is the feeling of aliveness that needs the strength and hope of youth.

SONG: KAMIEYEEM (No. 51)

LOVE

Newborn infants come into the world in helpless dependency, with only the knowledge of how to receive. As they grow up, as they cease to be children, they sense a new power—not the power to demand love, but rather the power to express love.

To sense that we not only need to be helped but also need to help, to feel that we not only require the care of others but also are able to give care, is the beginning of inner security. We do not transcend our loneliness by only finding others to love us. We transcend our sense of separation by finding others to love. In the act of being useful, in the work of fulfilling the desires and needs of other human beings, we feel our creative power and discover our strength. The more we help the stronger we feel, and the stronger we feel the more secure we become.

Love is the developed art of expressing our human power through the act of giving to others. It overwhelms our fears and gives us hope through the promise of our own strength.

SONG: SHEEM' OO (No. 83)

DIGNITY

Self-respect is never a gift. It is always an achievement. Neither the flattery of friends nor the reassurance of family will give us the feeling of self-worth. Neither the counseling of therapists nor the comforts of religion will elevate our dignity. Self-esteem is the child of competence. It is the offspring of personal skill. People who think that they are unable to help themselves or to help others cannot respect themselves.

People who like themselves believe that they have power. They believe that they have the power to determine the course of their own lives. They believe that they have the competence to be useful to others. They believe that they have the strength to make decisions even when the consequences of their decisions cannot early be predicted. They even know that when they give to others they do not threaten their own welfare. For their own security lies in no possession. It resides in their own creative skill.

SONG: LAM'TSAPPEEM (No. 56)

OPENNESS

Youth is not so much a condition of the body as it is a state of the mind. Many people are old at thirteen/sixteen, their curiosity chilled by fear. Others are young at eighty, their perceptions warmed by the courage to love surprise. Physical youth fades quickly, but the springtime of our mind lasts as long as we will it. To find in each new event a teacher and to see in each new day the excitement of hope is never to grow old. Wisdom is not the product of wintry age. It is the special gift of the eternally young.

SONG: EREV SHEL SHOSHANNEEM (No. 30)

FAMILY

Family and friendship are like the air we breathe. We cannot really live without them. We are not suited for loneliness. We crave the warmth of human concern. We need to give our love. We need to receive the love of others. Family and friends pay us the tribute of caring. Our pain becomes their pain; our pleasure becomes their pleasure. Through their love we come to love ourselves and find our self-respect.

There are many families to which we belong which deserve our love and devotion. There is the family of our mother and father, brothers and sisters, grandparents and cousins. Without them we would have no life. There is also the family of the Jewish people in which our ancestors grew up for over four thousand years with the help of many brave and wise teachers. Without them we would have no past. There is even the family of humanity into which every child is born, which reaches out to cover all the world, and which makes each of us the brother and the sister of the other. Without them we would have no future.

SONG: Y'ROOSHALIEYIM SHEL ZAHAV (No. 101)

LOYALTY

Loyalty is life. We live through the loyalty of others, not only the devotion of living family and friends, but also the loyalty of the past to the future. Countless numbers of our ancestors worked, saved, and gave up their pleasure to provide for generations yet unborn. They pursued distant goals which they knew they would never reach, in order that their children and grandchildren could enjoy the fruit of their efforts. The mountain of human culture is built out of many layers of human achievement, each generation resting on the work of the one before.

We are here today because the people of the past did not forget us. Our ancestors have planted and we have reaped. Let us also live for more than the present. Let us also work for those who will follow.

SONG: HINNAY MA TOV (No. 47)

WOMEN

Women have a tradition all their own. It is a tradition which has often been ignored in a world governed by men. Against the persecution, exploitation, and boorishness of masculine power—against the self-demeaning consent of women themselves to their own subservience—many women throughout history have sought to affirm their dignity and their equality.

Jewish women have a tradition all their own. It is more than a tradition of loyal wife and devoted mother. It is more than a history of self-sacrificing love and menial service. It is a proud adventure of achievement, mastery, and wisdom.

In the days when the men of Israel cowered before the armies of the Canaanite kings and were unable to defend their farms and their homes, the woman Deborah stood up to take command, to inspire their courage, and to lead them to victory.

Growing Up (Mitsva) 353

In the years when Israel was torn by civil war, when Greek and Roman armies threatened her security and her freedom, the woman Salomé emerged to become the queen and ruler of the Jews. She made peace among the warring men, brought justice to the people, and gave hope to those who despaired. Her will was loving and strong.

In a troubled hour of modern Israel's struggle for survival, with her leadership deeply divided among political rivals, with Arab enemies waiting for the moment of weakness, the woman Golda Meir was chosen to be the ruler of her people. She united her nation, inspired her citizens with trust and confidence, and revealed to the world the power of the Jewish will to live.

There are many women of dignity in the Jewish tradition.

There are many women of dignity in the human tradition.

SONG: HANAAVA (No. 36)

FUTURE

The future of women will be more interesting than their past. The world has awakened to the power and beauty of the female potential. Although the past has cruelly wasted some of its greatest human resources, the future will be wiser and more considerate.

Women will continue to be wives and mothers, but they will also be more. Deborah, Salomé, and Golda Meir will no longer be startling exceptions. They will be part of a sisterhood of self-respecting persons who will be able to share leadership and social decision with men.

Equality and dignity are human rights. They are the rights of Jews. They are the rights of women.

SONG: AYFO OREE (No. 14)

MITSVA PRESENTATION

RESPONSE

(From a representative of the community)

Growing Up (Mitsva)

CANDLELIGHTING

(Family and friends light the lights of the Menorah)

SONG: HAVA NAGEELA (No. 42)

3
EDUCATIONAL ACHIEVEMENT

SONG: NAASE SHALOM (No. 69)

EDUCATION

Education is life: From the moment we are born we begin to learn, and until the day we die we continue to learn.

We are born incomplete: Our possibility is so much greater than our reality. The infant is only an intimation of the adult to be. But neither instinct nor destiny are enough to guarantee our future. Our big brain and open mind respond to the world and help us go beyond our inheritance to understanding and wisdom. Something is always happening to us, and we change with every experience.

Long after our body ceases to grow, our mind continues to grow. Even when we become physical adults, the curious child never completely leaves us. Maturity is as elusive as perfection.

SONG: SAHAKEE (No. 78)

PASSAGE

Life is purpose. Without goals and aspirations, we would cease to be vital. We would also cease to be human.

Purpose comes from our needs, our instinct for survival, our desire for pleasure and dignity. They give us the motivation and the passion to go beyond our present condition and to strive to become more than we are. They are the fire which fuels our ambition.

No life is long enough to satisfy all our desires. There is so much we want to be, so much we need to be, that our years are inadequate to accommodate all our dreams. No sooner do we complete one task than another awaits us. Sometimes we have to make painful choices, choosing one path over another, forgoing one dream to fulfill another vision and never knowing for sure that the decision we made was the right decision.

Life is passage. We move from achievement to achievement, all of them linked by the striving which gives our existence meaning.

SONG: BAMAKOM (No. 19)

CURIOSITY

As human beings, we never need to lose the openness of childhood. Our taste for the freshness of things persists far beyond the youth of the body. Even in old age, the wonders of the world can still remain wondrous.

A lively curiosity enables us to change for the better. If we are too pleased with what we are and what we do and what we think, we close our minds to new opportunities and feed on our own self-satisfaction. If we are too afraid of shame and failure, we choose familiar tasks which are too easy for us and which never really test our possibility. Only when we are willing to explore new perspectives and new skills, only when we are willing to risk our self-esteem in climbing mountains we have never climbed before, do we discover the excitement of living.

The good life is more than safety and repetition. It is the risk of adventure. If we can control our fear, we will discover that we can climb higher than we ever imagined.

SONG: LAMTSAPPEEM (No. 56)

DISCIPLINE

Wishing is never enough. If we wait for success, it will most likely elude us. And if we rely on luck and destiny to get what we want, they will prove less dependable than their reputation suggests.

Dreams need work and self-control to become more than dreams. They also need planning and the postponement of pleasure. Running away from frustration and the tedium of daily tasks is only a momentary satisfaction. The wisdom we want, the skills we need, demand training. Our potential is a weak muscle that needs constant exercise. Our intention alone will never make it stronger. It requires an earnest discipline.

Talent is useful for the successes of life, but it is rarely sufficient. Too many talented people betray their promise by their laziness. Effort and the willingness to work make the difference. True education is not a gift. It is an achievement.

SONG: MEE HAHAM (No. 65)

GROWTH

When we are children, we want so desperately to grow up. We see the power and privileges of adults and we want them for ourselves.

When we are adults, we are less naïve. We see the obligations more than the privileges and we know that we have tasted only a small part of our power. In fact, we realize that we never really stop growing up.

Our power to learn and to change keeps us younger than our body suggests. Our self-awareness and our actions take longer than our limbs to reach maturity. Awkwardness is more than physical. It is also a mental condition, a roughness of the human spirit that comes from too little knowledge and too little experience. Grace is an inner strength and refinement which emerges out of hard striving and achievement. Every fulfilled dream makes it smoother and more satisfying.

Growing up does not end at thirteen—or sixteen—or twenty. It has barely begun.

SONG: BASHANA HABAA (No. 21)

SELF-ESTEEM

Self-esteem is our dignity. It is our sense of personal independence. It is the experience of turning the power of our possibility into reality.

There are times in our lives when we feel our self-esteem most strongly. When an important task is finished, when a course of study is completed, when a new skill is mastered, when the people we respect give us their respect for the things we do—our perception of our own dignity becomes bolder and fills our lives with a deep satisfaction. It is good to know that we can do what we want to do and that others can see our competence.

If we pause for a moment to congratulate ourselves, the acknowledgment is appropriate. But we must not linger too long on our achievements. There are many more mountains to climb.

SONG: AYFO OREE (No. 14)

MEMORIAL

We are not the first generation to strive for self-esteem. We are not the first people to dream dreams and to work hard to fulfill them. There are millions of people who came before, who lived in earlier times and in more primitive places. There are ancestors of long ago who gave us life and culture, who gave up the pleasures of the present to guarantee the survival of the future. There are loved ones who bore us and cared for us who left the marks of their achievement upon our lives.

We are the heirs to a legacy of learning. What we know rests on the discoveries of the people of the past. What we create builds on the inventiveness of those who preceded us. As others did not betray their potential, so must we not betray ours. Our achievements are our gifts to the future.

SONG: SHEEM'OO (No. 83)

HONORING OF GRADUATES

4
CONFIRMATION (CELEBRATION OF COMMITMENT)

SONG: NAASE SHALOM (No. 69)

COMMITMENT

Community is very important. Human nature resists aloneness. It prefers the company of other people. Belonging to a group, whether that group be a family, a congregation, a people, a nation, offers us advantages we cannot find in solitude.

A good community reinforces our sense of personal self-esteem. It makes us feel wanted, important, and honest. It gives us people who share our convictions and ideals and who make us feel comfortable to speak freely.

From time to time, it is good for us to confirm our membership in the community to which we belong—especially if we were born into the group and never had the chance to choose it on our own—especially if we have come to the community from somewhere else and want to celebrate our attachment—especially if we have studied the beliefs and principles of the group and want to renew our commitments.

The community of humanistic Judaism is our community. It is also a special part of our personal identity. When members of our congregation have enriched their awareness of being humanistic Jews through study and reflection, it is very important to celebrate this new awareness. Confirmation belongs to no particular age or time of life. It does not stop at thirteen—or at sixteen. It happens when we prepare for it and when we need it.

SONG: HINNAY MA TOV (No. 47)

HUMANISM

This evening we confirm our commitment to humanism.

Humanism is the way we see ourselves and the world we live in. It is the way we see our own power and our place in the order of things.

If we are humanists, we do not dwell on our weakness and our helplessness. We do not linger on our fears and anxieties. We are careful to remember that our limitations can become our excuses. If we think about them too often, we tend to exaggerate them. We become too timid for happiness.

If we are humanists, we start with our limitations, but we do not stop there. We move on to the power we have to improve our lives. We know that we can know more than we know. We know that we can do more than we do. Our mistakes are matched by our talents. Our anxieties are confronted by our strength.

If we are humanists, we recognize that life has more possibilities than our fears will allow. We do not indulge our fear. We resist it.

CONGREGATION

We confirm our commitment to humanism.

SONG: SAHAKEE (No. 78)

DIGNITY

This evening we confirm our commitment to human dignity.

Dignity is a human need, like survival and pleasure. It is also a human value which stands above all other values. It is the moral guide to our life.

If we pursue our dignity we do not hide from the reality of our own freedom. We do not run away from our own responsibility. We know that no one else can make our decisions for us, and that, in the end, we always consent to what we do. If we pursue our dignity, we seek to become the masters of our own lives. We do not embrace pleasure when it makes us more dependent. We do not avoid pain when it makes us more independent. Self-reliance is a virtue, even if it is difficult to achieve.

If we pursue our dignity, we do not strive to become the humble servants of any authority. We will not bow our heads in worship. But we will extend our hands in friendship.

CONGREGATION

We confirm our commitment to human dignity, both our own and that of others.

SONG: OUT OF THE NIGHT (No. 76)

JEWISH PEOPLE

This evening we confirm our commitment to the Jewish people.

The Jewish people is our extended family. It is the source of a compelling identity which we both inherit and choose. Although it began in one land, the world is now its home.

If we are part of the Jewish people, we have roots that go back four thousand years. We have memories that embrace almost every historic age, almost every civilization. Not very much in human awareness has failed to touch the Jewish experience.

If we are part of the Jewish people, we are the heirs to an old and powerful culture. Prose and poetry, music and dance, holidays and ceremonies emerged from our history and made us unique. Other nations shared our values, but our ancestors gave them a Jewish flavor.

If we are part of the Jewish people, we feel humanism in the bones of our history. Our leaders told us that the universe offers us justice and compassion, but our experience told us that destiny is often cruel and unfair. In the end, if there is going to be any justice or compassion, it must come from us.

CONGREGATION

We confirm our commitment to the value of Jewish identity and to the survival of the Jewish people.

SONG: AM YISRAEL HIE (No. 9)

HUMANITY

This evening we confirm our commitment to all humanity.

The human race is also our extended family. More than any piece of land, more than any natural environment, humanity is our home. Endowed with self-awareness, reason, and hope, we stand separate from all other creatures, bound together by our own uniqueness.

If we confirm our human identity, we confirm the reality of human nature. Although each individual is unique, although each culture is special, there is a common humanity that defines us all. Love and anger, compassion and hate, reason and intuition are not the possession of any one people. They belong to us all and build the human condition we all share.

If we confirm our human identity, we confirm our power to cross the boundaries of family, race, and nation and to identify with the humanness of people beyond. Our human connection does not diminish the value of our individuality or the importance of our Jewishness. It enriches them and gives them an appropriate setting, a context where the similarities are far more important than the differences.

CONGREGATION

We confirm our commitment to the unity of all people.

SONG: AHEE ADAM (No. 4)

COMMUNITY

This evening we confirm our commitment to our community.

Our community is more than a building. It is more than a congregation. It is our extended family. It is our humanistic Jewish home where we can celebrate the identities we feel so strongly, where we can work together to help each other, where we can make friendship grow.

If we are part of our community we know that we do not stand alone. Other people share our thoughts and feelings. Other people share our beliefs and convictions. In a world that often does not share our point of view, there is a comfort in togetherness. Solidarity is a welcome pleasure.

If we are part of our community we know that we are better together than we are alone. In solitude we cannot really discover who we are and what we do. Only the stimulus of other people who prod us through friendship, challenge, and shared work can awaken us to our potential. We are social beings made more real by the presence and love of others.

CONGREGATION

We confirm our commitment to the welfare of our community.

SONG: AYFO OREE (No. 14)

MEMORIAL

This evening we confirm our gratitude to the heroes of our past.

The heroes of our past are the human roots of our present commitments. They are the many Jews who valued their power, their responsibility, and their identity. They are the numberless non-Jews who bequeathed their thoughts and deeds to the progress of humanity.

If we truly confirm our roots, we do not do so slavishly. The past is not well-served when it is worshiped. Our heroes were neither gods nor saints. They were eminently human, striving to reach goals they often never reached. Their legacy, like all legacies, is an imperfect wisdom. Just as they took their past and changed it for the better, so must we do the same with our own heritage.

If we truly confirm our roots, we do not do so pretentiously. Not all of our heroes were famous men and women. Not all of them wrote books and became the leaders of noble causes. Many of them were patient workers and loyal followers. Many of them were caring ancestors who spoke their humanism more through their deeds than through their words. Many of them were family and friends who day by day, undramatically, revealed the truth through example.

CONGREGATION

We confirm our commitment to the heroes of our past, and to the better world which they strove to achieve.

SONG: SHEEM'OO (No. 83)

5 MARRIAGE

ORDER OF CELEBRATION

1. **WELCOME**
2. **REFLECTIONS ON MARRIAGE**
3. **REMARKS**
4. **VOWS**
5. **RING EXCHANGE**
6. **CUP OF UNITY**
7. **ANNOUNCEMENT**
8. **BREAKING GLASS**

1. WELCOME

(Choose One)

LOVE

SHEEM'OO SHEEM'OO OHAVAY AHAVA
KEER'OO KEER'OO MOSHEEAY Y'SHOOA
KEE AYN Y'SHOOA B'LEE AHAVA
O AHAVA AHAVA KAYN T'HEE

Listen now you lovers of love
Here this you seekers of happiness
There is no happiness without love.

LIFE

We affirm the power of love and life in all the world. We affirm the power of love and life in every human being. On this day, we reaffirm the power of love and life in (groom) and (bride).

JOY

ASHRAY HABAEEM B'SHEM HAHIEYEEM.
ASHRAY HABAEEM B'SHEM HAAHAVA.

Happy are those who come in the name of life.
Happy are those who come in the name of love.

---

2. REFLECTIONS ON MARRIAGE

(Choose One)

CHALLENGE

Marriage is an opportunity for happiness. It is also risky business. Two people who choose the partnership of love and loyalty need many skills to make it work. They need patience, kindness, generosity, good humor, and the ability to compromise. They need persistence, nurturing, trust, discretion, and the willingness to be vulnerable.

But almost nothing offers a greater possibility for living life well. When marriage works it justifies all the effort. Life is richer when experience is shared. We are more ourselves when we are responding to the stimulus of others, especially when we are responding to the gift of love. Good lovers bring out the best in each other.

If romance leads to friendship, if coming together makes room for individual space, if dreams turn into realistic expectations, if the dazzle of beginnings yields to long-run commitment, if one is always willing to demand of oneself what one demands of others, then love becomes more profound and the bond of marriage is strengthened.

To choose marriage is to accept a challenge, the challenge that love provides when it wants to grow.

COMMITMENT

Marriage is never easy. For two people to blend their personalities into a lasting relationship is no mean feat. Much more than falling in love is required. Intelligence, patience, compassion, and good humor are indispensible. Even discretion and compromise have their time and place.

Good marriages do not happen all by themselves. They require human determination and commitment. They require the willingness to go beyond momentary frustration to pursue common goals and shared unions. They need the wisdom to distinguish between the trivial and the unimportant, between the time to laugh and the time to be serious. They need more nurturing than lecturing, more kindness then self-righteousness, more listening then bossing. In a good marriage falling in love becomes loving—something less noisy and much more profound.

LOVE

Love is so popular that it is sometimes drowned in clichés. Yet no human emotion is more important for happiness. Without the opportunity to love or be loved, we turn inward and become absorbed with ourselves. Or we turn to fantasy, praise our independence, and deny our loneliness. We are ironic beings. Our self-reliance needs other people. Our lovers make us strong because they help us respond to the world, because they draw us outward from ourselves and move us to care and to hope.

True marriage is the outer sign of inner love. It does not steal our personhood. It does not compromise our independence. It gives a warm and comfortable setting in which to grow, to share, to explore. In the presence of each other, lovers discover themselves. Husband and wife, man and woman, give themselves more generously to life, because they are more generous one to the other. Hope comes from love. In the intimacy of mutual commitment we learn that the world can be good.

MATURITY

Marriage is a labor of love. It is also a labor of intelligence, patience, compassion, and good humor. Human relations that last require more than passion. They require a commitment to share the pain as well as the pleasure. They need the sensitivity to know when it is time to complain and when it is time to be supportive. They demand the insight to see through foolish mistakes and uncontrolled anger to the loyalty beyond. Marriages grow and change like all living things. When relationships are mature, husband and wife are the best of friends, desiring and enjoying each other, without any need for pretense, and without clutching and desperation. Marriages that last add respect and honesty to love.

PARTNERSHIP

Marriage is a partnership. It is not a merger in which two people lose their individual identities. It is not a union of master and servant. It is a commitment, reinforced by love, of equals who discover that they are more fulfilled together than they are apart. In a good marriage husband and wife are aware of how much they need each other—of how much they transform each other. Joy, laughter, caring, tenderness, and hope are the gifts of love. In the presence of loneliness and strangers it is difficult to express all that we are. In the presence of love we feel our power and experience life in a new way. And you are partners in love who taste life more fully because you have found each other.

SELF-DISCOVERY

Loneliness is not the best of human conditions. Although being alone is sometimes necessary and desirable, being alone all the time undermines the human spirit and prevents us from being what we ought to be. We are people needing people. We are social beings in search of human contact. We are persons reaching out, seeking completeness in the encounter with those we love. In the presence of friends and lovers we discover more about ourselves. We come to understand our need to touch, our need to communicate, our need to share.

Marriage is the celebration of our basic human needs. If it is good, it does not limit us. It does not restrict our freedom; rather it fulfills us. It takes our power to love and to share and channels it into long-run satisfaction. Bonds of loyalty and commitment allay our fear of being vulnerable and open up to us the pleasures of intimacy. In marriage we become friends and partners in the exploration of ourselves and the world we live in.

3. REMARKS

(Choose One)

LOVE

(Groom) _____ and (Bride) _____, we are all standing here to celebrate the most important reality of your lives, the special relationship of love and loyalty that defines your friendship.

Love is more than a verbal promise. It is more than a feeling inside. Love, in its true sense, is a behavior. It is the way you strive to treat each other every single day of your experience together. Love is a set of personal skills that enables each of you to care for the other intimately and intensely.

It is, first of all, the skill of respect. (Groom) _____, you are a unique human being. There is no other (groom) _____ like you in the world. You have your own distinctive talents, ideas, and perspective. You are always entitled to be yourself. And (bride) _____ loves you because you are what you are. She knows that her project in life is not to turn you into (bride) _____, but to let you be (groom) _____.

(Bride) _____, you are a unique human being. There is no other (bride) _____ like you in the world. You have your own special power, values, and style of being. You are always entitled to be yourself. And (groom) _____ loves you because you are what you are. He knows that his project in your relationship is not to turn you into (groom) _____, but to let you be (bride) _____.

If you love each other, you respect each other; you respect each other's individual reality. You give each other enough space to grow as persons. But you stand close enough together so that you can share the adventure of life, one with the other.

Love is also the skill of trust. (Groom) _____, you are standing next to your best friend. She must be more than your wife. She must be the person in whom you place the greatest faith and confidence. (Bride) _____ is truly trustworthy. You can share with her your most intimate thoughts and feelings, thoughts and feelings you would share with no one else. As your best friend, she will treat them tenderly, because she cares what ultimately happens to you. She wants you to be fulfilled.

(Bride) _____, you are standing next to your best friend. (Groom) _____ must be more than your husband. He must be the person in whom you place your greatest faith and confidence. He is trustworthy. You can share with him your most intimate thoughts and feelings. As your best friend, he will not betray you because he cares what ultimately happens to you. He wants you to be fulfilled.

Love is, above all, the willingness to help. There will be days, (groom) _____, when you will feel very strong and self-sufficient, when you will feel that you need nobody. But there will also be times when you will feel very needy. And then you can turn to (bride) _____, your best friend, and say "I need you." And, because she loves you, she will say "Let me help you."

There will be days, (bride) _____, when you too will feel strong and completely in charge of your life. But there will be times when you will feel very needy. And then you can turn to (groom) _____, your best friend, and say "I need you." And because he loves you, he will respond "Let me help you."

No human being is fully independent. We need each other. We lean on each other. We help each other. Marriage is a sign of our mutual dependency. We are not happy when we are always alone. We crave the intimacy of reliable love.

DISCOVERY

(Groom) _____ and (bride) _____, we have all come together, your family and friends, to help you celebrate your love for one another and your decision to be husband and wife.

At this special time it is very important for you to remember the reasons why you are in love and why you belong together—and especially all the important discoveries you have made about each other. You have certainly discovered how good you are for each other. (Groom) _____, (bride) _____ has come into your life and transformed it. She has made an enormous difference. And you are a better person because she is there. (Bride) _____, (groom) _____ has come into your life and transformed it. He has made an enormous difference. And you are a better person because he is there.

Each of you is more complete because you have each other. That is the chemistry of love. True lovers evoke the best from those they love and make them aware of feelings and possibilities they never experienced before.

You have certainly discovered that you respect each other. Love needs respect to make it healthy. It needs the recognition that each of you gives the other, the recognition that a good marriage does not require you to give up your personal identity and to surrender your individual style.

The sign of your respect is the way you listen to each other. Each of you is unique and special. Each of you has the need to be the master of his or her own destiny. Each of you has the right to be treated with dignity. The thoughts and feelings of each of you is of ultimate importance to both of you. And you must always take the time to hear each other and to understand each other. In a humanistic marriage there are no masters and slaves, bosses and servants, rulers and subordinates. There are equals loving equals.

You have certainly discovered that you are the best of friends. You know that you can trust each other and depend on each other. No matter how old we may become, we still need nurturing and loyal support. We still need approval and encouragement to achieve what we want to achieve.

You nurture each other in many ways. You listen without being judgmental. You help without being self-sacrificing. You share without holding back. You resist fear without being naïve.

In short, you are a partnership in which the fulfillment of one depends on the fulfillment of the other.

Above all, you have discovered that you are responsible for your own lives. Bad-humored people go through life always imagining that what happens to them is the fault of destiny and other people. Good-humored people accept their limitations. They avoid excuses. They know that, despite all the intrusions of surprise, the quality of their life is up to them.

And the quality of your life will depend on the small decisions of daily existence that define your character and commitment. It will especially depend on your always being there when the other really needs you. It will especially depend on your willingness to direct your anger to those who deserve it and not to those who love you. It will especially depend on your ability to distinguish between the important and the trivial and to avoid giving important energy to petty concerns.

The task of determining your own future is a little bit frightening. But it is also exciting, especially since you are undertaking the adventure of life together. You share many hopes and dreams. Do not betray them. Find strength in yourself in each other.

4. VOWS

(Choose One)

LOVE

In the spirit of love and loyalty let me address this question to you (groom) _____.

Do you, (groom) _____ freely affirm that (bride) _____ is indeed your wife? And do you promise in the presence of your family and friends, to respect her, to trust her, and to care for her?

(Groom: I do.)

And in the same spirit of love and loyalty let me address this question to you (bride) _____.

Do you (bride) _____ freely affirm that (groom) _____ is indeed your husband? And do you promise, in the presence of your family and friends to respect him, to trust him, and to care for him?

(Bride: I do.)

COMMITMENT

This celebration is a public affirmation of a reality that already exists in your lives and of pledges you have already made privately. Therefore, let me ask you to share with your family and friends the commitment you have made to each other.

Do you (groom) _____ love (bride) _____? And have you pledged to her your caring respect and loyal support?

(Groom: I have.)

And do you (bride) _____ love (groom) _____? And have you pledged to him your caring respect and loyal support?

(Bride: I have.)

5. RING EXCHANGE

(Choose One)

STRENGTH

May I have the rings? (The leader takes the rings.)

These rings are strong. They are signs of your strength and your power, the power you have to practice the skills of love, the strength you possess to achieve your expectations, the determination you feel to fulfill the promise you have made to each other.

Take these rings and exchange them in the spirit of love. (Bride and groom take the rings and turn to each other.)

Groom: HARAY AT M'KOODESHET LEE B'TABBAAT ZOO K'DAT YISRAEL V'AHAVA. (Bride) _____, you are my wife in love and equality.

Bride: HARAY ATTA M'KOODASH LEE B'TABBAAT ZOO K'DAT YISRAEL V'AHAVA. (Groom) _____, you are my husband in love and equality.

SHARING

May I have the rings? (The leader takes the rings.)

These rings are reminders to you of an important power that you both possess— the power to give each other gifts of love. Every day of your life together presents you with the opportunity to share with each other the gifts of tenderness, understanding, and hope, the gifts of trust, respect, and loyalty.

Take these rings and exchange them in the spirit of generous love.

Groom: (Bride) _____, I give you this ring as a sign of my love, respect, and loyalty.

Bride: (Groom) _____, I give you this ring as a sign of my love, respect, and loyalty.

6. CUP OF UNITY

(Choose One)

SHARING

(Leader takes and holds goblet.)

This goblet is a single cup from which you both shall drink. It is a sign of your unity. Although you are two distinct persons, both respecting the equal dignity of the other, you have chosen to unite your lives and to seek your happiness together. You drink from the same cup to be reminded that you will share pain and pleasure, struggle and success.

ASHRAY HEHATAN V'HAKALLA SHEYIMTS'OO AHAVA B'NIS-SOOEEN.

Happy are a man and a woman who find love in marriage.

Take this cup and drink from it in the spirit of loving union.

(Bride and groom drink from the cup, each holding it for the other.)

This goblet is also a sign of your connection to others beyond yourselves. You live in a community of family and friends who support you with their love and who enrich your lives with the gifts of their own enthusiasm. Let them share in this cup as they share in your joy and fulfillment.

(Those standing in attendance share the cup.)

HAPPINESS

(Leader takes and holds goblet.)

This goblet is the cup of happiness, the happiness that you now seek together. Your individual joy will be all the greater because it is shared. Your individual fulfillment will be all the stronger because it rests in the fulfillment of the other.

In the culture of the Jewish people wine is the symbol of happiness. Take this goblet and drink the wine as an affirmation of your hope for the future, a future that welcomes your dreams and makes them real.

(Bride and groom drink from the cup, each holding it for the other.)

This goblet is also a reminder that you do not stand here alone. You are surrounded by family and friends who love you and whom you have invited to this celebration.

They have given you their loyal support in the past. They will continue to give you their love in the years to come. They will share your pleasure. They will help you deal with your pain. Their caring presence will give you strength and enrich your lives.

(Those standing in attendance share the cup.)

---

7. ANNOUNCEMENT

(Choose One)

I.

You have spoken your promise. You have exchanged the signs of your commitment to each other. You have drunk from the cup of unity. It is time for creativity.

Therefore, it is with great pleasure that I declare, that because of the special love and respect that you give to each other, that you (groom) _____ and you (bride) _____ are husband and wife.

May you find the happiness that you seek together.

II.

You have drunk from the cup of happiness and tested the wine of joy. And you have allowed us, your family and friends, to share in the celebration of your love.

Therefore, it is with great pleasure that we all declare that, because of your commitment one to the other that you (groom) _____ and you (bride) _____ are indeed husband and wife. You have married each other through your own design and determination. And we are your witnesses.

8. BREAKING GLASS

(Choose One)

GOOD LUCK

(Leader takes glass wrapped in napkin and places it under the foot of the groom.)

May the sound of this breaking glass be the sound of *mazeltov* (good luck).

EQUALITY

(Leader takes two glasses, each wrapped in its own napkin, and places one under the foot of the groom and one under the foot of the bride.)

May the sound of the glass you break together be the sound of *mazeltov* (good luck).

6
DEATH

ORDER OF MEMORIAL SERVICE

1. OPENING READING
2. EULOGY
3. SECOND READING
4. SILENT TRIBUTE
5. CLOSING WORDS

1. OPENING READING

(Choose One)

CONTINUITY

Death is something individual. Against the collective stream of life, it seems powerless. Particular flowers fade and die, but every spring repeats them in the cycle of nature. Individual man is a brief episode, but humanity bears the mark of immortality, renewed in every generation by the undying spark of life. We are, each of us, greater than ourselves. We survive in the children we create. We endure in the humanity we serve.

As an individual, separate and distinct, each of us is temporary, an ephemeral chapter in the saga of the universe. As a moment in the never-ending process of life, each of us is immortal, an expression of the persistent thrust of vital energy. The leaves of last year's summer have died and have vanished into the treasury of mother earth, but each one lives on in the renewal of every spring. Every person dies, but humanity survives. Every living thing perishes, but life persists.

COURAGE I

Human culture does not really thrive when everything is comfortable. Great civilizations have never emerged in the paradise of tropical islands and lush lagoons. They tend to grow where problems challenge human ingenuity. Flooded river valleys and rock-faced harbors, wintry plains and storm-assaulted coastlines—these are the settings for human progress and achievement. Where life is too easy, where leisure dulls ambition, the weather is more interesting than the people.

Our own striving builds on the striving of past generations. We are here today because pioneers crossed an ocean to build a new life in a new world, because immigrants believed that their lives and the lives of their children could be improved through dreams and hard work, because parents and grandparents disciplined their fear and their skepticism to risk new ventures and new careers. Although they talked a lot about safety and security, they were far bolder than they would choose to admit.

We can learn from their legacy of courage.

COURAGE II

Death needs courage. It is so overwhelmingly final that it fills our lives with dread and anxious fear. When it arrives at the end of a long and happy life it is never welcome, yet not deeply resented. But when it comes too soon, invading young lives, disrupting hopes and dreams, it adds anger to our fear. We cry out at the injustice of destiny and wait for answers that never seem to come.

Courage is the power to confront a world that is not always fair. It is the refusal to beg for what will never be given. It is the willingness to accept what cannot be changed.

Courage is loving life even in the face of death. It is sharing our strength with others even when we feel weak. It is embracing our family and friends even when we fear to lose them. It is opening ourselves to love, even for the last time.

Courage is self-esteem. It prefers quiet determination to whining. It prefers doing to waiting. It affirms that exits, like entrances, have their own dignity.

_____, whom I loved very much and still do, chose to die with dignity. We shall never forget his/her courage.

DIGNITY

Death is not always tragic.

If we have enough years to test our skills, if we can see and enjoy the results of our work, if we can nurture our family and have them near, if we can love our friends and share their pains and pleasures over many seasons, if we have the time to develop our own unique style and know that it will not easily be forgotten, if we can die quickly, without the agonies of prolonged suffering—well, then death is not tragic.

For some people, life scripts are never meaningful unless they last forever. Others derive their grace from the rhythm of growth, fulfillment, and decay. What never ends cannot be very precious. Today cannot be special if there is always a tomorrow.

In the flow of life, exits, like entrances, have their own dignity.

FAMILY

Life offers the gift of many blessings. None is more precious than the love of family and friends. In the strength and compassion of parents, in the mutual devotion of husband and wife, brother and sister, we find the security of love. For the landscape of our years is peopled by the presence of open hearts that exact no price for the gift of themselves.

When an intimate friend dies, sadness and despair are normal responses. Two people cannot share the best and worst of life in mutual experience and find that absence is trivial. The tribute of love is the pain of separation.

GIVING

Love is never self-sacrifice; it is never the act of giving up what belongs to us. Self-sacrifice is the twin of self-pity. If helping others means diminishing ourselves, then kindness is nothing more than the suicide of martyrdom. People who truly love may suffer, but they do not love in order to suffer. The heroes of our past gave us the best of their devotion and care without demanding our gratitude. They knew that the act of giving was its own compensation. They toiled beyond their energies and worked beyond their strength for the welfare of others. They saw that love was its own reward.

HOPE

We live and find it hard to live. We are consumed by the anxiety of desire and know that nature is stingy with satisfaction. We are terrified by the limits of our wisdom and shiver in the cold of human ignorance. Love touches us with the pleasure of fulfillment and runs away too soon. Pain squeezes the marrow of our bones and lingers with malice. If our suffering cries out for justice, the world answers with deaf defiance, and the darkness of evil is a persistent shadow.

We live and find it good to live. We feel the invitation of doing and rush to the surprise of new excitement. We sense the opportunity of our talents and plunge to taste their fulfillment. Bold events penetrate our mind and tease the ordering skills of our reason. Unselfish acts overwhelm our being and fill our hearts with the security of love. The world is an open door to vital variety; it stuns our hopes with boundless promise. For the light of our possibility shines through to dispel the darkness.

LOVE

Newborn infants come into the world in helpless dependency, with only the knowledge of how to receive. As they grow up, as they cease to be children, they sense a new power—not the power to demand love, but rather the power to express love. To gradually sense that we not only need to be helped but also need to help, to steadily feel that we not only require the care of others but also are able to give care, is the beginning of inner security. We do not transcend our loneliness by only finding others to love us. We transcend our sense of separation by finding others to love.

In the act of being useful, in the work of fulfilling the desires and needs of other human beings, we feel our creative power and discover our strength. True love is an ironic deed. It binds us closer to other people while it awakens within us the thrill of independence. The more we help, the stronger we feel. And the stronger we feel, the more secure we become.

Love is the developed art of expressing our human power through the act of giving to others. It overwhelms our fears and gives us hope through the promise of our own strength.

PARENTS

Friendship is possible when we know how to trust, when we know that others can be faithful and honest. In the earliest experiences of our childhood, in the first awakening of our infant minds, we discover the security of love. Families may scold and complain. Parents may lecture and cry. But their deeds are usually sweeter than their words. In the hour of need they do not judge. They help.

When parents die they leave us more than memory. The leave us the well-being of acceptance, the possibility of trust, and the reassurance of unconditional love. Without their gifts we would stand alone in fear. We would not be able to reach out to other people in friendship.

SELF-RESPECT

Self-respect is never a gift. It is always an achievement. Neither the flattery of friends nor the reassurance of family will give us a feeling of self-worth. Neither the counseling of therapists nor the comforts of religion will elevate our dignity. Self-esteem is the child of competence. It is the offspring of personal skill. People who think that they are unable to help themselves or to help others cannot respect themselves.

People who like themselves believe that they have power. They believe that they have the power to determine the course of their own lives. They believe that they have the strength to make decisions even when the consequences of their decisions cannot easily be predicted. They even know that when they give to others they do not threaten their own welfare. For their own security lies in no possession. It resides in their own creative skill.

TRAGEDY

The past is unchangeable. What happened yesterday is beyond our control. We can cry and shout, we can scream and complain, but the events of just a moment ago are as far from our reach as the farthest star. Fools never forgive the past. They devote every present moment to worrying about it, scolding it and wishing it were different. Wise people release the past. They do not need to assault what cannot be taken. They do not need to forgive what cannot be altered. They simply accept what they are not able to change. Since the future is open to human decision, they turn their energies forward and choose to create rather than to regret.

People of self-respect do not dwell on helplessness. They do not assault what cannot be taken. Since death is irreversible, they accept it and turn to the living.

UNEXPECTED DEATH

Death is an intrusion.

Sometimes it arrives at the end of a long life when we are waiting for it. But sometimes it comes unexpectedly, interrupting young lives and wasting hopes and dreams. People we love are taken from our midst too soon, and we struggle to deal with their absence.

Destiny is often unkind. Since it is a mindless force, we cannot praise it or blame it. We simply accept what we cannot change.

But people are different from destiny. We have hearts and minds. We have hopes and dreams. We have love and loving attachments. Above all, we have the power of courage—the courage to affirm the value of life in the face of death.

The fates are beyond our control. But our response to the fates is in our hands. We do not know what will happen, but we do know that amid all the uncertainty, we have the courage to love.

Those we remember also had that courage. Love is the power that binds the living and the dead.

2. EULOGY

(A tribute [or tributes] is now offered by the leader of the service or by family and friends.)

3. SECOND READING

(Choose One)

AUTUMN

Autumn leaves are more useful than they seem. Although in final glory they fall to the ground in a wistful descent of death, the fertile earth pays them tribute. She embraces their forms and turns their hidden energies into the evolution of new life. In the drama of human love, a similar pattern prevails. The thoughts and ideals of those we admire survive death. They fall on the fertile earth of our minds and hearts and renew our lives through inspiration.

AWARENESS

Our families and our friends are so close to us that we often take for granted what they do. What is familiar has a tendency to appear ordinary. We lose our perspective. We imagine that what is far away is superior to what is close at hand. People are only heroic when we cannot experience them.

We need to pay attention. We need to notice the extraordinary in the ordinary. We need to see the special in the familiar. There are parents who give us love. There are children who give us hope. There are friends who give us courage. In their own unique way—without the privilege of spoken philosophy—they make us feel worthwhile.

In this hour of remembering, we offer them our tribute and our recognition.

CHANGE

The glories of our universe are never eternal. They shine for a while and are then consumed by the darkness. All things change. All life yields to death. If the beauties of nature endured for ever, they would not be precious. We cannot love what we do not fear to lose.

CONTINUITY

After every spring comes the fullness of summer. After every summer comes the color of autumn. Beyond every autumn lies the serenity of winter. And beyond every winter appears the freshness of spring.

The circle of human existence reflects this return. It sweetens death with hope. Old people yield to the child. Old life is forever the prelude to the new.

DEEDS

When we think of philosophy we tend to think of words and spoken ideas. We tend to think of articulate men and women who write profoundly about the human condition.

But philosophy is not confined to those who can talk about it. It is also the intimate possession of those who live it.

Most of the people who have touched our lives in a positive way cannot fully explain their vision of truth, reality, and moral virtue. But they speak through their deeds and grant us the gifts of integrity.

We honor all people of conviction who have made their humanism an act of living, who have turned their feelings and ideas into visible commitment.

DEFIANCE

Death is a reminder of human frailty. We are very vulnerable creatures. And we have so many natural enemies. Floods and earthquakes, disease and famine, heat and cold take their toll and thin our ranks. Even in the time of science, the ancient enemies of aging and decay still creep up on us uninvited and make us mortal.

In a world of peace there is still a war to be fought—not a war of people against people—but a war against death and all its friends. If we must fight, let us fight poverty. If we must enter battle, let us battle with disease. If we must assault the enemy, let us assault the poisons of our environment. There are many real foes to face.

Let our tribute to the dead be our struggle against death.

DIGNITY

The value of life does not lie in mere survival. Lasting eternally is never enough. The value of life lies in personal dignity. Self-respect, however brief, gives human existence its meaning.

The long life of cautious boredom is inferior to the short life of bold adventure. Many of us who believe ourselves to be living are already dead. And many who have died live on in the memory of their courage.

HOPE

We live through hope. Where there is darkness we wait for the light. Where there is pain we anticipate pleasure. Where there is boredom we yearn for the arrival of new excitement.

Living without hope is living without dignity. It is a denial of everything vital. It is an abject surrender to evil. It is a humiliating affirmation of the darkness, the pain, and the dullness of human experience. If the future holds no promise of better things to come, then the present weighs us down like an intolerable burden.

Persons of self-respect, people who esteem their own power, do not welcome despair. In the darkest hour, they resist the self-pity that paralyzes action. Even when the night seems more than eternal, they plead for the morning.

IMMORTALITY

Immortality is not an illusion.

The selfish kind of immortality is the vision that imagines that each of us is indestructible, exempt from the laws of nature, immune to personal death.

But there is a natural immortality. It finds its source in the two billion-year-old chain of life, in the experience of parents and children, in the sentimental power of human memory.

Each of us is an extension of the past. Each of us is an intimation of the future.

We are more than individuals. We have connections. That is how we are born. That is why we never completely die. We receive our inheritance, we leave our legacy.

_____ is part of that chain of life. It still continues.

May we regard the life of _____ as a special link in the chain of vital existence. May we honor him/her always with the gift of remembrance.

INHERITANCE

Death is real. In the world of changing nature it is inevitable. It may be postponed, but it cannot be avoided.

Loved ones do not pass away. They die. They do not escape the rhythm of life.

But they leave their gifts. We still bask in their love. We still use their instruction. We are still inspired by their deeds. We still linger on the memories of their style.

Immortality is very intimate. It is part of our mind. It is as close as our power to remember.

In the real world death is part of the drama of life. So is the loving tribute of remembrance.

LIFE

We often run away from life. We think of death and are obsessed by it. The threat of aging fills us with dread and casts a shadow over all our youthful pleasures. The end of our story ruins the middle and sours the taste of our happiness. Why bother to pursue what must pass away? Why bother to value what must cease to be?

To love life is to dismiss death. It is to risk every possible joy, every chance for vitality, every invitation to beauty.

It is to affirm the dignity of the human struggle and the victory of human survival. Death is real and inevitable. But we do not have to prepare for it. It will happen all by itself.

LOYALTY

Loyalty is life. We live through the loyalty of others, not only the devotion of having family and friends but also the loyalty of the past to the future. Our ancestors worked, saved, and gave up their pleasure to provide for generations yet unborn. They pursued distant goals which they knew they would never reach so that their children and their grandchildren could ultimately achieve them. The mountain of human culture is built out of many layers of human achievement, each generation resting on the work of the one before.

We are here today because the people of the past did not forget us. Our ancestors have planted and we have reaped. Like them, we must live for more than the present. Like them, we must work for those who will follow.

MEANING

Death makes us angry. It seems to cheat us of what we work so hard to secure. Many of our loved ones spent their years in struggle. They knew poverty, disease, and deprivation in the battle for survival. They dreamed of so much for themselves and their families and lived to taste so little of their vision. How painfully aware we are of our limits and how fearfully conscious that, in a moment, the blind hand of circumstance can also steal our future. But anger and fear are inappropriate. No person, however young, is fully denied the opportunities of the good life. If we cannot find in the worry of the present the intrinsic beauties of life, we will never find them. Indeed death can never deny us and those we love what life bestows in every moment.

MEMORY

Memory is a precious possession. It captures the past and trains it to our need. The harshness of old events is softened by vagueness and the pleasures of happy moments are sharpened by vivid imagination. Loved ones linger on in the glory of their individual uniqueness. In life they willed to live and hewed the path of their personal difference. In death they transcend decay and find their niche in fond remembrance. No person is defined by the sameness of another. If it were so, memory would die from generalities.

In the particular grace of _____ lies his/her immortality.

May the memory of _____, whom we loved in life and still love in death, bless our thoughts and actions. May the special grace of his/her years reach out to touch our hearts and to give us hope.

WINTER

Winter is a cruel season. It reminds us of how hostile nature can sometimes be.

It also reminds us of the power of human love and human connection.

In the winter, we become aware of how we derive our warmth from one another, of how much we depend on the loving care of parents and children and friends.

When it is cold outside, we must create our own human fires. When one flame is extinguished, we must light another.

388   *Death*

May this moment make us sensitive to our need for one another.

May the death of one we love encourage us to foster life.

May we regard the life of _____ as a special link in the chain of vital existence. May we honor him/her always with the gift of remembrance.

4. SILENT TRIBUTE

Let us all rise and stand for a moment of silent tribute to the life and memory of _____.

5. CLOSING WORDS

(Choose One)

MEMORY

ZAY-KHER TSA-DEEK-KEEM LEE-V-RA-KHA

Let the memory of good people bless us.

May the memory of _____, whom we loved in life and still love in death, continue to bless our thoughts and our actions.

LOVE

SHEEM'OO SHEEM'OO OHAVAY AHAVA
KEER'OO KEER'OO MOSHEEAY Y'SHOOA
KEE AYN Y'SHOOA B'LEE AHAVA
O AHAVA AHAVA KAYN T'HEE.

Listen now, you lovers of love.
Hear this, you seekers of happiness.
There is no happiness without love.

7
MEMORIAL STONE DEDICATION

MEMORY

We live and we die. That is the pattern of nature. Sometimes death comes too early, spoiling hopes and dreams. Sometimes it comes when we least expect it, interrupting success and stability. Sometimes it comes in old age, concluding what is already complete.

Although death is relentless, we do not surrender to it. We pay our tribute to life. No matter how brief, no matter how long, life is supremely important. Every person is unique. Every biography is special.

Our tribute to those we loved is that we do not forget. They always have a place in our minds and in our hearts. They always survive in the freshness of our memories.

This service of memorial is an expression of our loyalty.

Let us pause for a moment of silent tribute to the life of ―――――, who lives on in the power of our remembering.

SILENT TRIBUTE

DEDICATION

This stone is a sign of our determination to remember. ――――― has died. But his/her memory is alive. Sometimes it makes us painfully aware of his/her absence. But at other times, it fills our thoughts with sweet remembrances.

Memorial Stone Dedication

Because we loved him/her, we shall not forget him/her. Nor shall we betray his/her will to live. In the presence of death, we shall help each other to live—and to hope.

We dedicate this stone to the memory of _____. Although the stone remains here, its meaning as a loving tribute travels with us wherever we go.

CLOSING WORDS

ZAYKHER TSADDEEKKEEM LEEV'RAKHA.

May the memory of good people continue to bless our lives.

SONGS

No celebration would be complete without music, especially without song. Singing reinforces the sense of solidarity that groups need to feel in order to be effective. Singing carries emotion far more powerfully than spoken prose or poetry.

For humanistic Jews the language of the song is important. In North America, in an English speaking environment, where the daily use and understanding of Jewish languages is very difficult, Hebrew and Yiddish songs become the best way to introduce the flavor of ethnicity into Jewish celebrations. Important ideas are universal. Prose reflections need to be understood. But the music of a song carries its own meaning, even when all the words are not fully comprehended.

The songs I have chosen to include in the following collection are the songs I have used and liked. After each reading, in every theme program, there is a suggested song. If you do not like the song I have chosen, please choose your own.

The words of only a few of the songs have been written by me. Most of the poetry comes from the traditional sources or from contemporary Israeli culture. Many of the songs are famous poems set to music.

1. ADAMA

A-DA-MA A-DA-MA
BA-SH'-FAY-LA OO-VA-RA-MA
BA-MA-TAR OO-VA-HA-MA.

A-DA-MA A-DA-MA
BA-RA-AV OO-VA-BA-MA
BAKH M'-KOR HA-NE-HA-MA.

A-DA-MA A-DA-MA
HA-G'-LOO-YA V'-HA-TA-MA
LA HA-GOOF V'-HA-N'-SHA-MA

AT IM-MAY-NOO A-DA-MA
AYM A-DAM AD-MAT KOL HIE.

אדמה אדמה
בשפלה ובדמה
במטר ובחמה.

אדמה אדמה
ברעב ובצמא
בך מקור הנחמת.

אדמה אדמה
הגלויה והתמה
לה הגוף והנשמת

את אמנו אדמה
אם אדם אדמת כל חי.

Land, Land
In the plain and on the heights
With the dew and with the heat.

Land, Land
In the plain and on the high place
In you is the source of consolation.

You are with us, O Land
The mother of humanity, the earth of every living being.

—*Abraham Broides*

---

2. ADEER HOO

A-DEER HOO
Y'-HEE HOF-SHEE B'-KA-ROV
BEE-M'-HAY-RA V'-YA-MAY-NOO
B'-KA-ROV
A-DAM HOF-SHEE B'-K-KA-ROV

אדיר הוא
יהי חפשי בקרוב
במהרה בימינו
בקרוב
אדם חפשי בקרוב.

Sing aloud, strong and proud, freedom's wondrous glory
Sing aloud, strong and proud, Israel's famous story
As we hear, year by year, the tale of our victory.

—*Traditional (Adapted)*

3. AHAVA OOVEENA

A-HA-VA OO-VEE-NA
L'-YOM HA-KIP-POO-REEM
SHA-NA TO-VA SHA-NA M'-TOO-KA

אהבה ובינה
ליום הכפורים.
שנה טובה שנה מתוקה.

> Love and understanding for Yom Kippur
> May we have a good year.
> May we have a good year.
>
> —*Folk Song (Adapted)*

---

4. AHEE ADAM

A-HEE A-DAM
AR-TSEE O-LAM
DA-TEE YO-FEE

אחי אדם.
ארצי עולם.
דתי יופי.

> My family is humanity.
> My homeland is the world.
> My religion is beauty.
>
> —*M. J. Leibensohn*

---

5. AL HOMOTIEYIKH

AL HO-MO-TIE-YIKH
Y'-ROO-SHA-LIE-YIM
HIF-KAD-TEE SHO-M'-REEM
KOL HA-YOM V'-KHOL HA-LIE-LA

על חומותיך
ירושלים
הפקדתי שומרים
כל היום וכל הלילה.

> Upon your walls, Jerusalem
> Watchmen stand night and day.
>
> —*Isaiah 62:6*

6. AL KOL AYLE

AL HA-D'-VASH V'-AL HA-O-KETS
AL HA-MAR V'-HA-MA-TOK
AL BIT-TAY-NOO HA-TEE-NO-KET
NISH-MOR ET HA-TOV
AL HA-AYSH HA-M'-VO-ERET
AL HA-MIE-YEEM HA-ZA-REEM
AL HA-EESH HA-SHAV HA-BIE-TA
MIN HA-MER-HA-KEEM.

AL KOL AY-LE
AKH SHAV NISH-MOR ET HA-TOV
AL HA-D'-VASH V'-AL HA-O-KETS
AL HA-MAR V'-HA-MA-TOK
AL NA-A-KOR NA-TOO-A
AL NISH-KAKH ET HA-TIK-VA
NA-SHOO-VA, KAYN KAYN, NA-SHOO-VA
EL HA-A-RETS HA-TO-VA.

על הדבש ועל העוקץ
על המר והמתוק
על בתנו התינוקת
נשמור את הטוב.
על האש המבוערת
על המים הזרים
על האיש השב הביתה
מן המרחקים.

על כל אלה
עכשיו נשמור את הטוב.
על הדבש ועל העוקץ
על המר והמתוק
אל נעקור נטוע
אל נשכח את התקוה.
נשובה כן כן
נשובה
אל הארץ הטובת.

For the honey and the bee sting
For the bitter and the sweet
For the pleasures and the sorrows
That make life complete.
For the fire that keeps on burning
For the water clean and pure
For the father who's returning
From a distant shore.
For all these now, these our blessings
We must hold them in our keep
As we think about the good life
Both the bitter and the sweet.
May we see the growth of our children
May we keep them safe and sound
May our eyes behold our homeland
Free and peaceful once again.
We shall not uproot the planting.
We must not give up our hope.
NA-SHOO-VA, KAYN KAYN, NA-SHOO-VA
EL HA-A-RETS HA-TO-VA.

—Naomi Shemer

7. AL SH'LOSHA D'VAREEM I

AL SH'-LO-SHA D'-VA-REEM
HA-O-LAM O-MAYD
AL HA-TO-RA V'-AL HA-A-VO-DA
V'-AL G'-MEE-LOOT HA-SA-DEEM

על שלשה דברים
העולם עומד.
על התורה ועל העבודה
ועל גמילות חסדם.

> On three things the world stands—
> On wisdom, on service, on kindness.
>
> —*Simon the Righteous*

8. AL SH'LOSHA D'VAREEM II

AL SH'-LO-SHA D'-VA-REEM
HA-O-LAM O-MED.
AL HAD-DEEN, V'-AL HA-E-MET,
V-AL HA-SHA-LOM.

על שלשה דברים
העולם עומר.
על הדין ועל האמת
ועל השלום.

> On three things the world stands—
> On justice, on truth, and on peace.
>
> —*Shimon Ben Gamliel*

9. AM YISRAEL HIE

AM YIS-RA-EL HIE.

עם ישראל חי.

> The Jewish people lives.
>
> —*Folk Song*

10. ANEE MAAMEEN

A-NEE MA-A-MEEN BE-E-MOO-NA
SH'-LAY-MA
B'-VEE-AT HA-MA-SHEE-AKH.
V'-AF AL PEE SHE-YIT-MA-MAY-A
IM KOL ZE A-NEE MA-A-MEEN.

אני מאמין באמונה
שלמה
בביאת המשיח.
ואף על פי שיתמהמה
עם כל זה אני מאמין.

> I believe with perfect trust
> In the coming of the golden age.
> And even though it has not come
> I still believe.
>
> —*Maimonides*

---

11. ANEE NOTAYA

A-NEE NO-TAY-A SH'-KAY-DEE-A
SH'-KAY-DEE-A YA-FA

אני נוטע שקדיה
שקדיה יפה.

> I plant an almond tree.
> A beautiful almond tree.
>
> —*Folk Song*

---

12. ARTSA ALEENO

AR-TSA A-LEE-NOO
K'-VAR HA-RASH-NOO V'-GAM
ZA-RA-NOO
A-VAL OD LO KA-TSAR-NOO.

ארצה עלינו.
זרענו.
כבר חרשנו וגם
אבל עוד לא קצרנו.

> We have gone up to our land.
> Already we have plowed and also planted.
> But we have not yet reaped.
>
> —*Folk Song*

13. ASHRAY HAGAFROOR

ASH-RAY HA-GAF-ROOR SHE-NIS-RAF
V'-HITS-TSEET LE-HA-VOT.
ASH-RAY HA-LE-HA-VA SHE-BA-A-RA
B'-SIT-RAY L'-VA-VOT.
ASH-RAY HA-L'-VA-VOT SHE-YA-D'-OO
LAH-DOL B'-KHA-VOD.
ASH-RAY HA-GAF-ROOR SHE-NIS-RAF
V'-HITS-TSEET LE-HA-VOT.

אשרי הגפרור שנשרף
והצית להבות.
אשרי הלהבה שבערה בסתרי
לבבות.
אשרי הלבבות שידעו
לחדול בכבוד.
אשרי הגפרור שנשרף
והצית להבות.

    Happy is the match which is consumed and ignites the flame
    Happy is the flame which burns in the secret places of the heart
    Happy are the hearts which know how to stop with honor
    Happy is the match which is consumed and ignites the flame.

                                                 —Hannah Szenes

14. AYFO OREE

AY-FO O-REE? O-REE BEE.
AY-FO TIK-VA-TEE? TIK-VA-TEE BEE.
AY-FO KO-KHEE? KO-KHEE BEE.
V'-GAM BAKH.

איפה אורי? אורי בי.
איפה תקותי? תקותי בי.
איפה כוחי? כוחי בי.
וגם בך.

    Where is my light? My light is in me.
    Where is my hope? My hope is in me.
    Where is my strength? My strength is in me.
    And in you.

                                                 —Sherwin Wine

15. AYIT

A-YIT AL S'-DO-TAY-NOO
BEE-V'-SA-RAY-NOO TSIP-POR-NAV
KOO-MOO KOO-MOO BA-HOO-RAY-NOO
KOO-MOO TS'-OO LEE S'-DAY HA-K'-RAV

עיט על שדותינו
בבשרנו צפרניו.
קומו קומו בחורינו
קומו צאו לי שדי הקרב.

    The bird of prey is in our fields
    Its claws are in our flesh
    Arise young men
    Go forth to the field of battle.

                                      —Avraham Shlonsky

16. AYLEEYAHOO HANAVEE

AY-LEE-YA-HOO HA-NA-VEE
AY-LEE-YA-HOO HA-TISH-BEE
AY-LEE-YA-HOO HA-GIL-A-DEE.

אליהו הנביא
אליהו התשבי
אליהו הגלעדי.

> Elijah the prophet
> Elijah the Tishbite
> Elijah the Gileadite
>
> —*Traditional*

---

17. AYTS HIEYEEM

AYTS HIE-YEEM HEE
LA-MA-HA-ZEE-KEEM BA.
V'-TO-M'-KHE-HA M'-OO-SHAR
D'-RA-KHE-HA DAR-KHAY NO-AM.
V'-KHOL N'-TEE-VO-TE-HA SHA-LOM.

עץ היים היא
למחזיקים בת
ותומכיה מאושר.
דרכיה דרכי נועם
וכל נתיבותיה שלום.

> Wisdom is a tree of life.
> Its ways are pleasant ways.
> All its paths are peace.
>
> —*Proverbs 3:17–18*

---

18. AYZE HOO GIBBOR

AY-ZE HOO GIB-BOR?
A-DAM HA-KO-VAYSH ET YITS-RO RA
A-DAM HA-KO-VAYSH ET ZA-MO RA
A-DAM SHEL KA-VOD ATS-MEE.

איזה הוא גבור?
אדם הכובש את יצרו רע
אדם הכובש את זעמו רע
אדם של כבוד עצמי.

> Tell me who is strong.
> A person who subdues his evil desire
> A person who subdues his anger's fire
> This is the one who is strong.
>
> —*Ben Zoma (Adapted)*

19. BAMAKOM

BAMAKOM SHE-AYN A-NA-SHEEM
HISH-TA-DAYL LEE-H'-YOT EESH.

במקום שאין אנשים
השתדל להיות איש.

> In a place where there are no real people
> Strive to be a *mensch*.
>
> —*Gamliel Ben Yehuda*

---

20. BAROOKH HAOR

BA-ROOKH HA-OR BA-O-LAM.
BA-ROOKH HA-OR BA-A-DAM.
BA-ROOKH HA-OR BA-SHAB-BAT.
    BA-SUK-KOT.
    BA-HA-NOOK-RA.
    BA-PE-SAKH.

ברוך האור בעולם.
ברוך האור באדם.
ברוך האור בשבת.
בסוכות.
בחנוכה.
בפסח.

> Radiant is the light of the world.
> Radiant is the light within people.
> Radiant is the light of the Shabbat.
>   Sukkot.
>   Hanukka.
>   Pesakh.
>
> —*Sherwin Wine*

21. BASHANA HABAA

BA-SHA-NA HA-BA-A
NAY-SHAYV EL HA-MIR-PE-SET
V'-NIS-POR TSIP-PO-REEM NO-D'-DOT
Y-LA-DEEM B'-HOF-SHA
Y'-SA-HA-KOO TO-FE-SET
BAYN HA-BIE-YIT OO-VAYN
HA-SA-DOT

OD TIR-E OD TIR-E
KA-MA-TOV YEE-H'-YE
BA-SHA-NA HA-BA-A

בשנה הבאה
נשב אל המרפסת
ונספור צפורים נודדות.
ילדים בחפשה
ישחקו תופסת.
בין הבית ובין
השדות.

עוד תראה
כמטוב יהיה.
בשנה הבאה.

     In the year just ahead
     We'll sit outside our windows
     Counting birds as they fly through the sky.
     Counting birds, no more planes
     This will be our tomorrow
     And our children will not have to cry.

     Soon you'll see, soon you'll see
     Just how good it will be
     In the year ahead, just ahead.

                             —*Ehud Manor*

22. B'AYLE HAYADIEYIM

B'-AY-LE HA-YA-DIE-YIM
OD LO BA-NEE-TEE K'-FAR
OD LO MA-TSA-TEE MIE-YIM
B'-EM-TSA HA-MID-BAR
OD LO TSEE-YAR-TEE PE-RAKH
OD LO GEE-LEE-TEE AYKH
TO-VEEL O-TEE HA-DE-REKH
OO-LAN'-A-NEE HO-LAYKH.

AI, OD LO A-HAV-TEE DIE
HA-ROO-AKH V'-HA-SHE-MESH AL PAN-NAI.
AI, OD LO A-MAR-TEE DIE
V'-EEM LO EEM LO AKH-SHAV AY-MA-TIE?

באלה הידים
עוד לא בניתי כפר.
עוד לא מצאתי מים
באמצא המדבר
עוד לא ציירתי פרח.
עוד לא גליתי איך.
תוביל אותי הדרך
ולאן אני הולך.

אי עוד לא אהבתי די.
הרוח והשמש על פני.
אי עוד לא אמרתי די.
ואם לא עכשיו אימתי.

With these hands
I have not yet built a city
I have not yet found water in the heart of the wilderness
I have not yet painted a flower
I have not yet discovered that way I need to go.

I have not yet loved enough—
The wind and the sun are on my face—
I have not said enough—
And, if not now, when?

—*Naomi Shemer*

23. BEHAREEM

BE-HA-REEM K'-VAR
HA-SHE-MESH MIL-HE-TET
OO-VA-AY-MEK OD-NO-TSAYTS HA-TAL
A-NOO O-HA-VEEM O-TAKH, MO-LE-DET
B'-SIM-HA B'-SHEER OO-V'-A-MAL.

MIM-MO-R'-DOT HA-L'-VA-NON
AD YAM HA-ME-LAKH
NA-A-VOR O-TAKH B'-MA-HA-RAY-SHOT
A-NOO OD NIT-TA LAKH V'-NIV-NE LAKH
A-NOO N'-YAP-PE O-TAKH M'-OD.

NAL-BEE-SHAYKH SAL-MAT
BE-TON VA-ME-LET
V'-NIF-ROS LAKH MAR-VA-DAY
GAN-NEEM
AL AD-MAT S'-DO-TIE-YIKH
HAN-NIG-E-LET
HA-DA-GAN YAR-NEEN PA-A-MO-NEEM

HA-MID-BAR A-NOO DE-REKH
BO NAKH-TSO-VA
HAB-BITS-TSOT A-NAKH-NOO
N'-YAB-SHAYN
MA NIT-TAYN LAKH OD L'-HOD VA-SO-VA
MA OD LO NA-TA-NOO V'-NIT-TAYN

BE-HA-REEM, BE-HA-REEM ZA-RAKH
O-RAY-NOO
A-NOO NA-PEE-LA EL HA-HAR
HA-ET-MOL NISH-AR
MAY-A-HO-RAY-NOO
AKH-RAB-BA HAD-DE-REKH
LAM-MA-HAR

EEM KA-SHE HEE HAD-DE-REKH
OO-VO-GE-DET
EEM GAM LO E-HAD YIP-POL HAL-LAL
AD O-LAM NO-HAV O-TAKH, MO-LE-DET
A-NOO LAKH BAK-K'-RAV OO-VE-A-MAL.

בהרים כבר
השמש מלחתת
ובעמק עוד נוצץ הטל.
אנו אוהבים אותך, מולדת,
בשמחה בשיר ובעמל.

ממורדות הלבנון
עד ים המלח.
נעבור אותך במתרשות.
אנו עוד נטע לך ונבנה לך
אנו ניפה אותך מאד.

נלבישך שלמת
בתון ומלט.
ונפרש לך מרבדי
גנים.
על אדמת שדותיך
הנגלת.
הדגן ירנין פעמונים.

המדבר אנו דרך
בו נחצואה
הבצות אנחנו
ניבשן.
מה נתן לך עוד להוד ושובע.
מה עוד לא נתנו ונתן.

בהרים בהרים זרח
אורנו
אנו נפילה אל ההר.
האתמול נשאר
מאחורנו
אך רבה הדרך
למחר.

אם קשה היא הדדך
ובוגדת.
אם גם לו אחד יפול חלל.
עד עולם נאהב אותך מולדת
אנו לך בקרב ובעמל.

> In the mountains the sun already sets
> And in the valley the dew still glistens
> We love you, motherland
> With joy, with song, and with work.
>
> —*Natan Alterman*

24. B'KHOL ADAM

B'-KHOL A-DAM A-HA-VA V'-SIN-A
TOV VA-RE-SHA HIE-YEEM VA-MA-VET

בכל אדם אהבה ושנאה
טוב ורשע חיים ומות.

> In every person there is love and hate
> Good and evil, life and death.
>
> —*Mahzor (Adapted)*

25. B'ROOKHEEM HAHIEYEEM

B'-ROO-KHEEM HA-HIE-YEEM BA-O-LAM.
B'-ROO-KHEEM HA-HIE-YEEM BA-A-DAM.

ברוכים החיים בעולם.
ברוכים החיים באדם.

> Marvelous is life in the world.
> Marvelous is life within us.
>
> —*Sherwin Wine*

26. DIEYAYNOO

EEM YAYSH LA-NOO HAY-ROO-TAY-NOO.
DIE-YAY-NOO.
EEM YAYSH LA-NOO SIM-HA-TAY-NOO.
DIE-YAY-NOO.
EEM YAYSH LA-NOO TIK-VA-TAY-NOO.
DIE-YAY-NOO.

אם יש לנו חרותנו.
דינו.
אם יש לנו שמחתנו.
דינו.
אם יש לנו תקותנו.
דינו.

> If we only have our freedom. Dieyaynoo.
> If we only have our Seder. Dieyaynoo.
> If we only have our hope. Dieyaynoo.
>
> —*Haggada (Adapted)*

27. DODEE LEE

DO-DEE LEE VA-A-NEE LO
HA-RO-E BA-SHO-SHAN-NEEM.

OO-REE TSA-FON OO-VO-EE TAY-MAN

דודי לי ואני לו
הרועה בשושנים.

אורי צפון ובואי תימן.

> My beloved is mine and I am his
> Who pastures among the lilies.
>
> Arise, north wind; come, south wind.
>
> *—Song of Songs 6:3*

---

28. EEM AYN

EEM AYN A-NEE LEE MEE LEE?
OO-KH'-SHE-A-NEE L'-ATS-MEE MA A-NEE?
V'-EEM LO AKH-SHAV AY-MA-TIE?

אם אין אני לי מי לי?
וכשאני לעצמי מה אני?
ואם לא עכשיו אימתי?

> If I am not for myself, who will be for me?
> And if I am only for myself, what am I?
> And if I do not act now, when?
>
> *—Hillel*

---

29. EMET L'YISRAEL

E-MET E-MET L'-YIS-RA-EL.
E-MET E-MET LA-A-DAM.
E-MET E-MET LA-O-LAM.

אמת לישראל.
אמת לאדם.
אמת לעולם.

> Let all people pursue the truth.
>
> *—Sherwin Wine*

30. EREV SHEL SHOSHANNEEM

E-REV SHEL SHO-SHAN-NEEM
NAY-TSAY-NA EL HA-BOOS-TAN
MOR B'-SA-MEEM OO-L'-VO-NA
L-RAG-LAYKH MIF-TAN.

LIE-LA YO-RAYD L'-AT
V'-ROO-AKH SHO-SHAN NO-SH'-VA
HA-VA EL KHASH LAKH SHEER BA-L'-AT
ZE-MER SHEL A-HA-VA

ערב של שושנים
נצאנה אל הבוסתן
מור בשמים ולבונה
על רגלך מפתן.
לילה יורד לאט.
ורוח שושן נושבת
הבה אל חש לך שיר בלאט.
זמר של אהבת

> Evening of roses
> Let us go down to the garden
> Myrrh and spices
> On the threshold
>
> Night descends
> With the fragrance of roses
> Come, let us sing a song
> A song of love.
>
> —*Moshe Dor*

31. HAD GADYA

HAD GAD-YA
DEE-Z'-VAN AB-BA BIT-RAY ZOO-ZAY
HAD GAD-YA.

חד גדיה
דזבן אבא בתרי זוזי
חד גדית,

> One kid.
> My father bought for two zuzim.
> One kid.
>
> —*Haggada*

32. HAEMET YOTSAYT

HA-E-MET YO-TSAYT LO MIN HA-PE
A-VAL MIN HA-YA-DIE-YEM.

האמת יוצאת לא מן הפה.
אבל מן הידים.

> Truth goes forth from the hands
> Not from the mouth.
>
> —*Sherwin Wine*

33. HAG POOREEM

HAG POO-REEM
HAG GA-DOL HOO LA-Y'-HOO-DEEM
MA-SAY-KHOT RA-A-SHAN-NEEM
Z'-MEE-ROT V'-RIK-KOO-DEEM.

HA-VA NA-REE-SHA RASH RASH RASH
BA-RA-SHAN-NEEM.

חג פורים
חג גדול הוא ליהודים
מסכות רעשנים
זמירות ורקודים.

הבה נרישה רש רש רש
ברעשנים.

        Purim day
        Joyous gladsome holiday
        Happy throngs singing songs
        Laughing and dancing gay

                —Folk Song

34. HAKH PATEESH

HAKH PA-TEESH A-LAY OO-TS'-NAKH
K'-VEE-SHAY B'-TON BA-HOOTS NIM-TAKH
OO-REE SH'-MA-MA DEE-NAYKH NEKH-TAKH
A-NOO BA-EEM LIKH-BOSH O-TAKH

DOOD BO-AYR HA-AYSH
HA-MAKH-BESH KO-VAYSH
HAL-A HAL-A RAYSH
KO-AKH YAYSH VA-YAYSH

DOOD HA-ZE-FET HAM
YAD-NO-TE-FET DAM
KA-KHA BEN A-DAM
BA-MID-BAR NIL-HAM

הך פטיש עלה וצנח.
כבישי בטון בחוץ נמתח.
עורי שממה דיניך נכתח.
אנו באים לכבוש אותך.

דוד בוער האש
המכבש כובש.
הלאת, הלאה ריש
כוח יש ויש.

דוד חופת חם
יד נוטפת דם
ככה בן אדם
במדבר נלחם.

    Strike, strike with hammer in your hand
    As we lay concrete roads on sand.
    Arise and bloom, O desert land
    For we have come to take command.

    Pitch boils on the fire
    New roads we desire.
    Onward we aspire!
    Strong men never tire!

    The pitch blazes and
    Blood drips from our hand.
    Thus an earnest band
    Wars with desert land.

                              —*Natan Alterman*

---

35. HALBEESHEENEE

HAL-BEE-SHEE-NEE, IM-MA K'-SHAY-RA
K'-TO-NET PAS-SEEM L'-TIF-E-RET
V'-EEM SHA-HA-REET HO-VEE-LEE-NEE
E-LAY A-MAL

הלבישיני, אמא כשרה
כתנת פסים לתפארת
ואם שחרית הובילני
אלי עמל.

    Dress me, good mother, in a splendid coat of many colors
    And with dawn lead me to work.

                              —*Avraham Shlonsky*

36. HANAAVA

HA-NA-A-VA BA-BA-NOT
A-NA HA-EE-REE PA-NIE-YIKH AY-LIE

הנאוה בבנות
אנה האירי פניך אלי.

> Fairest of women
> Raise up your face to me.
>
> —*Traditional*

---

37. HANOOKKA

HA-NOOK-KA, HA-NOOK-KA
HAG YA-FE KOL KAKH.
OR HA-VEEV MIS-SA-VEEV
GEEL L'-YE-LED RAKH.
HA-NOOK-KA, HA-NOOK-KA
S'-VEE-VON SOV SOV.
SOV SOV SOV
MA NA-EEM VA-TOV.

חנוכה חנוכה
חג יפה כל כך
אור חביב מסביב
גיל לילד רך.

חנוכת, חנוכה
סביבון סוב סוב
סוב סוב סוב
מה נעים וטוב.

> Hanukka, Hanukka, feast of dedication
> Hanukka, Hanukka, freedom for the nation
> Hanukka, Hanukka, time for jubilation
> Candle light, candle bright
> Gifts for this occasion.
>
> —*Folk Song*

38. HAOLAM MALAY YOFEE

HA-O-LAM MA-LAY YO-FEE
HA-O-LAM MA-LAY SIM-HA
EEM HA-AY-NIE-YEEM TIR-E-NA
ET HA-YO-FEE
EEM HA-OZ-NIE-YEEM TISH-MA-NA
ET HA-SIM-HA

העולם מלא יופי.
העולם מלא שמחה.
אם העינים תראינה
את היופי.
אם האזנים תשמענה
את השמחה.

    The world is filled with beauty.
    The world is filled with joy.
    If only my eyes would see the beauty.
    If only my ears would hear the joy.

                               —*Sherwin Wine*

39. HAOR SHEL HAYOFEE

HA-OR SHEL HA-YO-FEE
HAY-EER ET HA-O-LAM

האור של היופי
האיר את העולם.

    The light of beauty illumines the world.

                        —*Sherwin Wine*

40. HATIKVA

KOL OD BA-LAY-VAV P'-NEE-MA
NE-FESH Y'-HOO-DEE HO-MEE-YA.
OO-L'-FA-A-TAY MIZ-RAKH KA-DE-MA
A-YIN L'-TSEE-YON TSO-FEE-YA.

OD LO A-V'-DA TIK-VA-TAY-NOO.
HA-TIK-VA SH'-NOT AL-PIE-YIM.
LEE-H'-YOT AM KHOF-SHEE B'-AR-TSAY-NOO
E-RETS TSEE-YON BEE-ROO-SHA-LIE-YIM.

כל עוד בלבב פנימה
נפש יהודי הומית.
ולפאתי מזרח קדימה
עין לציון צופיה.

עוד לא אבדה תקותנו
התקוה שנות אלפים.
להיות עם חפשי בארצנו
ארץ ציון בירושלים.

    The soul of the Jew yearns for Zion
    The hope of two thousand years
    To be a free people
    In the land of Israel, in the city of Jerusalem.

                            —*N. Imber*

41. HATOV O HARA

HA-TOV O HA-RA
ZOT HA-SH'-AY-LA.
ZOT HA-B'-A-YA.
LA-A-DAM HA-B'-RAY-RA.

הטוב או הרע
זאת השאלה.
זאת הבעיה.
לאדם הברירה.

> Good or evil.
> That is the question.
> That is the problem.
> The decision is ours.
>
> —*Felice Friedman*

---

42. HAVA NAGEELA

HA-VA NA-GEE-LA V'-NIS-M'-HA.
HA-VA N'-RAN-N'-NA V'-NIS-M'-HA.
OO-ROO A-HEEM B'-LAYV SA-MAY-AKH.

הבה נגילה ונשמחת.
הבה נרננה ונשמחת.
עורו אחים בלב שמח.

> Come and rejoice
> Come sing and rejoice
> Awake, brothers and sisters, and be happy.
>
> —*Folk Song*

43. HAYAMEEM HOL'FEEM

HA-YA-MEEM HO-L'-FEEM
SHA-NA O-VE-RET

A-VAL HA-MAN-GEE-NAH
A-VAL HA-MAK-HAY-LA
A-VAL HA-HEV-RA-YA TA-MEED
NISH-E-RET.

הימים חולפים
שנה עוברת.

אבל המנגינה
אבל המקהלה
אבל החבריה תמיד
נשארת.

>   Days pass and years go by
>   Ever and ever.
>
>   And as your voices ring
>   Ring with our songs we sing
>   Life is a joyous thing
>   Ever and ever.
>   —*Folk Song (Adapted by Daniel Friedman)*

44. HAYVAYNOO SHALOM ALAYKHEM

HAY-VAY-NOO SHA-LOM A-LAY-KHEM

הבאנו שלום עליכם.

>   Let there be peace.
>   —*Folk Song*

45. HAZAK

HA-ZAK HA-ZAK V'-NIT-HA-ZAYK

חזק חזק ונתחזק.

>   Be strong, be strong, and let us strengthen each other.
>   —*Deuteronomy 32:23*

46. HEVAY MITTALMEEDAV

HE-VAY MIT-TAL-MEE-DAV SHEL A-HA-RON
O-HAYV SHA-LOM V'-RO-DEF SHA-LOM.
O-HAYV ET HAB-B'-REE-YOT
OO-M'-KA-R'-VAN LA-TO-RAH

הוה מתלמידיו של אהרון
אוהב שלום ורודף שלום.
אוהב את הבריות
ומקרבן לתורת.

Be of the disciples of Aaron
Loving peace and pursuing peace
Loving all people
And bringing them near to wisdom.

—*Hillel*

47. HINNAY MA TOV

HIN-NAY MA TOV OO-MA-NA-EEM
SHE-VET A-HEEM GAM YA-HAD.

הנה מה טוב ומה נעים
שבת אחים גם יחד.

How good and how pleasant it is
For brothers and sisters to celebrate together.

—*Psalms*

48. HOSHANA

HO-SHA-NA. הושענת

Let us save ourselves.

Mahzor

---

49. I HAVE A LITTLE DRAYDEL

I have a little draydel
I made it out of clay
And when it's dry and ready
Then draydel I will play.

O draydel, draydel, draydel
I made it out of clay
And when it's dry and ready
My draydel I will play.

—*F. Grossman*

50. KALLANEEYOT

HA-E-REV BA, SH'-KEE-A BA-HAR YO-KE-DET.
A-NEE HO-LE-MET V'-RO-OT AY-NIE.
AH-GIE-A, NA-A-RA K'-TA-NA YO-RE-DET
OO-V'-AYSH KAL-LA-NEE-YOT LO-HAYT HA-GIE.

ET HA-P'-RA-HEEM LEE-TS'-ROR HEE
T'-LAK-KAYT LAH.
OO-VASH-VEE-LEEM HAM-MIT-KAS-SEEM BAT-TAL
EL IM-MA HEE NEH-PE-ZET V'-KO-RET LAH.
HAB-BEE-TEE MA HAY-VAY-TEE LAKH BAT-TAL.

KAL-LA-NEE-YOT, KAL-LA-NEE-YOT,
KAL-LA-NEE-YOT
A-DAM-DAM-MOT AD-MO-NEE-YOT
KAL-LA-NEE-YOT, KAL-LA-NEE-YOT,
KAL-LA-NEE-YOT
M'-TOOL-LA-LOT HIN-NA-NEE-YOT.

SH'-KEE-OT BA-HAR TIV-AR-NA V'-TID-AKH-NA
A-VAL TA-MEED KAL-LA-NEE-YOT TIF-RAH-NA.
SOO-FOT LA-ROV TAY-HOM-NA V'-TIS-AR-NA
AKH MAY-HA-DASH KAL-LA-NEE-YOT TIV-AR-NA

KAL-LA-NEE-YOT, KAL-LA-NEE-YOT,
KAL-LA-NEE-YOT
A-DAM-DAM-MOT AD-MO-NEE-YOT

הערב בא שקיעה בהר יוקדת
אני חולמת ורואות עיני.
הגיאה נערה קטנה יורדת
ובאש כלניות לוהט הגיא.

את הפרחים לצרור
היא תלקט לך.
ובשבילים המתכסים בטל.
אל אמא היא נחפזת וקוראת לך
הביטי מה הבאתי לך בטל.

כלניות כלניות
כלניות
אדמדמות ארמוניות
כלניות כלניות
כלניות
מטוללות הנניות.

שקיעות בהר תבערנה ותראכנה
אבל תמיד כלניות תפרחנה.
סופות לרוב תהומנה ותסערנה
אך מחדש כלניות תבערנת

כלניות כלניות
כלניות
אדמדמות ארמוניות.

    The evening comes, the sun sets over the mountain
    I dream and my eyes see
    I arrive: a small girl descends
    And in the fire of the poppies, the valley glows.

                              —*Natan Alterman*

---

51. KAMIEYEEM

KA-MIE-YEEM HA-PA-NEEM LA-PA-NEEM
KAYN LAYV HA-A-DAM LA-A-DAM.

כמים הפנים לפנים
כן לב האדם לאדם.

      Face to face
      Each person reflects the heart of the other.

                             —*Sherwin Wine*

52. KAN AL P'NAY ADAMA

כאן על פני אדמה
לא בעבים מעל
על פני אדמה הקרובה האם.

KAN AL P'-NAY A-DA-MA
LO VE-A-VEEM MAY-AL
AL P'-NAY A-DA-MA HA-K'-RO-VA, HA-AYM.

לא ארפלי מחר
היום הממומש ביד
היום הממוצק
החם האיתן.
לראות את היום הזה
הקצר האחד.
על פני אדמתנו כאן.

LO AR-FIL-LAY MA-HAR
HIE-YOM HAM-M'-MOO-MASH VIE-YAD
HIE-YOM HAM-M'-MOO-TSAK,
HE-HAM, HA-AY-TAN.
LEE-R'-OT ET HIE-YOM HAZ-ZE,
HAK-KA-TSAR, HA-E-HAD,
AL P'-NAY AD-MA-TAY-NOO KAN.

בטרם עתה הליל
בואו בואו הכל
מאמץ מאוחד
עקשני ועד.
של אלף זרועות
האמנם יבצר לגול.
את האבן מפי הבאר.

B'-TE-REM A-TA HA-LAYL
BO-OO, BO-OO HAK-KOL!
MA-A-MATS M'-OO-HAD
AK-SHA-NEE VA-AYD
SHEL E-LEF Z'-RO-OT,
HA-OOM-NAM YIB-BA-TSAYR LAG-GOL
ET HA-E-VEN MEE-PEE HAB-B'-AYR?

> Here on earth
> Not in high clouds
> On this mother earth that is close
>
> Not nebulous tomorrow but today: solid, warm, mighty.
> Today materialized in the hand
> Of this single short day to drink deep
> Here in our own land.
>
> Before night falls—come, oh come all!
> A unified stubborn effort, awake
> with a thousand arms. Is it impossible to roll
> The stone from the mouth of the well?

—Rachel Bluwstein

---

53. KEE NAYR MITSVA

כי נר מצוה ותורה אור.
ודרך חיים תוכחות מוסר.

KEE NAYR MITS-VA V'-TO-RA OR
V'-DE-REKH HIE-YEEM TO-KHA-HOT MOO-SAR.

> For a good deed is a flame and wisdom is a light.
> And the path of life is the discipline of morality.

—Proverbs (Adapted)

54. KEE V'SIMHA

KEE V'-SIM-HA TAY-TSAY-OO
OO-V'-SHA-LOM TOO-VA-LOON
HE-HA-REEM V'-HA-G'-VA-OT
YIF-TS'-HOO LIF-NAY-KHEM RIN-NA
V'-KHOL A-TSAY HA-SA-DE YIM-HA-OO KHAF

כי בשמחה תצאו.
ובשלום תובלון
ההרים והגבעות
יפצחו לפניכם רנה
וכל עצי השדה ימחאו כף.

> You shall go forth with joy
> And in peace shall you be led.
> The mountains and the hills shall burst into song before you
> And all the trees of the field shall applaud.

—Siddur

55. KOL NID-RAY

KOL NID-RAY VE-E-SA-RAY
VA-HA-RA-MAY V'-KO-NA-MAY
V'-KIN-NOO-YAY V'-KIN-NOO-SAY
OO-SH'-VOO-OT.
DEE-N'-DAR-NA OO-D'-ISH-TAB-BA-NA
OO-D'-A-HA-RIM-NA
V'-DEE-A-SAR-NA L'-MA-AN
A-HA-VA OO-TS'-DA-KA
YEE-H'-YOO KIE-YA-MEEM.

כל נדרי ואסרי
יחרמי וקונמי
וקנוסי
ושבעות
דנדרנא ודאשתבענא
ודאחרימנא
ודאסרנא למען
אהבה וצדקה
יהיו קימים.

> We affirm all promises and resolutions
> Which we have made for the sake of love.

—Mahzor (Adapted)

56. LAM'TSAPPEEM

LA-M'-TSAP-PEEM HA-T'-HIL-LA
KEE LA-HEM HE-A-TEED.
HA-O-M'-DEEM MOOL HA-HAR
V'-AY-NAM NIR-TA-EEM
YA-A-LOO EL PIS-GA-TO.

למצפים התהלה
כי להם העתיד.
העומדים מול ההר ואינם נרתאים
יעלו אל פסגתו.

> For the expectant is the glory
> The future is theirs.
> Whoever stands against the mountain without recoil
> Shall ascend its summit.

—David Rokeach

57. LEE-R'-DOF BAEMET

LEE-R'-DOF BA-E-MET
LEE-M'-TSO HA-E-MET
L'-DAB-BAYR HA-E-MET
AY-LE HA-MA-A-SEEM SHEL HA-TSAD-DEEK

לרדוף באמת
למצוא אמת
לדבר אמת
אלה המעשים טובים של הצדיק.

> To pursue the truth
> To find the truth
> To speak the truth
> These are the deeds of the noble person.
>
> —*Sherwin Wine*

---

58. L'MAAN TSEEYON LO EHESHE

L'-MA-AN TSEE-YON LO E-HE-SHE
OO-L'-MA-AN Y'ROO-SHA-LIE-YIM LO ESH-KOT.
AD YAY-TSAY KHA-NO-GA TSID-KA
VEE-SHOO-A-TA K'-LAP-PEED YIV-AR

למען ציון לא אחשה.
ולמען ירושלים לא אשקוט.
עד יצא כנוגע צדקה.
וישועתה כלפיד יבער.

> For the sake of Zion I will not be quiet
> And for the sake of Jerusalem I will not be silent
> Until her justice shall go forth as a beacon
> And her redemption like a burning torch.
>
> —*Isaiah 62:1*

59. LOO Y'HEE

OD YESH MIF-RASH LA-VAN BA-O-FEK
MOOL A-NAN SHA-HOR KA-VAYD
KOL SHE-N'-VA-KESH—LOO Y'-HEE.
V'-EEM BA-HA-LO-NOT HA-E-REV
OR NAY-ROT HA-HAG RO-AYD
KOL SHE-N'-VA-KESH—LOO Y'-HEE

LOO Y'-HEE—LOO Y'HEE—A-NA LOO Y'-HEE
KOL SHE-N'-VA-KESH—LOO Y'-HEE

עוד יש מפרש לבן באופק
מול ענן שחור כבד.
כל שנבקש — לו יהי.
ואם בחלונות בערב
אור נרות החג רועד.
כל שנבקש — לו יהי.

לו יהי לו יהי אנא לו יהי
כל שנבקש לו יהי.

    Still there is a white sail on the horizon
    Against a heavy black cloud.
    All that we want—let it be.
    And if in the windows in the evening
    The holiday lights burn.
    All that we want—let it be.

    Let it be, let it be,
    All that we want, let it be.

—Naomi Shemer

60. LO YISSA GOY

LO YIS-SA GOY EL GOY HE-REV.
LO YIL-M'-DOO OD MIL-HA-MA.

לא ישא גוי אל גוי חרב.
לא ילמדו עוד מלחמת.

    Nation shall not lift up sword against nation.
    Neither shall they learn war anymore.

—Isaiah 2:4

61. MAASEEM TOVEEM

MA-A-SEEM TO-VEEM MID-D'-VAREEM.
DAB-BAYR M'-AT VA-A-SAY HAR-BAY.

מעשים טובים מדברים.
דבר מעט ועשה הרבה.

    Deeds are better than words.
    Speak little, do much.

—Shammai (Adapted)

62. MACCABEES OF OLD

Maccabees of old did rise
To defy the wicked king
They fought hard to help all men
And through courage freedom bring.

They brought a message cheering
That the time was nearing
Which will see all men free
Tyrants disappearing.

— *Traditional (Adapted)*

63. MAHAR

MA-HAR OO-LIE NAF-LEE-GA BA-S'-FEE-NOT
MAY-HOF AY-LAT AD HOF SHE-N'-HAV.
V'-AL HA-MISH-HA-TOT HA-Y'-SHA-NOT
YAT-EE-NOO TA-POO-HAY ZA-HAV.

KOL ZE AY-NO MA-SHAL V'-LO HA-LOM
ZE NA-KOHN KA-OR BA-TSO-HO-RIE-YEEM.
KOL ZE YA-VO MA-HAR EEM LO HA-YOM
V'-EEM LO MA-HAR AZ MOKH-RA-TIE-YEEM.

מחר אולי נפליגה בספינות
מחוף אילת עד חוף שנהב
ועל המשחתות הישנות
יטעינו תפוחי זהב.

כל זה אינו משל ולא חלום
זה נכון כאור בצהרים
כל זה יבוא מחר אם לא היום
ואם לא מחר אז מחרתים.

Tomorrow will bring a new dawn of peace
And if not tomorrow, then surely the following day.

— *Naomi Shemer*

64. MA TOVOO

MA TO-VOO O-HA-LE-KHA YA-A-KOV
MISH-K'-NO-TE-KHA YIS-RA-EL

מה טובו אוהליך יעקב
משכנותיך ישראל.

How pleasant are the tents of Jacob
And the dwelling places of Israel.

— *Numbers 24:5*

65. MEE HAHAM

MEE HA-HAM? HA-MAY-VEEN ET ATS-MO.
MEE GIB-BOR? HA-MO-SHAYL B'-ATS-MO.
MEE HOF-SHEE? HE-HA-HAM V'-HA-GIB-BOR.

מי חכם? המבין את עצמו.
מי גבור? המושל בעצמו.
מי חפשי? החכם והגבור.

Who is wise? He who understands himself.
Who is strong? He who rules himself.
Who is free? He who is wise and strong.

—Sherwin Wine

66. MEE YITT'NAYNEE OF

MEE YIT-T'-NAY-NEE OF
TSIP-POR KA-NAF K'-TAN-NA
BEE-N'-DOO-DAY AYN-SOF.

MEE YIT-T'-NAY-NEE OF
TSIP-POR KA-NAF K'-TAN-NA
A-SHER BA-KAN HA-TOV
TA-NOO-AKH SHA-A-NAN-NA.

A-HA, K'-OF N'-DOD
A-GOOD A-NEE GAM KAYN.
AKH AYT EE-AF MA-OD
LA-NOO-AH AYN LEE KAN

מי יתנני עוף?
צפור כנף קטנה
בנדודי אין סוף.

מי יתנני עוף?
צפור כנף קטנה
אשר בכן הטוב
תנוח שאננת.

אהה, כעוף נדוד
אגוד אני גם כן
אך את איעף מאוד
לנוח אין לי כן

Who will give me a bird.
A bird of small wing
Who wanders endlessly?

—David Shimoni

67. MEE Y'MALLEL

MEE Y'-MAL-LEL G'-VOO-ROT YIS-RA-EL
O-TAN MEE YIM-NE?
KAYN B'-KHOL DOR YA-KOOM HA-GIB-BOR
GO-EL HA-AM

מי ימלל גבורות ישראל
אותן מי ימנה?
כן בכל דור יקום הגבור
גואל העם.

> Who can retell the things that befell us?
> Who can count them?
> In every age a hero or sage
> Comes to our aid.
>
> *—Traditional*

68. MISSAVEEV

MIS-SA-VEEV Y'-HOM HA-SA-AR
AKH RO-SHAY-NOO LO YEE-SHAKH.
LIF-KOO-DA TA-MEED
A-NAKH-NOO TA-MEED
A-NOO A-NOO HA-PAL-MAKH.

MEE-M'-TOO-LA AD HA-NE-GEV
MIN HA-YAM AD HA-MID-BAR
KOL BA-KHOOR V'-TOV LA-NE-SHEK
KOL BA-KHOOR AL HA-MISH-MAR

N'-TEEV LA-NE-SHER BA-SHA-MIE-YIM
SH'-VEEL LA-FE-RE BAYN HA-REEM
MOOL O-YAYV DAR-KHAY-NOO YA-AL
BAYN NIK-ROT OO-VAYN TSOO-REEM

REE-SHO-NEEM TA-MEED A-NAKH-NOO
L'-OR HA-YOM OO -VA-MAKH-SHAKH
LIF-KOO-DA TA-MEED A-NAKH-NOO
TA-MEED A-NOO A-NOO HA-PAL-MAKH.

מסביב יהום הסער.
אך ראשנו לא ישך.
לפקודה תמיד
אנחנו תמיד
אנו אנו הפלמ״ח.

ממטולה עד הנגב
מן הים עד המדבר
כל בחור וטוב לנשק
כל בחור על המשמר.

נתיב לנשר בשמים.
שביל לפרא בין הרים
מול אויב דרכנו יעל
בין נקרות ובין צורים.

ראשונים תמיד אנחנו
לאור היום ובמחשך.
לפקודה תמיד אנחנו
תמיד אנו הפלמ״ח.

    Though the wind around is howling
    Darkness reigns upon the trail
    The Palmach will march without fear or doubt
    For the land of Israel.

    Like the eagle in the skyways
    We shall soar to heights unknown
    Not for us are roads and highways
    Proudly we shall march along.

    Fear not the Palmach is coming
    To the rescue of the frail
    We are kings of hills and deserts
    Knowing every hill and dale.

    Everytime that we are needed
    The Palmach is ready for the call
    We are proud to be defenders
    And friends to our brethren one and all.

                                    —Zerubavel Gilad

69. NAASE SHALOM

NA-A-SE SHALOM BA-O-LAM.
NA-A-SE SHA-LOM A-LAY-NOO
V'-AL KOL HA-O-LAM.
V'-EE-M'-ROO SHALOM.

נעשה שלום בעולם
נעשה שלום עלינו
ועל כל העולם.
ואמרו שלום.

Let us make peace and friendship for all the world.

—*Siddur (Adapted)*

70. NAE HAOR

NA-E HA-OR BA-A-DAM.
NA-E HA-OR MIK-KOL KO-KHA-VEEM
NA-E HA-OR MIK-KOL O-LA-MEEM
NA-E HA-OR BA-A-DAM.

נאה האור באדם
נאה האור מכל כוכבים
נאה האור מכל עולמים
נאה האור באדם.

Marvelous is the light within us
More wonderful than all the stars
More wonderful than all the galaxies
Marvelous is the light within us.

—*Sherwin Wine*

71. N'TAHAYR LIBBAYNOO

N'-TA-HAYR LIB-BAY-NOO
L'-RA-D'-FA E-MET.
N'-TA-HAYR LIB-BAY-NOO
L'-RA-D'-FA SHA-LOM.

נטהר לבנו
לרדפה אמת.
נטהר לבנו
לרדפה שלום.

Let us purify our heart to pursue the truth
Let us purify our heart to pursue peace.

—*Sherwin Wine*

72. O BEAUTIFUL

> O beautiful for heroes proved
> In liberating strife,
> Who more than self their country loved
> And mercy more than life.
>
> America! America!
> May we thy gold refine
> Till all success the nobleness
> And all our gains combine.
>
> *—Katherine Lee Bates*

73. OIFN PRIPETSHOK

אויפן פריפעטשאק ברענט א פייערעל

OI-FN PRI-PE-TSHOK BRENT A FIE-E-REL
UN IN SHTUB IZ HAYS
UN DER REB-RE LE-RENT
KLAY-NE KIN-DER-LAKH
DEM A-LEF BAYS.

און אין שטוב איז היים.
און דער רבי לערענט
קליינע קינדערלאך
דעם אלף בית.

SAYT SHE KIN-DER-LAKH
GE-DENKT SHE TIE-E-RE
VOS EER LE-RENT DO
ZOGT SHE NOKH A-MOL
UN TA-KE NOKH A-MOL
KO-METS A-LEF O

זייט שע קינדערלאך
גערענקט שע טייערע
וואס אהיר לערענט דא
זאגט שע נאך אמאל
און טאקע נאך אמאל
קמץ אלף א.

> On the Pripet burns a fire
> And in the small house it is hot
> And the rabbi teaches small children
> The alphabet.
>
> *—Folk Song*

74. OOSH'AVTEM MIEYIM

OO-SH'-AV-TEM MIE-YIM B'-SA-SON
MEE-MIE Y'-NAY HA-Y'-SHOO-A

ושאבתם מים בששון
ממעיני הישועה.

> Joyfully shall you draw water
> From the fountains of deliverance.
>
> *—Isaiah*

75. OOTSOO AYTSA

OOTSOO AY-TSA V'-TOO-FAR
DAB-B'-ROO DA-VAR V'-LO YA-KOOM
KEE IM-MA-NOO TSE-DEK.

עוצו עצה ותופר
דברו דבר ולא יקום.
כי עמנו צדק.

> Though hateful men conspire to do evil
> Their will will not prevail
> For justice is with us.
>
> *—Traditional (Adapted)*

---

76. OUT OF THE NIGHT

> Out of the night that covers me,
> Black as the pit from pole to pole,
> I thank whatever gods may be
> For my unconquerable soul.
>
> In the fell clutch of circumstance
> I have not winced nor cried aloud.
> Under the bludgeonings of chance
> My head is bloody but unbowed.
>
> Beyond this place of wrath and tears
> Looms but the horror of the shade,
> And yet the menace of the years
> Finds, and shall find me, unafraid.
>
> It matters not how strait the gate,
> How charged with punishments the scroll,
> I am the master of my fate
> I am the captain of my soul.
>
> *—W. Henley*

---

77. RAYSHEET HOKHMA

RAY-SHEET HOKH-MA K'-NAY HOKH-MA.
RAY-SHEET BEE-NA K'-NAY VEE-NA.

ראשית חכמה קנה חכמת
ראשית בינה קנה בינת.

> The beginning of wisdom is to seek wisdom.
>
> *—Proverbs (Adapted)*

78. SAHAKEE

SA-HA-KEE SA-HA-KEE AL HA-HA-LO-MOT
ZOO A-NEE HA-HO-LAYM SAKH.
SA-HA-KEE KEE VA-A-DAM A-A-MEEN
KEE O-DEN-NEE MA-A-MEEN BAKH.

שחקי שחקי על החלומות
זו אני החולם שח.
שחקי כי באדם אאמין
כי עודני מאמין בך.

> Laugh, laugh at all my dreams
> But this I the dreamer proclaim
> That I believe in man
> That I believe in you.
>
> —*Shaul Tchernikhovsky*

79. SEE-SOO V-SEE-M'-HOO

SEE-SOO V'-SEE-M'-HOO B'-SIM-HAT HAG.
MA-HA-OO KA-PIE-YIM.
NA-G'-NOO SHEER B'-KOL HA-ZAK.
OO-VEE-M'-TSIL-TIE-YIM.

שישו ושמחו בשמחת חג
מחאו כפים
נגנו שיר בקול חזק
ובמצלתים.

> Rejoice and be happy on this joyous holiday.
> Clap your hands.
> Sing your song in a strong voice.
> And with special instruments.
>
> —*Folk Song*

80. SHAALOO SH'LOM Y'ROOSHALIEYIM

SHA-A-LOO SH'-LOM Y'-ROO-SHA-LIE-YIM
YISH-LA-YOO O-HA-VIE-YIKH
Y'-HEE SHA-LOM B'-HAY-LAYKH.
SHAL-VA B'-AR-M'-NO-TIE-YIKH.

שאלו שלום ירושלים
ישליו אוהביך.
יהי שלום בחילך.
שלוה בארמנותיך

> Seek the peace of Jerusalem
> Let all who love her be secure
> Let peace be in her ranks.
>
> Let peace be in her ranks.
> Tranquility in her palaces.
>
> —*Psalms 122:6–7*

81. SHALOM LARAHOK

SHA-LOM LA-RA-KHOK V'-LA-KA-ROV.　　　שלום לרחוק ולקרוב.

    Let us make peace for everybody.

                            —*Mahzor*

---

82. SHA-LOM L'-YIS-RA-EL

SHA-LOM L'-YIS-RA-EL　　　שלום לישראל.
SHA-LOM LA-A-DAM　　　שלום לאדם.
SHA-LOM LA-O-LAM　　　שלום לעולם.

    Let there be peace for the Jewish people
    Let there be peace for humanity
    Let there be peace for all the world.

                            —*Sherwin Wine*

---

83. SHEEM'OO

SHEE-M'-OO SHEE-M'-OO O-HA-VAY A-HA-VA.　　　שמעו שמעו אוהבי אהבה.
KEE-R'-OO KEE-R'-OO MO-SHEE-AY Y'-SHOO-A.　　　קראו קראו מושיעי ישועה.
KEE AYN Y'-SHOO-A B'-LEE A-HA-VA.　　　כי אין ישועה בלי אהבה.
O A-HA-VA A-HA-VA KAYN T'-HEE.　　　או אהבה אהבה כן תהי.

    Listen now you lovers of love
    Hear this, you seekers of happiness
    There is no happiness without love.

                            —*Sherwin Wine*

84. SHOSHANNAT YAAKOV

SHO-SHAN-NAT YA-A-KOV
TSA-HA-LA V'-SA-MAY-KHA
BEE-R'-O-TAM YA-HAD
ES-TAYR OO-MOR-D'-KHIE.

שושנת יעקוב
צהלה ושמחה
בראותם יחד.
אסתר ומרדכי

> The Jews of Shushan shouted with joy
> When they saw Mordecai and Esther.
>
> — *Traditional*

85. TAPOOHEEM OO-D'-VASH

TA-POO-HEEM OO-D'-VASH L'-ROSH HA-SHA-NA
SHA-NA TO-VA SHA-NA M'-TOO-KA

תפוחים ודבש לראש השנה
שנה טובה שנה מתוקה.

> Apples and honey for the New Year
> May we have a good year
> May we have a sweet year
>
> — *Folk Song*

86. TAYN SHABBAT

TAYN SHAB-BAT
V'-TAYN SHA-LOM
BA-EER Y'-ROO-SHA-LIE-YIM

תן שבת
ותן שלום
בעיר ירושלים.

> Let peace and serenity reign in the city of Jerusalem.
>
> — *Traditional*

87. TEEK'OO BASHOFAR

TEE-K'-OO BA-SHO-FAR.
HASH-MEE-OO E-MET.
HASH-MEE-OO VEE-NA.

תקעו בשופר.
השמיעו אמת.
השמיעו בינה.

> Blow the shofar.
> Proclaim truth and understanding.
>
> —*Sherwin Wine*

---

88. TEER'OO BASHOFAR

TEE-R'-OO BA-SHO-FAR
HASH-MEE-OO BEE-NA
HASH-MEE-OO E-MET

תרעו בשופר.
השמיעו בינה.
השמיעו אמת.

> Sound the ram's horn
> Announce understanding and truth.
>
> —*Sherwin Wine*

89. TIKVA B'HEERA

תקוה בחירה.
לא נמצאת.
לא נתנה.
תמיד נלקחת.

TIK-VA B'-HEE-RA
LO NIM-TSA-A
LO NIT-TAN-NA
TA-MEED NIL-KA-HA.

יש אנשים
שממתינים להתפס בה.
הם יושבים כאסירי יאוש.

YAYSH A-NA-SHEEM
SHE-MAM-TEE-NEEM L'-HIT-TA-PAYS BAH.
HAYM YO-SH'-VEEM KA-A-SEE-RAY YAY-OOSH.

יש אחרים שמחפסים אותה
הם מוצאים חזרת זעמם לבדה.

YAYSH A-HAY-REEM SHE-M'-HAP-P'-SEEM O-TA
HAYM MO-TS'-EEM HEZ-RAT ZA-MAM L'-VAD-DA.

תקוה מעשה כוח רצון.
מאשרת לפני הרע שהטוב יקרה.
בוחרת לפני הכשלון
בכבוד עצמי מרחמנות.

TIK-VA MA-A-SE KO-AKH RA-TSON
M'-A-SHE-RET, LIF-NAY HA-RA, SHE-HA-TOV YIK-RE
BO-HE-RET, LIF-NAY HAK-KISH-SHA-LON,
B'-KHA-VOD ATS-MEE MAY-RAKH-MA-NOOT.

אופטומיסים משחקים
אפילו בחושך.
הם יודעים
שתקוה דרך חיים
לא ערובה.

OP-TO-MEE-SEEM M'-SA-HA-KEEM,
A-FEE-LOO BA-HO-SHEK.
HAYM YO-D'-EEM
SHE-TIK-VA DE-REKH HIE-YEEM
LO A-ROOB-BA.

> Hope is a choice
> Never found
> Never given
> Always taken
>
> Some wait to be captured by it.
> They sit as the prisoners of despair.
>
> Others search for it.
> They find only the reflection of their own anger.
>
> Hope is an act of will.
> Affirming, in the face of evil, that good things will happen
> Preferring, in the face of failure, self-respect to pity.
>
> Optimists laugh, even in the dark.
> They know that hope is a lifestyle
> Not a guarantee.

—*Sherwin Wine*

90. TOV LEEH'YOT

TOV LEE-H'-YOT EEM HA-MA-VET
BA-AY-NIE-YEEM
TOV LA-DA-AT: KOL RE-GA A-HA-RON.
A-NAKH-NOO BO-NEEM ET Y'-ROO-SHA-LIE-YIM
K'-O'LEEM L'-GAR-DOM.

TOV LA-HA-ZOT HA-DO-ROT SHE-YA-VO-OO
TOV L'-HO-SHEET LA-R'-HO-KEEM ET HA-YAD.
LA-HEM HA-NA-TEEV SHE-DA-RAKH-NOO
BA-TO-HOO.
YA-HAD KOO-LA-NOO BA-DAD.

NA-SHEER LA-O-M'-DEEM AY-TAN-NEEM
AL HA-HE-RES
NA-SHEER LA-LO-HA-MEEM B'-AYN
MA-GEN LE-HA-ZE
NA-SHEER LA-LA-PEED HA-SHO-KAY-A,
LA-HE-RES—
KEE YA-AL MAY-AY-VER MIZ-ZE.

טוב להיות עם המות
בעינים.
טוב לדעת כל רגע אחרון
אנחנו בונים את ירושלים
כעולים לגרדום.

טוב לחזות הדורות שיבואו.
טוב להושיט לרחוקים את היד
להם הנתיב שדרכנו
בתוהו
יחד כולנו בדד.

נשיר לעומדים איתנים
על ההרם.
נשיר ללוחמים באין
מגן לחזה.
נשיר ללפיד השוקע
לחרם—
כי יעל מעבר מזה.

    It is good to live with death in your eyes.
    It is good to know every moment may be the last.
    We build Jerusalem
    As those who ascend to the scaffold.

    It is good to see the generations which are coming.
    It is good to hold out the hand to those far away.
    For them is the path which we hewed in the void
    Together all of us alone.

    Let us sing to those who stand against destruction.
    Let us sing to those who fight a shield for the beast.
    Let us sing to the torch which is setting, to the sun
    As it crosses the sky.

—Shin Shalom

91. TS'REEKHEEM

TS'-REE-KHEEM A-NAKH-NOO
L'-TA-HAYR LIB-BAY-NOO
KEE AYN BA-NOO MA-A-SEEM

צריכים אנחנו
לטהר לבנו
כי אין בנו מעשים.
תהי עמנו צדקה וחסד
ויושיענו.

We look for the right thing to do
The right thing to do is to love one another
That is the right thing to do.

—*Sherwin Wine*

---

92. TUM BALALAIKA

SHAYT A BO-KHER
UN ER TRAKHT
TRAKHT UN TRAKHT DEE
CAN-TSE NAKHT
VE-MEN TSOO NE-MEN
UN NIT FER-SHE-MEN.

שטייט א בחור און ער טראכט
טראכט און טראכט די
גאנצע נאכט.
וועמען צו נעמען און ניט פערשעמען.

TUM-BA-LA TUM-BA-LA
TUM-BA-LA-LAI-KA
TUM-BA-LA-LIE-KA SHPEEL
BA-LA-LAI-KA.
TUM-BA-LA-LIE-KA
FRAY-LAKH ZOL ZIEN.

טום באלא
טום באלאלייקא
טום באלאלייקא שפיל
באלאלייקא
טום באלאלייקא פריילאך זאל זיין.

Tell me, tell me, tell me true,
What can grow without the dew?
What can burn for years and years?
What can cry and shed no tears?

Listen to the answer true.
A stone can grow without the dew.
Love can burn for years and years.
A heart can cry and shed no tears.

—*Folk Song*

93. V'AHAVTA

V'-A-HAV-TA L'-RAY-A-KHA KA-MO-KHA.

ואהבת לרעך כמוך.

And you shall love your neighbor as yourself.

—*Leviticus 19:18*

94. V'RAK ANAKNOO

V'-RAK A-NAK-NOO, HA-LOO MAY HAP-PA-HAD
G'-ZOO-LAY HA-LOM AY-DAY HAT-TAV-AY-RA,
NIS-SA ET AD-MA-TAY-NOO HAP-PO-RA-HAT
K'-NAY-ZER A-VAY-LOOT E-LAY-K'-VOO-RA

ורק אנחנו הלומי הפחד
גזולי חלום עדי התבערה.
נשא את אדמתנו הפורחת.
כנזר אבלות אלי קבורת

And only we, by the terror hit,
Dream-robbed witnesses from the fire saved,
Our blossoming land we will lift
Like a wreath of mourning unto the grave.

—*Leah Goldberg*

95. V'SHOOV ITKHEM

V'-SHOOV IT-KHEM
NAY-TSAY LEE-R'-OT BA-OR
V'-SHOV IT-KHEM
NIR-KOD ET KOL HA-LIE-LA
KEE A-LAY-KHEM RA-TSEE-NOO
LA-HA-ZOR.

V'-SHOOV IT-KHEM
EEM E-REV NIT-O-RAYR
V'-SHOOV IT-KHEM
NIS-MAKH KOO-LA-NOO YA-HAD
OO-L'-SHEER-KHEM NA-SHOOV
PIZ-MON HO-ZAYR.

V'-SHOOV IT-KHEM
V'-SHA-LOM A-LAY-KHEM
V'-A-LAY-NOO AL KOO-LA-NOO
V'-SHOOV IT-KHEM
A-NAKH-NOO SHE-LA-KHEM
V'-KHOL HA-SHEE-REEM SHE-LA-NOO.

ושוב אתכם
נצא לראות באור.
ושוב אתכם
נרקוד את כל הלילה.
כי עליכם רצינו
לחזור.

ושוב אתכם
עם ערב נתעורר
ושוב אתכם
נשמח כולנו יחד
ולשיריכם נשוב
פזמון חוזר.

ושוב אתכם
ושלום עליכם
ועלינו על כולנו
ושוב אתכם
אנחנו שלכם
וכל השירים ש׳

Again with you
Let us go out to see the light
Again with you
Let us dance all night
For to you we want to return.

—*Ehud Manor*

96. WE SHALL BROTHERS BE

We shall brothers be
Some day
For deep in my heart
I do believe
We shall brothers be someday.

We shall sisters be
Some day
For deep in my heart
I do believe
We shall sisters be someday.

—*Folk Song*

97. A WICKED, WICKED MAN

Once there was a wicked, wicked man
And Haman was his name, sir.
He would have murdered all the Jews
Though they were not to blame, sir.

Oh, today we'll merry merry be
And nash some hamentaschen.

And Esther was the lovely queen
Of King Ahashuerus
When Haman said he'd kill us all
Oh my how he did scare us.

Oh, today we'll merry merry be
And nash some hamentaschen.

— *Folk Song*

---

98. Y'HEE SHALOM

Y'-HEE SHA-LOM TO-VA OO-V'-RA-KHA
HAYN VA-HE-SED V'-RA-HA-MEEM.

יהי שלום טובה וברכה
חן וחסד ורחמים.

Let there be peace, good and blessing
Grace and kindness and compassion.
— *Siddur (Adapted)*

---

99. Y'MAY HANOOKKA

Y'-MAY HA-NOOK-KA
HA-NOOK-KAT MIK-DA-SHAY-NOO
B'-GEEL OO-V'-SIM-HA M'-MAL-EEM
ET LIB-BAY-NOO
LIE-LA VA-YOM S'-VEE-VO-NAY-NOO
YIS-SOV
SOOF GA-NEE-YOT NO-HAL
BAM LA-ROV.

ימי חנוכה
חנוכת מקדשנו
בגיל ובשמחה ממלאים
את לבנו.
לילה ויום סביבננו
יסוב.
סוף גניות נוחל
בם לרוב.

The days of Hanukka
Fill our hearts with joy and happiness.
Night and day our draydels turn.

— *A. Avronin*

100. Y'ROOSHALIEYIM

MAY-AL PIS-GAT HAR HA-TSOFEEM
ESH-TA-HA-VE L'-KHA A-PIE-YEEM.
MAY-AL PIS-GAT HAR HA-TSOFEEM
SHA-LOM LAKH Y'-ROO-SHA-LIE-YEEM.
MAY-A DO-ROT HA-LAM-TEE A-LIE-YIKH
LEE-Z'-KOT LEE-R'-OT B'-OR PA-NIE-YIKH.
Y'-ROO-SHA-LIE-YIM
HA-EE-REE PA-NIE-YIKH LIV-NAYKH.
Y'-ROO-SHA-LIE-YIM
MAY-HOR-VO-TIE-YIKH EV-NAYKH.

מעל פסגת הר הצופים
אשתחוה לך אפים.
מעל פסגת הר הצופים
שלום לך ירושלים.
מאה דורות הלמתי עליך
לזכות לראות באור פניך.
ירושלים, האירי פניך לבנך.
ירושלים, מחרבותיך אבנך.

    From the top of Mount Scopus
    I greet you Jerusalem
    For a hundred generations I have dreamed
    Of basking in the light of your presence
    O Jerusalem I will rebuild you from your ruins.

                             —*Avigdor Ameiri*

101. Y'ROOSHALIEYIM SHEL ZAHAV

A-VEER HA-REEM TSA-LOOL KIE-YIE-YIN
V'-RAY-AH O-RA-NEEM
NIS-SA B'-ROO-AH HA-AR-BIE-YIM
EEM KOL PA-A-MO-NEEM.

OO-V'-TAR-DAY-MAT EE-LAN VA-E-VEN
SH'-VOO-YA BA-HA-LO-MA
HA-EER A-SHER BA-DAD YO-SHE-VET
OO-V'-LIB-BA HO-MA.

Y'-ROO-SHA-LIE-YIM SHEL ZA-HAV
V'-SHEL N'-HO-SHET V'-SHEL OR
HA-LO L'-KHOL SHEE-RIE-YIKH
AN-NEE KIN-NOR.

אויר הרים צלול כיין
וריח אורנים.
נשא ברוח הערבים
עם קול פעמונים.

ובתרדמת אילן ואבן.
שבויה בחלומה.
העיר אשר בדד יושבת
ובלבה חומה.

ירושלים של זהב
ושל נחושת ושל אור
הלא לכל שיריך
אני כנור.

        O Jerusalem of gold
        Of brass and of light
        For all your songs I will be your harp.

                       —*Naomi Shemer*

Songs 437

102. Y'VARAYKH ADAM

Y'-VA-RAYKH A-DAM E-MET.
Y'-VA-RAYKH A-DAM BEE-NA.
Y'-VA-RAYKH A-DAM DAY-A.

יברך אדם אמת.
יברך אדם בינה.
יברך אדם דעת.

Let us praise truth, understanding, and wisdom.

—*Sherwin Wine*

103. ZAYKHER

ZAY-KHER TSAD-DEEK-KEEM LEE-V'-RA-KHA

זכר צדיקים לברכת

May the memory of good people bless us.

—*Traditional*

104. ZEMER LAKH

ZE-MER, ZE-MER LAKH
ZE-MER, ZE-MER LAKH
ZE-MER LAKH M'-KHO-RA-TEE,
M'-KHO-RA-TEE.
HA-MA-GAL SO-VAYV
ZE-MER LAKH DO-VAYV
ZE-MER LAKH, M'-KHO-RA-TEE,
M'-KHO-RA-TEE

זמר זמר לך
זמר לך מכורתי.
המגל סובב
זמר לך דובב
זמר לך מכורתי.

HA-RA-RIE-YIKH HAY-MA YIS-MA-HOO
ET M'-KHOL HA-HO-RA YIS-AR.
E-LEF P'-RA-HEEM L'-FE-TA YIF-RA-HOO
Y'-KHAS-SOO ET AYN HA-MID-BAR.

הרריך המה ישמחו
את מחול ההורה יסער.
אלף פרחים לפתע יפרחו
יכסו את עין המדבר.

HO-RA, HO-RA LAKH
HO-RA, HO-RA LAKH
HO-RA LAKH, M'-KHO-RA-TEE,
M'-KHO-RA-TEE
HA-MA-GAL SO-VAYV
HO-RA LAKH DO-VAYV
HO-RA LAKH, M'-KHO-RA-TEE,
M'-KHO-RA-TEE

הורה הורה לך
הורה לך מכורתי.
המגל סובב
הורה לך דובב
הורה לך מכורתי.

A song, a song for you
A song for you, my native land.

—*Avraham Ben-Z'ev*

105. ZOG NIT KAYNMOL

ZOG NIT KAYN-MOL
AZ DOO GAYST DEM LETS-TE VEG
KHOTSH HIM-LEN BLIE-E-NE
FAR-SHTELN BLOY-E TEG
KU-MEN VET NOKH
UN-DZER OYS-GE-BENK-TE SHO
ES VET A POYK TON UN-DZER TROT:
MIR ZIE-NEN DO

FUN GREE-NEM PAL-MEN LAND
BEZ VIE-TN LAND FUN SHNAY
MIR KU-MEN ON MIT UN-DZER PIEN,
MIT UN-DZER VAY.
UN VOO GE-FA-LN SIZ A SHPRITS
FUN UN-DZER BLUT.
SHPRO-TSN VET DORT
UN-DZER GVU-RE UN-DZER MUT.

DOS LEED GE-SHRI-BEN IZ
MIT BLUT UN NIT MIT BLIE.
SIZ NIT A LEE-DL
FUN A FOY-GL OYF DER FRAY.
DOS HOT A FOLK
TSVI-SHN FA-LN-DI-KE VENT
DOS LEED GE-ZUN-GEN
MIT NA-GA-NES IN DEE HENT.

זאג ניט קיינמאל
אז דו גייסט דעם לעצטע וועג.
חאטש הימלען בלייענע
פארשטעלן בלייע טעג.
קומען וועט נאך
אונדזער אויסגעבענקטע שעה
אז וועט א פויק טאן אונדזער טראט.
מיר זיינען דא.

פון גרינעם פאלמען לאנד
ביז ווייטן לאנד פון שניי
מיר קומען אן מיט אונדזער פיין,
מיט אונדזער ווײ
און וואו געפאלן ס׳איז א
שפריטס פון אונדזער בלוט
שפראצן וועט דורט
אונדזער גבורה אונדזער מוט

דאס ליד געשריבען איז
מיט בלוט מיט בלײ
ס׳איז ניט א לידל
פון א פייגל אויף דער פרײ
דאס האט א פאלק
צווישן פאלנדיקע ווענט.
דאס ליד געזונגען
מיט נגנית אין די הענט.

Never say that you are on your final road
Though overhead dark skies of lead may death forbode
The long awaited hour's surely drawing near
When with a roar our steps will thunder we are here.

From land of palm tree to the far-off land of snow
Our people come together crushed by pain and woe
But where a drop of our blood has touched the ground
There our strength and our courage will resound.

This song was written with our blood and not with lead.
This is no song of free birds flying overhead
But a people amid crumbling walls did stand
They stood and sang this song with rifles held in hand.

—*Hirsh Glik*

106. ZOOM GALEE

ZOOM GA-LEE
HE-HA-LOOTS L'-MA-AN A-VO-DA
A-VO-DA L'-MA-AN HE-HA-LOOTS

זום גלי
החלוץ למען עבודה
עבודה למען החלוץ.

Rejoice
The pioneer needs his work
Work needs the pioneer.

—Folk Song

Reprint permission granted for the lyrics of the songs by the following:

1.	Alterman, Natan	KALLANEEYOT	© author; Acum, LTD., Israel
		BEHAREEM (Sheer Boker)	© Miralei Tarbut Vechinuch; Acum LTD., Israel
		HAKH PATEESH (Sheer Hak'veesh)	© Miralei Tarbut Vechinuch; Acum LTD., Israel
2.	Ameiri, Avigdor	Y'ROOSHALIEYIM	© Edition Negen; Acum LTD., Israel
3.	Avronin, A.	Y'MAY HANOOKKA	© author; Acum LTD., Israel
4.	Ben-Z'ev, Avraham	ZEMER LAKH	© Miralei Tarbut Vechinuch; Acum LTD., Israel
5.	Bluwstein, Rachel	KAN AL P'NAY ADAMA	© author; Acum LTD., Israel
6.	Broides, Abraham	ADAMA	Reprint permission granted by Leah Broides for the late Abraham Broides; Israel
7.	Dor, Moshe	EREV SHEL SHOSHANEEM	© author; Acum LTD., Israel
8.	Gilad, Zerubavel	MISSAVEEV (Sheer Hapalmakh)	© Miralei Tarbut Vechinuch; Acum LTD., Israel
9.	Manor, Ehud	BASHANA	© author; Acum, LTD., Israel
		V'SHOOV ITKHEM	© Ilanot Music Publishers; Acum LTD., Israel
10.	Rokeakh, David	LAM'TSAPEEM	© author, Acum LTD., Israel
11.	Szenes, Hannah	ASHRAY HAGAFROOR	Acum LTD., Israel
12.	Shalom, Shin	TOV LEEH'YOT	© author; Acum LTD., Israel
13.	Shemer, Naomi	AL KOL AYLE	© author; Acum LTD., Israel
		LOO Y'HEE	© author; Acum LTD., Israel
		MAHAR	© author; Acum LTD., Israel
		B'AYLE HAYADIEYIM	© author; Acum LTD., Israel
		Y'ROOSHALIEYIM SHEL ZAHAV	© author; Chappel Music, LTD., London
14.	Shimoni, David	MEE YITT'NAYNEE OF	© Miralei Tarbut Vechinuch; Acum LTD., Israel
15.	Shlonsky, Avraham	HALBEESHEENEE (Amal)	© author; Acum LTD., Israel
trs.	Shlonsky, Avraham	AYIT (Sheer Hapartizaneem)	© Miralei Tarbut Vechinuch; Acum LTD., Israel.
16.	Tchernikhovsky, Shaul	SAHAKEE	© author; Acum LTD., Israel
17.	Traditional	TAYN SHABBAT	© Acum LTD., Israel

If you wish to acquire the music for the words used in traditional songs, or for songs with lyrics written by Felice Friedman, Daniel Friedman, or Sherwin Wine, please write to: The Society for Humanistic Judaism, 28611 W. 12 Mile Rd., Farmington Hills, MI 48018.